Above All Things
Essays on Christian Ethics and Popular Culture

ADAM BARKMAN

Above All Things:
Essays on Christian Ethics and Popular Culture
Copyright © 2011 Adam Barkman

Winged Lion Press
Hamden, CT

All rights reserved. Except in the case of quotations embodied in critical articles or reviews, no part of this book may be reproduced or transmitted in any form or by any means, electronic or mechanical, including photocopying, recording, or by any information storage or retrieval system, without written permission of the publisher.
For information, contact Winged Lion Press www.WingedLionPress.com

Winged Lion Press titles may be purchased for business or promotional use or special sales.

Cover Design: Ashley Barkman

10-9-8-7-6-5-4-3-2-1

WINGED LION PRESS

ISBN-13 978-1-936294-16-9

*This book is dedicated to
my precious daughter Heather.*

Sweetheart,

By the time you can read this book, "Daddy" will have become "Dad." So much will be different, but some things will never change, especially my love for you.

Just a few weeks before my hero, C. S. Lewis, died he gave this advice – a summary of all the wisdom of man – to a little girl; he wrote, "If you continue to love Jesus, nothing much can go wrong with you, and I hope you may always do so." This is my advice and hope for you as well.

Love,
Dad

ACKNOWLEDGEMENTS

Many thanks to those who read and commented on earlier drafts of this book, in particular, my wife, Ashley, my colleagues Al Wolters and Kevin Flatt, and my TA, Taylor Kraayenbrink.

I'd like to express my thanks also to April Marratto, who helped index this book, and to Redeemer University College for awarding me a Grant in Aid of Publication to finance this task.

Many of the chapters in this book are based – either very loosely (*The Big Bang Theory and Philosophy*) or quite closely (*The Philosophy of J. J. Abrams*) – on essays written for the popular culture and philosophy series of books published by Open Court, Wiley-Blackwell and the University Press of Kentucky. I acknowledge their claim to the original versions of these chapters, and am grateful to be able to publish modified versions of these chapters herein.

Thanks again to my editor, Robert Trexler, who is, as always, supportive of my work.

Above all, I'm grateful to God not just for helping me write this book, but for revealing Himself to be the Good and the True, so that man can worship with real joy.

TABLE OF CONTENTS

INTRODUCTION		ix
CHAPTER 1	The Lion, the Witch and TULIP: C. S. Lewis Engages the Calvinist Worldview	1
CHAPTER 2	From Teaching to Hypnosis to *Inception*: Reflections on the Ethics of Idea-Giving	22
CHAPTER 3	"Evolution Isn't an Opinion, It's a Fact"? Evolution and the Ethics of Belief in *The Big Bang Theory*	30
CHAPTER 4	"I Don't Think Those Rules Apply Anymore": Law and Theft in *The Walking Dead*	44
CHAPTER 5	Do We All Need to Get Shot in the Head? *Regarding Henry*, Rights and Ethical Transformation	54
CHAPTER 6	"I'm the King; That's What I Do": King Neptune and the Duties of Kingship	62
CHAPTER 7	"No Other Gods Before Me": God, Ontology and Ethics in *The Avengers*	69
CHAPTER 8	"The Power to Go Beyond God's Boundaries"? *Hulk*, Human Nature and Some Ethical Concerns Thereof	83

Chapter 9	Superman: From *Anti-Christ* to Christ-Type	93
Chapter 10	"Do You Believe You Will Meet Them Again?" *Gladiator*, Gender and Marriage in the Next Life	107
Chapter 11	"It's Arbitrary"? *Breaking Bad* and the Ethics of Drugs	121
Chapter 12	"The Gods Hate Incest": Nature and Consanguine Unions in *A Game of Thrones*	130
Chapter 13	"All of This Is Wrong": Roman Thoughts on Slavery and *The Hunger Games*	140
Chapter 14	"Make What You Can of It If You Are a Philosopher": Sherlock Holmes Investigates Necromancy	151
Chapter 15	Is a Tattoo a Sign of Impiety?	161
Chapter 16	*Winnie the Pooh* and the Four Loves	169
Index		179

INTRODUCTION

This book is a sequel of a sort to *Through Common Things: Philosophical Reflections on Global Popular Culture*. As with that previous volume, this current collection of essays uses popular culture to advance important (or at least interesting) philosophical topics. The major differences between *Through Common Things* and *Above All Things* are that the latter is both more obviously Christian and more specifically concerned with ethical issues. Nevertheless, in each I've attempted "to take every thought captive to Christ."

Of course, it would be misleading to suggest that my views over both volumes have remained static. I've changed, even in the span of two years.

I have little respect for Christians who are quick to sell their orthodox birthright for a bowl of progress – who surrender key truths to accommodate the Spirit of the Age. Satan is always switching tactics after all. Yet that said, I have the deepest respect for Christians who, while maintaining what is essential, develop their thought to accommodate new evidence or better reasoning. Alvin Plantinga and Nicholas Wolterstorff – the founders of so-called "Reformed epistemology" – came, over the course of their lives, to reject certain beliefs that are difficult to reconcile with righteousness, such as the compatibilist understanding of free will or the notion that love abolishes justice. Or again, C. S. Lewis moved from materialism to idealism to Christianity, and his own Christian ideas grew deep and strong like the roots of a mighty oak over time. In my opinion, these are examples of proper intellectual development.

Of course, all three of these men are imperfect. They continued to hold onto some erroneous beliefs throughout their lives and also accepted a few new ones as well. Take gender, for example. Plantinga and Wolterstorff lately came to believe that gender-inclusive language ("humankind") is more proper or just than orthodox language ("man"), and Lewis could never bring himself to affirm the equality of men and women *qua* rational souls, spirits or persons. The orthodox view, which I see no reason to challenge, has usually insisted that men and women are equal in respect to the image of God (as rational souls, spirits or persons) and yet unequal in respect to their gender roles (hence it's quite proper to use the masculine term "man," which has a sense of authority about it, to refer to the general class of humanity).

Nonetheless, when I examine the thoughts of these men, I see, for the most part, progress toward, and within, orthodox Christianity, and my hope is that readers will see this in me and my books as well.

CHAPTER ONE

THE LION, THE WITCH AND TULIP:
C. S. LEWIS ENGAGES THE CALVINIST WORLDVIEW

Few would disagree with philosopher Peter Kreeft when he declares C. S. Lewis "the best apologist for the Christian faith in the twentieth century."[1] Indeed, according to some figures, the Oxford Don is "the best-selling . . . and the most quoted Christian author of all time."[2] Evangelicals, Anglicans, Lutherans, Catholics and even Eastern Orthodox Christians have found Lewis, an Anglican "mere" Christian, to be an invaluable mentor and interlocutor.

However, there is one branch of Christianity – Calvinism – that has had little to say, or at least little positive to say, about Lewis's theological writings.[3] As a Lewis scholar writing from within a Calvinist community, I find this troubling, for though there are differences between Lewis and Calvinists, these differences have been exaggerated, partly by Calvinists who have misunderstood Lewis, such as Cornelius van Til,[4] and partly by a few

---

1   Peter Kreeft, *Heaven: The Heart's Deepest Longing* (San Francisco: Ignatius Press, 1989), 210.
2   Philip Ryken, "Winsome Evangelist: The Influence of C. S. Lewis," in *C. S. Lewis: Lightbearer in the Shadowlands*, ed. Angus Menuge (Wheaton, IL: Crossway Books, 1997), 56.
3   You can, of course, be a Calvinist who is Anglican (the Puritans were such), but even then, Calvinist Anglicans, with the exception of N. T. Wright, typically ignore Lewis.
4   Van Til once questioned Lewis, asking, "Is it orthodox to hold that man must seek to ascend in the scale of being from animal life to participation in the life of the triune God?" to which Lewis replied through a friend, "As to Professor Van Til's point it is certainly scriptural to say that 'as to many as believed He gave power to become sons of God' and the bold statement 'God became Man that men might become gods' is patristic. Of course Van Til's wording 'that man must *seek* to *ascend* in the scale of life' with its suggestions (a) That we could do this by our own efforts (b) That the difference between God and Man is a difference of position on a 'scale of life' like the difference between a (biologically) 'higher' and a (biologically) 'lower' creature, is wholly foreign to my thought." C. S. Lewis, *The Collected Letters of C. S. Lewis: Volume III; Narnia, Cambridge, and Joy 1950-1963*, ed. Walter Hooper (San Francisco: HarperSanFrancisco, 2007), 1013-1014 [January 20, 1959].

misleading things Lewis believed true of, and thus said about, certain Calvinist thinkers, such as Karl Barth, John Knox and even John Calvin himself.

Consequently, I want to compare and contrast Lewis and Calvinist thinkers – not just theologians but philosophers as well – on some key issues pertaining to creation, fall and redemption. Of course, since Calvinist thinkers (be they Reformed, Presbyterians, Reformed Baptists or others) differ from each other as much as any particular thinker in any particular group, my selection of thinkers will appear a bit arbitrary. Nevertheless, my goal is largely to select Calvinist thinkers who come closest to agreeing with Lewis, thus achieving an important Christian task: greater understanding and unity in the one, undivided body of Christ.

CREATION

Lewis and Calvinists agree that before we can talk about creation, we first need to talk about its *Creator*. Thus, Reformed theologian R. C. Sproul maintains, "Reformed theology is first and foremost theocentric rather than anthropocentric,"[5] and in nearly every story Lewis ever wrote, God the sovereign Creator and King receives powerful expression.[6] When Dutch Reformed statesman Abraham Kuyper declares, "There is not one square inch of the entire creation about which Jesus Christ does not cry out, 'Mine!'"[7] he asserts precisely what Lewis proclaims at nearly the same time just across the Channel: "There is no neutral ground in the universe: every square inch, every split second, is claimed by God [its rightful Lord] and counter-claimed by Satan."[8]

Thus, Lewis and Calvinists agree that God is the transcendental cause

---

5   R. C. Sproul, *What Is Reformed Theology?* (Grand Rapids, MI: Baker Books, 2005), 25.
6   See Adam Barkman, "C. S. Lewis and the Enduring Relevance of Monarchy," *CSL: The Bulletin of the New York C. S. Lewis Society* 37, no. 4 (July-August 2006): 1-15. Of course, while Lewis understands God's sovereignty and omnipotence to refer to His being able to do all that is logically possible (meaning, among other things, God can't do nonsense), a few Calvinists understand God to be able to do anything, even nonsense (God could make $1 + 1 = 3$, create a square circle and even, apparently, do evil).
7   Abraham Kuyper, "Sphere Sovereignty," in *Abraham Kuyper, A Centennial Reader*, ed. James Bratt (Grand Rapids, MI: Eerdmans, 1998), 488.
8   C. S. Lewis, "Christianity and Culture," in *C. S. Lewis: Essay Collection & Other Short Pieces*, ed. Lesley Walmsley (London: HarperCollins, 2000), 90. Cf. "Christianity is the story of how the rightful king has landed, you might say landed in disguise, and is calling us all to take part in a great campaign of sabotage." C. S. Lewis, *Mere Christianity*, in *C. S. Lewis: Selected Books* [Long Edition] (London: HarperCollins, 1999), 349.

and ground of all creation: without God, nothing in creation would be possible, for nothing created can literally do anything without the Creator's strength and permission (though not necessarily His *approval*). Hence, Lewis envisions Satan "sawing off the branch he is sitting on,"[9] and Reformed theologian Vern Poythress asserts the same thing somewhat crudely when he says, "*All* scientists – atheists and theists alike – believe in God. They have to to do their work."[10]

Furthermore, because Lewis and Calvinists acknowledge God as the perfection of Power, Justice, Love, Rationality and so on, all of creation – that is, all of God's kingdom – was declared *good*, and, in the language of Reformational philosophy, is "subject" to, and rationally ordered by, the Only Wise and Benevolent King's "creational laws."[11] These laws are either norms, such as "don't murder," or the laws of nature, such as gravity, and these laws may be either general, such as "don't murder" or gravity, or particular, such as "sacrifice your son, Isaac" or "Jesus walked on water." Although Calvinists are (sometimes rightly, sometimes wrongly) distrustful of the language of Natural Law (often fearing that such implies an ethical absolute *separate* from God), the ethical norms of God's creational laws are precisely this provided that they are understood as Lewis understands them, namely, as being inextricably linked to God's nature, thus implying that these norms are in fact the voice of the Holy Spirit directly revealing something of Himself to us in our conscience: "Is not the [Natural Law] the Word Himself considered from a particular point of view?"[12] And, of course, something similar is true of the laws of nature, "If God directs the course of events at all, then He directs the movement of every atom at every moment.... The 'naturalness' of natural events does not consist in being somehow outside God's providence."[13]

Furthermore, Lewis and Calvinists agree that the crown of earthly creation, man, was created in the image of God, meaning, among other things, that he was more loved by God than the rest of earthly creation.[14] Being more loved by God, man was given a greater charge or destiny than

---

9   C. S. Lewis, *A Preface to Paradise Lost* (Oxford: Oxford University Press, 1969), 96.
10 Vern Poythress, *Redeeming Science: A God-Centered Approach* (Wheaton, IL: Crossway Books, 2006), 13.
11 Albert Wolters, *Creation Regained*, 2nd edition (Grand Rapids, MI: Eerdmans, 2005), 16.
12 C. S. Lewis, *The Collected Letters of C. S. Lewis: Volume III; Narnia, Cambridge, and Joy 1950-1963*, ed. Walter Hooper (San Francisco: HarperSanFrancisco, 2007), 1227 [January 11, 1961].
13 C. S. Lewis, *Miracles*, in *C. S. Lewis: Selected Books* [Long Edition] (London: HarperCollins, 1999), 1232.
14 Nicholas Wolterstorff, *Justice: Rights and Wrongs* (Princeton, NJ: Princeton University Press, 2008), 352.

the rest of earthly creation. For Lewis, just as much as for Calvinists, this destiny is best expressed in the words of the Westminster Confession, namely, that man is "to glorify God and enjoy Him forever."[15] Of course in order to achieve this great calling, God had to give man the necessary equipment for the task – rational cognitive faculties, desires and free will – for only if man has free will can man bless God in this special way (that is, the love of free creatures is more meaningful than coerced creatures), and man, in turn, being made by God, for God, was created such that he can only find real happiness in a (proper or just) covenantal relationship with Him. Man, therefore, was created to *know* and *love* God. Of course, each person should love God in *all* that he or she does (embodied in neo-Calvinism's "cultural mandate" or Lewis's "We can play, as we can eat, to the glory of God"[16]); however, since all people have been designed differently (Christians are *unique* members in the one body of Christ), each person needs to love God according to what he or she is (as rational souls, of course, but also as men, as women, as elder, as younger, etc.) and also according to his or her fluctuating vocation in God's creation (as professors, as students, etc.).

Of course, God's knowledge of, and love for, man come *prior* to anything that man knows or does. However, regarding man, he must first know that God exists and something of the divine nature in order to love God: a person cannot love something he knows nothing about. In other words, some revelation of God to man (we will discuss the types of revelation later) is necessary in order for man to achieve his purpose. Thus in Romans 1, Paul tells us that knowledge of God's existence (in Calvin's phrase, a *sensus divinitatis*[17])

---

15 "Now the disquieting thing is not simply that we skimp and begrudge the duty of prayer. The real disquieting thing is that it should have to be numbered among duties at all. For we believe that we were created to 'glorify God and enjoy Him forever.'" C. S. Lewis, *Prayer: Letters to Malcolm*, in *C. S. Lewis: Selected Books* [Short Edition] (London: HarperCollins, 2002), 631.

16 C. S. Lewis, "Christianity and Literature," in *C. S. Lewis: Essay Collection & Other Short Pieces*, ed. Lesley Walmsley (London: HarperCollins, 2000), 419.

17 "'There is within the human mind, and indeed by natural instinct, an awareness of divinity.' This we take to be beyond controversy. To prevent anyone from taking refuge in the pretence of ignorance, God himself has implanted in all men a certain understanding of His divine majesty. Ever renewing its memory, He repeatedly sheds fresh drops.... There is, as the eminent pagan says, no nation so barbarous, no people so savage, that they have not a deep-seated conviction that there is a God.... From this we conclude that it is not a doctrine that must first be learned in school, but one of which each of us is master from his mother's womb and which nature itself permits no one to forget.... Lest anyone, then, be excluded from access to happiness, He not only sowed in men's minds that seed of religion of which we have spoken, but revealed Himself and daily discloses Himself in the whole workmanship of the universe... . Even the common folk and the most untutored, who have been taught only by the

can be known by *all* people. Moreover, because this knowledge makes people "without excuse" for failing to worship God, having a moral duty to worship God – that is, having general awareness of justice (the ethical norms of the creational law of which I spoke of earlier) – can also be known by *all* people.

However, when it comes to discerning the precise nature of the knowledge of God's existence and the ethical norms of God's creational laws, Calvinists differ amongst themselves. Some Calvinists, including Sproul, B. B. Warfield and Emil Brunner, endorse natural theology, wherein God's existence is inferred by way of argumentation (the cosmological argument, for instance), while others – indeed the majority of Calvinists these days, not the least of whom is Alvin Plantinga – think that God's existence is properly basic, meaning that people immediately – without inference or induction – just *see* that God exists on certain occasions, such as when one sees the beauty of the world from the top of a mountain, when one is in dire need or when things are going perfectly: we are designed by God such that on all of these occasions a properly functioning human being will be aware of the existence of God and something of His nature, namely, that God is the author of all creation and the source of Happiness, Goodness and Truth.[18]

Although Lewis has often been included in the natural theology camp, this is not totally accurate. Yes, Lewis is famous for his formulations of the argument from morality, the argument from reason and the argument from joy.[19] And yes, all of these arguments, in one form or another, helped Lewis in his conversion to Christianity. However, Lewis, just as much as Plantinga, found the ontological argument, among others, helpful but wanting,[20] and, moreover, there is strong agreement between Lewis and Plantinga when we conjoin the two following quotes from the Oxford Don: "The *form* of the

---

aid of the eyes, cannot be unaware of the excellence of divine art, for it reveals itself in this innumerable and yet distinct and well-ordered variety of the heavenly host." John Calvin, *Institutes of the Christian Religion*, tr. Ford Lewis Battles (Philadelphia: Westminster Press, 1960), 43-44.

18   Alvin Plantinga, *The Analytic Theist: An Alvin Plantinga Reader*, ed. James Sennett (Grand Rapids, MI: Eerdmans, 1998), 141.

19   See Adam Barkman, *C. S. Lewis & Philosophy as a Way of Life* (Allentown, PA: Zossima Press, 2009).

20   "As for proof, I sometimes wonder whether the Ontological Argument did not itself arise as a partially unsuccessful translation of an experience without concept or words. I don't think we can initially argue from the *concept* of Perfect Being to its existence. But did they really, inside, argue from the experienced glory that it could not be generated subjectively?" C. S. Lewis, "The Language of Religion," in *C. S. Lewis: Essay Collection & Other Short Pieces*, ed. Lesley Walmsley (London: HarperCollins, 2000), 266. Also see the conclusion of Alvin Plantinga, *God, Freedom, and Evil* (Grand Rapids, MI: Eerdmans, 1996).

desired is in the desire,"[21] and, "If we are made for heaven, *the desire for our proper place will be already in us.*"[22] Although many Calvinists will want more clarification about the "desire" in the latter quotation (again, we will pick this up later), what is crucial to notice here is that since one cannot desire something that one does not have *any* knowledge of, these sentences imply that Lewis believes all people to have some basic (innate, acquired or occasioned) knowledge of God. Perhaps, then, Lewis belongs more to the Plantinga camp (or better, both are of the Augustinian or Christian Platonist camp[23]) in that they acknowledge God's existence (and the existence of God's moral law) as basic, yet at the same time endorse the use of natural theology not only to respond to challenges to Christianity (negative apologetics) but also to point out problems with alternatives to Christianity (positive apologetics).

Consequently, in regard to God (His existence and nature), His creational laws (which are inextricably linked to His very nature at every moment), and His creation (especially man: his destiny and means of achieving such) there is really no disagreement between Lewis and Calvinists as I have construed them. At this point in our discussion, both are merely orthodox in their Christianity.

FALL

Nevertheless, the Fall, true to its name, separates: man from God, of course, but also one theological interpretation from another. Yet even here Lewis is

---

21 C. S. Lewis, *Surprised by Joy*, in *C. S. Lewis: Selected Books* [Long Edition] (London: HarperColllins, 1999), 1371.
22 C. S. Lewis, "The Weight of Glory," in *C. S. Lewis: Essay Collection & Other Short Pieces*, ed. Lesley Walmsley (London: HarperCollins, 2000), 98. We should note that when Lewis says we were made for "Heaven," he is using Heaven as a synonym for "God."
23 Charles Taliaferro sees Plantinga writing in the vein of the Cambridge Platonists. Charles Taliaferro, *Evidence and Faith* (Cambridge: Cambridge University Press, 2005), 372. However, I see Plantinga writing in a vein older than the Cambridge Platonists, namely, that of Augustine (who inspired both Calvin and the Cambridge Platonists). We should note that while Plantinga uses *language* that often seems opposed to Lewis or Christian Platonists in general, this is just that: language. For example, though Plantinga speaks harshly about those seeking "evidence" for God's existence, he does not mean that belief in God is therefore groundless or irrational: he simply means we do not need a philosophical argument in order to be justified in believing in God's existence – something with which Lewis agreed: "And in fact, the man who accepts Christianity always thinks he has good evidence; whether like Dante, *fisci e metafisici argomenti*, or historical evidence, or the evidence of religious experience, or authority, or all these together." C. S. Lewis, "On Obstinacy in Belief," in *C. S. Lewis: Essay Collection & Other Short Pieces*, ed. Lesley Walmsley (London: HarperCollins, 2000), 208.

not nearly so far from Calvinist interpretations of the Fall as some – including Lewis himself – might think.

To begin with, since Lewis and Calvinists will generally agree that justice means treating each as it ought to be treated (wherein the value of each thing or person is given by either God's free choice or flow from a necessary aspect of God's very nature), God, being the greatest person, ought to be loved above all else. However, since man loved himself (the inferior) more than God (the superior), man committed injustice or sin. As a result, God justly cursed man in kind in that *all* that is subordinate to man now rebels against him: his mind, will and emotions rebel within; his body, once immortal, now rebels against his immortal soul in that his body is now susceptible to diseases and death; animals and the entire natural world threaten man and make his life difficult; and man's children – who are rightly subordinate to him – properly inherit the curse called original sin (of which, as we shall see, there are at least two views).

Now those who are familiar with Lewis's writings will want to stop me here, demanding to see the evidence of Lewis's supposed agreement with Calvinists in regard to the scope of the Fall – after all, did Lewis not explicitly reject the doctrine of Total Depravity?

> The doctrine of Total Depravity – when the consequence is drawn that, since we are totally depraved, our idea of good is worth simply nothing – may thus turn Christianity into a form of devil-worship. . . . [Consequently] I disbelieve [in Total Depravity] partly on the logical ground that if our depravity were total we should not know ourselves to be depraved, and partly because experience shows us much goodness in human nature.[24]

Quite rightly, Calvinists will be upset with Lewis's understanding and rejection of the "T" in their theological TULIP since what Lewis has described is *not* Total Depravity at all but rather *utter depravity*, which Calvinists, just as much as Lewis, reject.[25] That is, both Lewis and Calvinists agree that *all* that is below man was touched by the curse of the Fall ("Since the Fall, no organization or way of life whatsoever has a natural tendency to go right"[26]), yet both agree that in spite of this curse, fallen man and the rest of creation still bear the marks of their Creator.

Specifically in regard to man, Lewis believes that unregenerated man – *without* acknowledging God as the source of Truth – can still discover Truth:

---

24 C. S. Lewis, *The Problem of Pain*, in *C. S. Lewis: Selected Books* [Long Edition] (London: HarperCollins, 1999), 487, 503.
25 Sproul, *What Is Reformed Theology?* 117.
26 C. S. Lewis, "The Sermon and the Lunch," in *C. S. Lewis: Essay Collection & Other Short Pieces*, ed. Lesley Walmsley (London: HarperCollins, 2000), 343.

> As regards the Fall, I submit that the general tenor of Scripture does not encourage us to believe that our knowledge of the Law has been depraved in the same degree as our power to fulfill it. . . . Our righteousness may be filthy and ragged; but Christianity gives us no ground for holding that our perceptions of right are in the same condition. They may, no doubt, be impaired; but there is a difference between imperfect sight and blindness. A theology which goes about to represent our practical reason as radically unsound is heading for disaster.[27]

Some Calvinists, particularly presuppositionalists of the Van Tillian sort, will challenge this, claiming that without acknowledging God as the source of Truth, no one can say *anything* truthful. But surely this is a confusion between epistemology (believing that God exists) and metaphysics (God being the ground of all rationality).[28] Alvin Plantinga comments,

> According to John Calvin, 'As soon as ever we depart from Christ, there is nothing, be it ever so gross or insignificant in itself, respecting which we are not necessarily deceived.' Perhaps Calvin means only what we have already noted: one who doesn't know God fails to know the most important truth about anything else. He may mean to go even further, however: perhaps he means to say that those who don't know God suffer much wider ranging cognitive deprivation and, in fact, don't really have any knowledge at all. . . . That seems a shade harsh, particularly because many who don't believe in God seem to know a great deal more about some topics than most believers do. (Could I sensibly claim, for example, that I know more logic than, say, Willard van Orman Quine, even if I can't do any but the simplest logic exercises, on the grounds that at any rate I know *something* about logic and he, being an unbeliever, knows nothing at all about that subject or indeed anything else?). As it stands, this suggestion is desperately wide

---

27 C. S. Lewis, "The Poison of Subjectivism," in *C. S. Lewis: Essay Collection & Other Short Pieces*, ed. Lesley Walmsley (London: HarperCollins, 2000), 663.
28 As Reformed philosopher Kelly James Clark insists, "But many Christian apologists believe that even for the atheist to know something, her cognitive faculties must have been designed by God; even for the atheist the *ontological fact* of God's existence is necessary for knowledge (but not the *epistemological awareness* of God). It does not follow that atheists must be aware of God's existence or submit to God's authority in order to know things. Although they deny the existence of God, their other cognitive faculties were nonetheless designed by God to produce true beliefs. So the atheist can know that the sky is blue, that 2 + 2 = 4, and that she had porridge for breakfast, even if she does not believe that God exists." Kelly James Clark, "Reformed Epistemology Apologetics," in *Five Views on Apologetics*, ed. Stanley Gundry and Steven Cowan, 265-313 (Grand Rapids, MI: Zondervan, 2000), 258.

of the mark.²⁹

Thus, presumably what Van Tillians *want to say* is precisely what Lewis says: that God's existence is the necessary condition for human thought to be possible, but if one wants to grow in rationality, one needs to know that God exists, for knowledge without knowledge of God is always knowledge, in the ultimate sense, out of context and hence misleading in ultimate matters.

That is the *mind* of fallen or unregenerated man, but what about his *will*? Lewis was a libertarian in respect to the will, meaning he believed that created persons can, though usually will not, choose to act against their strongest desires. Thus, even if fallen man's corrupt or unjust desires were always stronger than his proper or just ones, he could still choose to act contrary to them.

But Lewis went further than this, insisting that fallen man's desire for injustice, falsity or the self-above-all-else isn't always stronger than his desire for Justice, Truth or God. Man is fallen – he is born with original sin – but original sin is neither the same as chosen sin nor is it irresistible. For instance, in *The Last Battle*, a pagan named Emeth, who, at least some of the time, *really* loved Truth and Justice ("*Emeth*" is the Hebrew word for "Truth"), was shown to have really loved Aslan / Christ indirectly.³⁰ And in essay after essay, Lewis wrote much the same thing:

> The Christian doctrine that there is no 'salvation' by works done according to the moral law is a fact of daily experience. . . . If the new Self, the new Will, does not come at His own good pleasure to be born in us, we cannot produce Him synthetically. The price of Christ is something, in a way, much easier than moral effort – it is to want Him. *It is true that the wanting itself would be beyond our power but for one fact.* The world is so built that, to help us desert our own satisfactions, they desert us. War and trouble and finally old age take from us one by one all those things that the natural Self hoped for at its setting out. Begging is our only wisdom, and want in the end makes it easier for us to be beggars. Even on those terms the Mercy will receive us.³¹

Now here many Calvinists (following the later Augustine) will probably disagree with Lewis, insisting that while fallen man still has free will, free will isn't libertarian, but is rather compatibilist, meaning that man must *always*

---

29 Alvin Plantinga, *Warranted Christian Belief* (Oxford: Oxford University Press, 2000), 217.
30 C. S. Lewis, *The Last Battle* (London: Fontana, 1985), 153-157. Cf. "We all know there have been good men who were not Christians; men like Socrates and Confucius . . ." C. S. Lewis, "Man or Rabbit?" in *C. S. Lewis: Essay Collection & Other Short Pieces*, ed. Lesley Walmsley (London: HarperCollins, 2000), 354.
31 C. S. Lewis, "Three Kinds of Men," in *C. S. Lewis: Essay Collection & Other Short Pieces*, ed. Lesley Walmsley (London: HarperCollins, 2000), 316 (emphasis mine).

act on his strongest desire, and, moreover, because man's strongest desire is *always* for injustice, falsity and the self-above-all-else, fallen man can never love Justice, Truth or God. As Calvin says, "In this way, then, man is said to have free will, not because he has a free choice of good and evil, but because he acts voluntarily, and not by compulsion."[32] The conclusion, then, appears to be that all acts of justice and mercy that a fallen man performs – including a father giving his life for his child – are not, in fact, acts of justice and mercy at all: these acts *appear* to be acts of justice and mercy but since the desire or intention behind them is still aimed at an *unjust* or *inordinate* love of self, such acts are not real acts of justice and mercy. They are acts of "civic virtue," not real virtue.[33]

Nevertheless, a minority of very prominent Calvinists, such as Alvin Plantinga and Nicholas Wolterstorff, side with Lewis in rejecting this interpretation. Seeing a legitimate analogy between the mind's fallen, but not utterly fallen, state, and the will's fallen, but not utterly fallen, state, Plantinga says of unregenerated man, "We are prone to hate God but, confusingly, in some way also inclined to love and seek him; we are prone to hate our neighbour, to see her as a competitor for scarce goods, but also, paradoxically, to prize her and love her."[34] Wolterstorff is even more blunt in rejecting compatibilism.[35]

As regards the Fall, then, there is some disagreement between Lewis and some Calvinists over unregenerated man's ability both to know things and to desire Truth, Justice and God. However, some Calvinists, like Plantinga and Wolterstorff, are on the same page as Lewis in this respect, and so the overall disagreement between Lewis and Calvinists on the Fall shouldn't be exaggerated.

REDEMPTION

All orthodox Christians, including Lewis and Calvinists, insist that the chief blueprint for determining how to live our lives is the Bible, the God-inspired text of special revelation. Nevertheless, all orthodox Christians, Lewis and Calvinists alike, will reject the "narrow scripturalism" that denies that God also reveals a lot of Himself and His creational laws through general revelation.[36]

---

32 Calvin, *Institutes of the Christian Religion*, 131.
33 Sproul, *What Is Reformed Theology?* 102.
34 Plantinga, *Warranted Christian Belief*, 210.
35 Nicholas Wolterstorff, *Justice in Love* (Grand Rapids, MI: Eerdmans, 2011), 268.
36 Lewis, *Poetry and Prose in the Sixteenth Century*, 459. Lewis never saw a conflict between special revelation and general revelation, though often these two might *appear* to be at odds. When asked by Calvin College trained philosopher John Beversluis whether he would be willing to apply God's absolute Goodness to the Old Testament, Lewis replied, "Yes. On my view one must apply something of the

Based on both special and general revelation, orthodox Christians agree *that* man cannot save himself. More specifically (and now based solely on special revelation), all orthodox Christians believe *that* God the Son became a man, died, rose, and offers, out of grace and mercy, forgiveness of sins to all who, out of faith, submit to Him. Genuine belief in this is probably what makes most Christians Christians – regardless of whether the person is Anglican, Catholic, Eastern Orthodox, Reformed or whatever.[37] Thus,

---

sort of explanation to, say, the atrocities of Joshua. I see the grave danger we run by doing so; but the danger of believing in a God whom we cannot but regard as evil, and then, in mere terrified flattery call Him 'good' and worship Him, is a still greater danger. The ultimate question is whether the doctrine of the goodness of God or that of the inerrancy of Scripture is to prevail when they conflict. I think the doctrine of the goodness of God is the more certain of the two. Indeed only that doctrine renders this worship of Him obligatory or even permissible. To this some will reply 'Ah, but we are fallen and don't recognize good when we see it.' But God Himself does not say we are as fallen as all that. He constantly, in Scripture, appeals to our conscience: 'Why do ye not of *yourselves* judge what is right?' – 'What fault hath my people found in Me?' and so on. Socrates' answer to Euthyphro is used in Christian form by Hooker. Things are not good because God commands them; God commands certain things because He sees them to be good. (In other words, the Divine will is the obedient servant of the Divine reason). The opposite view (Ockham's & Paley's) leads to the absurdity, if 'good' means simply 'what God wills' then to say 'God is good' can mean only 'God wills what He wills.' Which is equally true of you or me or Judas or Satan. But of course having said all this, we must apply it with fear and trembling. Some things which seem to us bad may be good. But we must not corrupt our consciences by trying to feel a thing as good when it seems to us totally evil. We can only pray that *if* there is an invisible goodness hidden in such things, God, in His own good time will enable us to see it. If we need to. For perhaps sometimes God's answer might be 'What is that to thee?' The passage may not be 'addressed to our (your or my) condition' at all." Lewis, *The Collected Letters of C. S. Lewis: Volume III*, 1437-1437 [July 3, 1963].

37 I say "most Christians" rather than "all Christians" since there is the important question about so-called "anonymous Christians," like the patriarchs of the Old Testament, for example, who didn't clearly know, and hence, believe, any of these things about Jesus. Their knowledge of God *qua* Jesus would have been lacking, but presumably they still loved God as God and Jesus, of course, is God. In this way, they would have loved, and had faith in, God directly, but God as Jesus indirectly. Knowledge of God as Jesus, it seems, is less important to salvation than the metaphysics of what God as Jesus did on Earth – hence the metaphysical statement: "I am the Way, the Truth and the Life, no one comes to the Father but through Me." If Jesus wasn't able to represent man, hadn't lived a morally perfect life, hadn't died and hadn't been resurrected, it wouldn't have mattered what people *believed*. The biblical evidence makes it clear: the metaphysics of Jesus's actions are more important than man's epistemological understanding of them.

keeping a clear distinction between the biblical *that* (the God-revealed fact) and the philosophical or theological *how* (the manmade explanation) is vital.

Now Calvinist theology is extremely systematic, which is what we should expect since its theological founder, John Calvin, was trained as a lawyer. Calvinist theology, therefore, prides itself "on understanding a doctrine in a coherent and unified manner . . . in discerning the interrelatedness of the teachings of Scripture itself."[38] Consequently, the *how* of saving faith is confidently extrapolated in Calvinism's TULIP, especially the U, L, I, and P of it. The idea is roughly this.

Before the creation of the world – before anyone was created, and *not* based on any foreknowledge He had about the *merit* or *desire* of future individuals – God elected, out of special grace, to save some, but not all, people from their injustice or sin: this is the "U" in TULIP – Unconditional Election. Connected to this is the flipside of the same coin: the doctrine of double predestination, wherein God simply chooses to pass over – not to extend a saving hand to – the rest of sinful humanity who *really* "sinned in Adam" (who are seen as having *chosen* Adam's injustice simply because they are his descendants), and so (even aborted children of non-Christian families) are *justly* damned. But even if the aborted child example is too much, it would still be the case that there are many who *never* had the ability to desire or choose God, and God, on this model, is considered *just* for damning them. These souls, so the logic goes, receive "justice," while the elect receive mercy. Consequently, Christ didn't die for *all* people, but only for those He elected to save: this is the "L" in TULIP – Limited Atonement. Moreover, the Holy Spirit inwardly testifies to the elect, giving them faith in terms of both saving knowledge of what Christ has done (namely, helping them to believe the most vital statements in the Bible) and a softened will such that they can – indeed, cannot do anything but – believe this testimony and knowledge: this is the "I" in TULIP – Irresistible Grace. And if the elect cannot – if it is beyond their free will to – resist God's grace, then it makes sense that the elect can never lose their salvation; they are eternally secure: this, of course, is the "P" in TULIP – the Perseverance of the Saints. Finally God's saints are those who enter into a covenant with Him – a covenant or agreement to be God's people and to continue the restorative work – the kingdom-building work, the work of regaining and healing *every aspect* of creation – which Christ began on the cross and will finish when He returns again.

What would Lewis say to all this, particularly the U, L, I and P of TULIP? On the surface, some might see him as a typical Arminian, believing that God wants to save all sinners but is frustrated in this because some sinners do not want to be saved; thus, Lewis writes things like, "I willingly believe

---

38 Sproul, *What Is Reformed Theology?* 23.

that the damned are, *in one sense,* successful rebels to the end; the doors of hell are locked on the inside."[39] However, those who have read the Oxford Don in more detail will soon see that this is not always clear.

To begin with, Lewis rarely used the biblical word "election," and when he did use it, it's not clear from his writings what he meant by it. Nevertheless, Lewis had no trouble admitting that God, being the perfection of Freedom, has the sovereign ability to assign greater or lesser value, or a greater or lesser destiny, to things He creates:

> It is idle to say that men are of equal value. If value is taken in a worldly sense – if we mean that all men are equally useful or beautiful or good or entertaining – then it is nonsense. If it means that all are of equal value as immortal souls then I think it conceals a dangerous error. The infinite value of each human soul is not a Christian doctrine. God did not die for man because of some value He perceived in him. The value of each human soul considered simply in itself, not of relation to God, is zero. As St Paul writes, to have died for valuable men would have been not divine but merely heroic; but God died for sinners. He loved us not because we were lovable, but because He is Love. It may be that He loves all equally – He certainly loved all to the death – and I am not certain what the expression means. If there is equality it is in His love, not in us.[40]

In keeping with this emphasis on God's sovereign choice, when a member of the Billy Graham Evangelistic Association asked Lewis, in true Arminian fashion, if he had "made a decision" to follow Jesus at the time of his conversion, Lewis replied in a Calvinistic manner, "I would not put it that way. What I wrote in *Surprised by Joy* was that 'before God closed in on me, I was in fact offered what now appears a moment of wholly free choice.' But I feel my decision was not so important. I was the object rather than the subject

---

39   Lewis, *The Problem of Pain*, 538.
40   C. S. Lewis, "Membership," in *C. S. Lewis: Essay Collection & Other Short Pieces*, ed. Lesley Walmsley (London: HarperCollins, 2000), 338. Cf. "We with our modern democratic and arithmetical presuppositions would so have liked and expected all men to start equal in their search for God. One has the picture of great centripetal roads coming from all directions, with well-disposed people, all meaning the same thing, and getting closer and closer together. How shockingly opposite to that is the Christian story! One people picked out of the whole Earth; that people purged and proved again and again. . . . The people who are selected are, in a sense, unfairly selected for a supreme honour; but it is also a supreme burden." C. S. Lewis, "The Grand Miracle," in *C. S. Lewis: Essay Collection & Other Short Pieces*, ed. Lesley Walmsley (London: HarperCollins, 2000), 7.

in this affair. *I was decided upon.*"[41] Clearly, Lewis perceived the Holy Spirit, through special grace (yes, he used the word[42]), making efforts to save him and having gone about doing so using whatever means – though particularly using his desire for Happiness (the argument from joy), Truth (the argument from reason) and Justice (the argument from morality) – to get him to the point of saving faith.

However, this is not Unconditional Election, for nowhere does Lewis say that desire or choice played *no* role in God's decision to set out to save him. Nevertheless, this silence on Lewis's part did *not* imply the Arminian opposite. It's significant that, true to "mere Christianity," Lewis intentionally tried not to take a strong position on this theological *how*, writing:

> What I *think* is this. Everyone looking back on *his own* conversion must feel – and I am sure the feeling is in some sense true – 'It is not *I* who

---

41 C. S. Lewis, "Cross-Examination," in *C. S. Lewis: Essay Collection & Other Short Pieces*, ed. Lesley Walmsley (London: HarperCollins, 2000), 553. Cf. "I never had the experience of looking for God. It was the other way round; He was the hunter (so it seemed to me) and I was the deer. He stalked me like a redskin, took unerring aim, and fired. . . . But it is significant that this long-evaded encounter happened at a time when I was making a serious effort to obey my conscience. No doubt it was far less serious than I supposed, but it was the most serious I had made for along time." C. S. Lewis, "The Seeing Eye," in *C.S. Lewis: Essay Collection & Other Short Pieces*, ed. Lesley Walmsley (London: HarperCollins, 2000), 60. Cf. "Only a bad person needs to repent: only a good person can repent perfectly. The worse you are the more you need it and the less you can do it. . . . Can we do it if God helps us? Yes, but what do we mean when we talk of God helping us? We mean God putting into us a bit of Himself, so to speak. He lends us a little of His reasoning powers and that is how we think: He puts a little of His love into us and that is how we love one another. When you teach a child writing, you hold its hand while it forms the letters: that is, it forms the letters because you are forming them. We love and reason because God loves and reasons and holds our hand while we do it. . . . I do not deny, of course, that on a certain level we may rightly speak of the soul's search for God, and of God as receptive of the soul's love: but in the long run the soul's search for God can only be a mode, or appearance . . . of His search for her, since all comes from Him, since the very possibility of our loving is His gift to us, and since our freedom is only a freedom of better or worse response. Hence I think that nothing marks off Pagan theism from Christianity so sharply as Aristotle's doctrine that God moves the universe, Himself unmoving, as the Beloved moves a lover. But for Christendom 'Herein is love, not that we loved God but that He loved us.'" Lewis, *Mere Christianity*, 356, 495.

42 "The operation of Faith is to retain, so far as the will and intellect are concerned, what is irresistible and obvious during the moments of special grace." C. S. Lewis, "Is Theism Important?" in *C. S. Lewis: Essay Collection & Other Short Pieces*, ed. Lesley Walmsley (London: HarperCollins, 2000), 57.

have done this. I did not choose Christ: He chose me. It is all free grace, which I have done nothing to earn.' That is the Pauline account: and I am sure it is the only true account of every conversion *from the inside*. Very well. It then seems to us logical & natural to turn this personal experience into a general rule 'All conversions depend on God's choice.'

But this I believe is exactly what we must not do: for generalizations are legitimate only when we are dealing with matters to which our faculties are adequate. Here, we are not. How our individual experiences are in reality consistent with (a) Our idea of Divine justice, (b) The parable [of the sheep and goats: Matt. 25:30-46, in which "all depends on works"] is not clear. What is clear is that *we* can't find a consistent formula. I think we must take a leaf out of the scientists' book. They are quite familiar with the fact that, for example, Light has to be regarded *both* as a wave in the ether and as a stream of particles. No one can make these two views consistent. *Of course reality must be self-consistent: but till (if ever) we can see the consistency it is better to hold two inconsistent views than to ignore one side of the evidence.*

The real inter-relation between God's omnipotence and Man's freedom is something we can't find out. Looking at the Sheep & the Goats every man can be quite sure that every kind act he does will be accepted by Christ. Yet, equally we all do feel sure that all the good in us comes from Grace. We have to leave it at that. I find the best plan is to take the Calvinist view of my own virtues and other people's vices: and the other view of my own vices and other people's virtues. But though there is much to be *puzzled* about, there is nothing to be *worried* about. It is plain from Scripture that, in whatever sense the Pauline doctrine is true, it is not true in any sense that *excludes* its (apparent) opposite.[43]

Writing as a literary historian, Lewis went further, insisting that the problem with Calvinism's Unconditional Election and subsequent Limited Atonement is that these doctrines are indicative of overconfidence in man's ability to discern theological truths from particular biblical statements. Thus, for example, Lewis speaks of "straw-splitting dialogues in Calvinist theology"[44] and considers the puritan Thomas Cartwright "twisted by dangerous

---

43 Lewis, *The Collected Letters of C. S. Lewis: Volume III*, 354-355 [August 3, 1953]. According to Lewis, the paradox of God's grace and man's free will is an instance of "transposition or adaption from a richer to a poorer medium." Because of God's perfect nature, there are countless examples of man not able to clearly perceive God and what He wants to say. C. S. Lewis, "Transposition," in *C. S. Lewis: Essay Collection & Other Short Pieces*, ed. Lesley Walmsley (London: HarperCollins, 2000), 271.
44 Lewis, *The Collected Letters of C. S. Lewis: Volume III*, 1265 [May 9, 1961].

certitude,"[45] for even though the Holy Spirit gives us faith in terms of deeper knowledge of Himself, this does not meant that every biblical statement will be equally apparent to the elect. Calvinists are right in asserting that God's creation is rationally ordered and that the elect will see more of this rational order than others (hence they are right in emphasizing *some* systematization), but they – or at least some, including Cartwright and even Calvin himself – are mistaken in thinking that the elect will therefore have knowledge – as opposed to mere opinion – of the true meaning of obscure biblical passages dealing with election and the scope of the atonement. Speaking of the early Reformers, Lewis remarks,

> Propositions originally framed with the sole purpose of praising the Divine compassion as boundless, hardly credible, and utterly gratuitous, build up, when extrapolated and systematized, into something that sounds not unlike devil-worship. . . . In it Calvin goes on from the original Protestant experience to build a system, to extrapolate, to raise all the dark questions and *give without flinching* the dark answers.[46]

Thus, in regard to election and the scope of the atonement, Lewis at once rejected the Calvinist understanding of divine justice yet also refused to embrace the Arminian alternative, preferring to relegate this to what theologians call "mystery" or remain temporarily agnostic in respect to the precise relation between God's and man's actions.

Unsurprisingly, therefore, Lewis was similarly divided in respect to the doctrine of Irresistible Grace. On the one hand, he does speak of God's "irresistible . . . grace" in certain respects,[47] but on the other hand, because he was a libertarian in respect to man's free will,[48] it seems more likely than not that he would have rejected the doctrine of Irresistible Grace (since a consistent libertarian would probably say that God can only *woo* the elect to saving faith, rather than *drag* them to it). However, since there are Calvinists who are libertarians – Plantinga and Wolsterstorff are two such – it seems that insofar as we allow Plantinga and Wolterstorff to call themselves Calvinists, that some Calvinists, too, can question some of the petals of TULIP.[49]

---

45 C. S. Lewis, *Poetry and Prose in the Sixteenth Century*, vol. 4, *The Oxford History of English Literature* (Oxford: Clarendon Press, 1997), 446.
46 Lewis, *Poetry and Prose in the Sixteenth Century*, 33, 43 (emphasis mine).
47 Lewis, "Is Theism Important?" 57.
48 "If what our will does [is] not 'voluntary,' and if 'voluntary' does not mean 'free,' what are we talking about?" Lewis, *The Collected Letters of C. S. Lewis: Volume III*, 237-238 [October 20, 1952].
49 "If a person is free with respect to a given action, then he is free to perform that action and free to refrain from performing it; no antecedent conditions and / or causal laws determine that he will perform the action, or that he won't." Plantinga, *The*

As regards the doctrine of the Perseverance of the Saints, Lewis, on the one hand, seems to deny it, saying things like

> The world does not consist of 100 percent Christians or a 100 percent non-Christians. There are people . . . who are slowly ceasing to be Christians but who still call themselves by that name. . . . There are other people who are slowly becoming Christians though they do not yet call themselves so. There are people who do not accept the full Christian doctrine about Christ but who are so strongly attracted by Him that they are His in a much deeper sense than they themselves understand. There are people in other religions who are being led *by God's secret influence* to concentrate on those parts of their religion which are in agreement with Christianity, and who thus belong to Christ without knowing it.⁵⁰

This said, on the other hand, there is nothing in this quotation at odds with the doctrine of the Perseverance of Saints *provided that* Lewis's "Christians" are only Christians so-called from man's perspective and not from God's. However, if Lewis means something stronger than this – that a man who at one point in his life had saving faith but that he has now lost it – then this quotation would be incompatible with the doctrine. As it stands, however, Lewis's precise meaning is ambiguous, though I think it can easily be read alongside the following words of a Calvinist like Plantinga:

> Those who don't share our commitment to the Lord are in transition, just as we are. As Calvin says, there is unbelief within the breast of every Christian; but isn't there also belief within the breast of every non-Christian? The antithesis is of course real; but at any time in history it is also less than fully articulated and developed. The City of God stands opposed to the City of the World: sure enough; but we all live in God's world, and those in the City of the World are subject to the promptings and blandishments of our God-given natures, of the *Sensus Divinitatis*, and of the Holy Spirit. Were the two cities completely formed and articulated, they could have little intellectual commerce or contact with each other. The believer would see the world a certain way, or perhaps in one of a certain range of ways; the unbeliever would see it quite differently, and feel no unease or discomfort in seeing it his way. . . . *But the cities, and the citizens therein, are not completely formed and developed.*⁵¹

Although Lewis ranges from temporarily agnostic to mildly hostile

---

Analytic Theist, 26.
50   Lewis, *Mere Christianity*, 455.
51   Plantinga, *The Analytic Theist*, 346-347 (emphasis mine).

toward the U, L, I and P of TULIP, this is also the case for some Calvinists, such as Plantinga and Wolterstorff. Perhaps the reason that Plantinga and Wolterstorff see themselves as free to reject parts of TULIP and still call themselves Calvinists is that they prefer to speak of themselves as "neo-Calvinists" or "Kuyperians." Neo-Calvinists are those who see Calvinism more about worldview or the total scope of creation, fall and redemption than about the particular theological doctrines of TULIP. Of course, the neo-Calvinist view of redemption usually does embrace TULIP, but it doesn't have to: biblical scope and Christian integrity are what matter more. As Wolterstorff recounts about his own experience:

> Doctrine and theological discussion have always been prominent in the Dutch Reformed tradition. But the professors who inspired me at Calvin College were not theologians.... [The professors who inspired me] had imbibed the mentality and spirituality of Abraham Kuyper.... What they instilled in us, their students, was Kuyper's neo-Calvinism. If I had to put into as few words as possible what that mentality and spirituality were, it would go something like this: God's call to those who are Christ's followers is to participate in the life of the church and to think, feel, speak, and act as Christians within the institutions and practices that we share with our fellow human beings.... Christian faith is not an add-on.[52]

In respect to redemption, Christ's redemptive work isn't just about saving souls, but is also about restoring all of creation. Redeemed man is supposed to play a part in regaining paradise – in furthering the kingdom of God and helping Him restore creation to its former splendour. And insofar as Calvinism in its neo-Calvinist form aims at this, Lewis completely agrees.

True, Lewis's conception of the New Earth may be more Lutheran than Calvinist (in that the Old Earth is destroyed and rebuilt, rather than being healed *per se*[53]); and true, Lewis, as a Christian Platonist,[54] had a slightly distorted idea of the afterlife, occasionally speaking of Christians "going to Heaven" rather than peopling the New Earth. Nevertheless, on the whole, Lewis and Calvinists agree that regenerate man becomes a creature infused

---

52   Nicholas Wolterstorff, *Hearing the Call: Liturgy, Justice, Church and World*, ed. Mark Gornik and Gregory Thompson (Grand Rapids, MI: Eerdmans, 2011), 431.
53   Lewis, *The Last Battle*, 141-161.
54   "Revelation does *not* give us a picture of Christians suddenly transported out of this world to live a spiritual existence in heaven forever.... This view of the end is the result of the combination of biblical teaching with pagan Greek philosophy in the early centuries of the church. It is especially in Augustine's early work, harmonizing Scripture with Neoplatonic philosophy." Craig Bartholomew and Michael Goheen, *The Drama of Scripture* (Grand Rapids, MI: BakerAcademic, 2004), 211, 231.

with new life and understanding with which he can act as God's agent in creational and cultural transformation.

This new knowledge or understanding – Herman Dooyeweerd's "the religious fullness of meaning,"[55] Dirk Vollenhoven's "Christian logic,"[56] or Lewis's "the correction of reason"[57] – needs to be applied to kingdom-building – to acting Christianly toward *all* aspects of creation. Thus, Lewis said things like, "What we want is not more little books on Christianity, but more little books by Christians on other subjects – with their Christianity *latent*;"[58] and,

> The work of a Beethoven, and the work of a charwoman, become spiritual on precisely the same condition, that of being offered to God, of being done humbly 'as to the Lord.' This does not, of course, mean that it is for anyone a mere toss-up whether he should sweep rooms or compose symphonies. A mole must dig to the glory of God and a cock must crow. We are members of one body, but differentiated members, each with his own vocation.[59]

In this way, Lewis and Calvinists oppose "a moderated religion" that falsely separates the world into realms where Christianity is appropriate and where it is inappropriate.[60] Since God is sovereign over all, all aspects of creation need to be subjugated to Him. Although Lewis and most Calvinists believe that Christians and non-Christians can find common ground (since both are made in the image of God and both retain something of that image and its ability to hear God's general revelation), Lewis and Calvinists vehemently reject the notion that Christianity is only for Sundays or only for priests: "The application of Christian principles, say, to trade unionism or education, must

---

55 Herman Dooyeweerd, *The Necessary Presuppositions of Philosophy*, vol. 4, *A New Critique of Theoretical Thought* (Lewistown, NY: Edwin Mellen Press, 1997), 101.
56 Vollenhoven uses this word in *The Necessity of a Christian Logic*. See Al Wolters, "Dutch neo-Calvinism: Worldview, Philosophy and Rationality," http://www.allofliferedeemed.co.uk/Wolters/AMWNeo_Cal.pdf (accessed on June 13, 2010).
57 C. S. Lewis, "*De Futilitate*," in *C. S. Lewis: Essay Collection & Other Short Works*, ed. Lesley Walmsley (London: HarperCollins, 2000), 678.
58 C. S. Lewis, "Christian Apologetics," in *C. S. Lewis: Essay Collection & Other Short Pieces* (London: HarperCollins, 2000), 150.
59 C. S. Lewis, "Learning in Wartime," in *C. S. Lewis: Essay Collection & Other Short Pieces*, ed. Lesley Walmsley (London: HarperCollins, 2000), 583.
60 As the devil Screwtape says, "A moderated religion is as good for us [devils] as no religion at all – and more amusing." C. S. Lewis, *The Screwtape Letters*, in *C. S. Lewis: Selected Books* [Long Edition] (London: HarperCollins, 1999), 759. Cf. "Jesus Christ did not say, 'go into all the world and tell the world that it is quite right.' The Gospel is something completely different. In fact, it is directly opposed to the world." C. S. Lewis, "Cross-Examination," 556.

come from Christian trade unionists and Christian schoolmasters: just as Christian literature comes from Christian novelists and dramatists – not from the bench of bishops getting together and trying to write plays and novels in their spare time."[61] Both Lewis and Calvinists seek to be in the world but not of the world and in all things to glorify God.

So in respect to redemption, Lewis agrees with Calvinists on the centrality of Scripture and the kingdom-building task, but has his reservations about the U, L, I and P of TULIP, preferring – because he strongly insists on separating biblical *thats* from philosophical and theological *hows* – to remain temporarily agnostic about many, though not all, of these doctrines. Thus, while Lewis disagrees with some Calvinists on some aspects of redemption, there are a few Calvinists – usually neo-Calvinist philosophers like Plantinga and Wolterstorff – who feel more or less the same as Lewis on these matters, and so, once again, differences between Lewis and Calvinists shouldn't be overstated.

CONCLUSION

Is C. S. Lewis, as he self-confesses, Calvinist "slush,"[62] or is he, as he says of Shakespeare in contrast to the Calvinists of his day, "gloriously anomalous?"[63] That is for the reader to decide. For my part, I have tried to emphasize Christian unity – to set aside misunderstandings and exaggerations in order to show that Lewis and Calvinists belong to the same orthodox family,[64] and,

---

61 Lewis, *Mere Christianity*, 374. Cf. "If any man, in some little corner out of the reach of the omnicompetent [government], can make or preserve a really Christian school . . . his duty is plain." C. S. Lewis, "On the Transmission of Christianity," in *C. S. Lewis: Essay Collection & Other Short Pieces*, ed. Lesley Walmsley (London: HarperCollins, 2000), 615.
62 C. S. Lewis, *The Collected Letters of C. S. Lewis: Volume II; Books, Broadcasts, and the War 1931-1949*, ed. Walter Hooper (San Francisco: HarperSanFrancisco, 2004), 351 [February 18, 1940].
63 "Of course not all Calvinists were puritans. Nor am I suggesting that the great fighting puritans who risked ruin and torture in their attack on the bishops were merely conforming to a fashion. We must distinguish a hard core of puritans and a much wider circle of those who were, at varying levels, affected by Calvinism. But a certain severity . . . was diffused even through the wider circle, in the sense that denunciation of vice became part of the stock-in-trade of fashionable and even frivolous writers. . . . The gentleness and candour of Shakespeare's mind has impressed all his readers. But it impresses us still more the more we study the general tone of sixteenth-century literature. He is gloriously anomalous." Lewis, *Poetry and Prose in the Sixteenth Century*, 43.
64 Thus, I agree with Alvin Plantinga, who writes, "The *Lebenswelt* of Richard Rorty or Jacques Derrida is quite different from that of Herman Dooyeweerd or C.

what's more, that their theological disagreements are not, or do not have to be, as large as Lewis and many Calvinists think. If we can get past both Lewis's uncharacteristic malice (saying that certain Calvinists are comparable to "devil worshippers" or "magicians"[65]), and certain Calvinist tendencies to exaggerate man's depravity, ignore problems of divine justice and exalt manmade theological formulae to the same level as clear biblical statements, then this chapter will have served its purpose.

S. Lewis. . . . We Christians have *real* enemies in the contemporary world; we do not need to fight each other." Plantinga, *The Analytic Theist*, 332, 349.
65 "In the magician and the astrologer we saw a readiness either to exaggerate or to minimize the power and dignity of Man. Calvinism perhaps satisfies both inclinations by plunging the unregenerate man as deep as the astrologers and exalting the elect as highly as the magicians." Lewis, *Poetry and Prose in the Sixteenth Century*, 49-50.

Chapter Two

From Teaching to Hypnosis to *Inception*: Reflections on the Ethics of Idea-Giving

Inception is a movie about idea-giving, specifically, about "inception" or the act of an "extractor" or dream navigator planting an idea in the mind of his unknowing, dreaming subject. Because idea-giving is a normative act or an act having to do with what's morally right or wrong, inception is also a normative act; as Dom Cobb tells Saito, "You asked me for inception. I do hope you understand the gravity of that request. The seed that we will plant in this man's mind will grow into an idea and this idea will define him. It may come to change everything about him."

In this chapter, I want to explore the ethics of inception vis-à-vis the ethics of idea-giving in general and teaching and hypnosis – arguably the two most important methods of idea-giving – in particular.

IS ALL TEACHING INDOCTRINATION?

Convinced by existential and postmodern epistemologies, some philosophers of education have argued that *all* forms of teaching – the most typical method of idea-giving – are immoral since *whatever* is selected to be taught is nothing but the subjective preference of a particular individual or culture. These philosophers would say, for example, that the mere fact that Cobb teaches his young children, James and Philippe, that "This world is the real world" or even "Tokyo is a city in Japan" is to violate his children's right to choose to believe whatever they want.

Wisely, few take this view too seriously, for to do so would be to point out an inherent contradiction, namely, that the philosophy that asserts "All forms of teaching are immoral" is a philosophy that asserts a proposition it thinks *true* and should be *imposed* on all: to insist that total freedom is the only way to avoid immoral idea-giving is to impose an idea ("All forms of teaching are immoral"), which, according to this view, is itself immoral.

It follows, then, that Cobb the parent can't avoid giving *some* ideas to his children. Moreover, the ideas he gives his children will unavoidably be filtered through his own worldview. For example, if Cobb were a Buddhist, he would believe that the goal of life is to escape the cycle of reincarnation or *samsara*, which can be achieved by adhering to the Eightfold Path, one principle of which states that knowledge of our circumstances is beneficial to such an escape; consequently, because Cobb, in our example, would be a Buddhist and not, for instance, a Hindu, he would likely think Buddhism to be truer or more correct than Hinduism (which is why he is a Buddhist and not a Hindu or even an agnostic, who thinks all religions are equally true and equally false). Thus, believing the Buddhist worldview to be truer than other worldviews, Cobb would very likely teach this worldview to James and Philippe.

However, educator I. A. Snook would argue that for Cobb to engage in this form of idea-giving is immoral since "teaching for belief in religious propositions is always indoctrination."[1] Snook's problem is that our hypothetical Cobb is immoral for teaching his children particular *content*, namely, religious content. Yet if teaching religious propositions were the problem, as Snook believes, then one would be faced with two huge difficulties. What is a religious proposition? And why is teaching these beliefs immoral?

To begin with, no one agrees what a religion *is*. If a religion is, as one dictionary has it, "a set of beliefs concerning the cause, nature and purpose of the universe, especially when considered as the creation of a superhuman agency or agencies," then how is metaphysical materialism – presumably Snook's worldview – not a religion? After all, it, just as much as Buddhism, Hinduism, Christianity and so on, maintains the world came to be through forces beyond human control and certainly has an account of the cause of the universe (the big bang theory), the nature of the universe (everything is material), and the purpose of the universe (there is no purpose). Even the agnostic – if Snook happened to be this – could easily be fitted into this definition of religion. Thus, it seems that *every* worldview is a religion, and so *every* proposition will be understood from one particular worldview or religious perspective or another.

Consequently, though eventually I will argue that teaching some *content* may be immoral, content isn't really the point. Philosopher R. M. Hare believes "indoctrination only begins when we are trying to stop the growth in our children of the capacity to think for themselves."[2] According to Hare, an indoctrinated child or person is one who has been given ideas and told to believe them regardless of the evidence – to slavishly accept a proposition or

---

1 I. A. Snook, *Indoctrination and Education* (London: Routledge & Kegan Paul, 1972), 74.
2 R. M. Hare, "Adolescents into Adults," in *Aims in Education: The Philosophic Approach*, ed. T. H. B. Hollins, 47-70 (Manchester: Manchester University Press, 1964), 52.

series of propositions in a fashion that disregards his or her autonomy and eliminates critical openness. For Hare, the problem isn't so much the *content* of the teaching, but rather the *method* of the teaching. For example, if Cobb were to teach his children that the Four Noble Truths are beyond question – to teach James and Philippe that it's unacceptable to reflect critically upon the truth of these claims – then, according to Hare, Cobb would be indoctrinating or engaging in immoral idea-giving.

While Hare certainly seems to be on the right path, he overlooks something that Plato, Aristotle and modern educational psychologists all insist upon: a child's rationality *develops*. Because a young child like James or Philippe – let's say a child under or around the age of five – can only reason on a very rudimentary level, the child won't really be able to challenge the beliefs given to him or her. James and Philippe wouldn't really be able to challenge the Buddhist ideas given to them by their dad, and so they would likely, for a time, make these beliefs their own. There is no avoiding this. Buddhism, then, would become James and Philippe's "plausibility structure," and this, in itself, would both be moral and, indeed, necessary for healthy growth: a tree can't grow in a vacuum; it needs soil, even, if it were the case, contaminated soil.[3]

However, what would be immoral is if Cobb failed to encourage rational development in his children – if he failed to give them the tools of logic that would allow them *eventually* to understand the reasons for and against Buddhism and then to accept or reject Buddhism based on their rational autonomy. "Eventually," of course, neither denotes a set age or time nor does it indicate a clear, black-and-white argument for-and-against. It's a process. Therefore, if, when James and Philippe are ready to start school, Cobb were to enrol them in a Buddhist school, he wouldn't necessarily be acting immorally since within the context of the Buddhist school, the children could learn how to reason critically while at the same time learning how a Buddhist might view history, literature, other worldviews, and so on. Secular humanist parents could send their children to secular humanist schools, Christians to Christian schools, Hindus to Hindu schools and, provided that they were being taught by the schools (and, of course, the parents) to reflect critically on what is being taught and given the freedom to accept or reject what is taught, none of these parents and schools should, in themselves, be seen as indoctrinating.

Nevertheless, if Cobb were a Buddhist, then he would very likely also believe certain Buddhist propositions or content which, if *taught*, could easily be seen as immoral, namely, any content maintaining that the principles of logic are relative and autonomy illusionary (Buddhists teach that principles of logic, such as the Law of Identity, are subjective, and that there is no self and

---

3   Peter Berger and T. Luckmann, *The Social Construction of Reality: A Treatise on the Sociology of Knowledge* (New York: Doubleday, 1966), 154.

hence no free will). Thus, if teaching is to be separated from indoctrination, some objective truths must be asserted and passed on, for if not, then the children won't be given the tools needed to challenge the worldview they are raised in.

Some, of course, will argue that to assert any objectivity, much less genuine autonomy, is to assert something that is relative or subjective to a particular worldview. I deny this. While all work from within a worldview, not all truth claims asserted from within a worldview are relative or dependent on that worldview being true as whole. If nothing is self-evident, nothing can be proven. Some truths such as 1 + 1 = 2, "It's always wrong to torture a child for fun," and the Law of Identity are immediately seen to be self-evident once we understand the terms, and there is no way for these propositions to be false. Even if everyone on the planet thought 1 + 1 = 2 is a social construct, this would not make it so. They would be wrong. Even if some, such as serial killers, thought it okay to torture children for fun, they would be *wrong* – not because most of society agrees, but because it is plainly and simply wrong. We know these truths by what the ancient Egyptians called *Ma'at*, the ancient Iranians, *Asha*, the ancient Hindus', *Rita*, Confucius, "the Way of Heaven" or *Tao*, Plato, the Form of Goodness, the Stoics, Natural Law, and Protestants, the general revelation of God. C. S. Lewis considers educating people in these truths as natural as "grown birds . . . teaching young birds to fly," and surely he is right.[4]

Cobb, then, ought to teach James and Philippe objective truths, especially the principles of critical reasoning, since either to suppress these or simply to neglect them would be directly, or indirectly through negligence, to indoctrinate. Moreover, if Cobb were to teach his children that free will is an illusion, this would seriously discourage his children from thinking about what they have been taught: if all is illusionary or determined, then why bother even trying to change what you've been taught? Indeed, here we could even agree with Descartes and others that the proposition "I have free will" is a truth clearly and distinctly perceived.

IS ALL HYPNOTISM IMMORAL?

Since *critical openness* and *autonomy* are essential in separating teaching from indoctrination, we have nearly all the tools and examples needed to tackle the ethics of inception itself. Nevertheless, one more example, this time from a more extreme idea-giving method – hypnotism – will crystallize what has been argued thus far.

---

4   C. S. Lewis, *The Abolition of Man; or, Reflections on Education*, in *C. S. Lewis: Selected Books* [Short Edition] (London: HarperCollins, 2002), 407.

Just as most people have the wrong idea about the connection between indoctrination and religion, so most have the wrong idea about hypnotism and control. Because of popular culture, most imagine the hypnotist to be akin to a magician who through sheer personality or magical ability seizes control of his subject and then force-feeds an idea to him or her. The hypnotist is seen as wholly active; the subject, wholly passive. But this view of hypnotism is an exaggeration, and arises due to misunderstanding, to some extent, its forerunner: spirit-possession and exorcism.[5]

In the ancient (and not so ancient) world, there are recorded cases of people being possessed or overcome by spirits, apparently against their wills. There is nothing philosophically impossible about this since naked spirits have of themselves (though always with the permission, if not the desire, of God) the ability to manipulate lower nature (including human nature). For example, in the Bible, we read both about the Spirit of God coming over certain men in moments of spontaneous prophecy,[6] and about the occasional evil spirit or demon possessing people, including young girls.[7] In none of these cases do the possessed appear to have agreed to be indwelt (God's indwelling being just, the demon's, unjust[8]).

However, for the most part, these are the exceptions, not the rule. Much more commonly, people who were possessed or indwelt by spirits weren't forced against their will to give their bodies and minds over to the more powerful spirit: typically, the shaman *invites* the spirit to take control of him; the witch makes an *agreement* with the demon; and the Christian *asks* the Holy Spirit to live in him. Likewise, in hypnotism, the subject must *be open* to the hypnotist: "Without the right attitude – motivation, expectations and willingness – the subject will not experience hypnosis."[9]

---

5   Burkhard Peter, "Gassner's Exorcism – Not Mesmer's Magnetism – Is the Real Predecessor of Modern Hypnosis," in *International Journal of Clinical and Experimental Hypnosis*, 53: 1-12.
6   1 Samuel 19:23.
7   Mark 7:25.
8   Does God act immorally or unjustly by speaking through a man against his will? I think the answer is clearly no. God has decided that in order for free will to matter, He will usually not override it; thus, He heartbreakingly watches as children are kidnapped, raped and murdered. If He stopped every evil choice from being made (He could do so), then free will would vanish and with it meaningful relationships with people. However, just because God doesn't usually override free will, it hardly follows that He can't or is unjust in doing so: He sets limits to freedom all the time (we can't imagine a square circle or decide that today I'm going to jump to the moon) and God, as the Creator of our voices, does have the moral right to claim use of them provided that He hasn't given us absolute ownership of them (which He hasn't).
9   Amanda Barnier and Michael Nash, "Introduction," in *The Oxford Handbook of*

Nevertheless, what makes hypnotism a more extreme form of idea-giving than teaching is that once the subject – let's say, Robert Fischer, here – has consented to be hypnotised, many of the suggestions given to the hypnotized subject cannot be critically reflected upon. That is, although the subject Fischer is neither asleep nor unconscious when hypnotized, he is in a consented-to state wherein his imagination is active but his experience of the events are felt to be involuntary. If the hypnotist – let's call him, Cobb – suggests that there is a helium balloon in the subject Fischer's hands, then the subject feels as if there is a balloon in his hands and could not have felt otherwise. Even more remarkable is the phenomenon of post-hypnotic suggestion, whose essence is that the subject will feel the *urge*, for example, to weep every time he sees a picture of his father but will neither *know* why he feels this way nor will *remember* the suggestion.

The question then becomes whether all hypnotism is immoral since in the hypnotized state of consciousness the subject – Fischer – isn't free to reflect critically upon what is going on. The Hypnotist Code of Ethics states that hypnotism is immoral if, among other things, the hypnotist places anything above the subject's "welfare, rights, and dignity."[10] This suggests that hypnotism could be seen as moral provided that the subject knows what he's getting into and consents to the general aim of the hypnotist, namely, to help the subject while at all times being, above all, respectful of the subject's right to be treated as an end in himself. If this is so, then Cobb the hypnotist giving Fischer the subject suggestions that are at all times respectful, and for the benefit, of Fischer shouldn't be seen as immoral and indeed should be seen as analogous to a surgeon who, at all times respectful of, and motivated by the benefit for, his patient, tells his patient generally what he is going to do – for example, perform heart surgery – while at the same time feeling no need to explain *every* detail to the patient and getting the patient's permission for *each* cut of the knife.

THE ETHICS OF INCEPTION

Our discussion of the ethics of teaching and hypnosis strongly indicate that the person to whom an idea is being given should, all things being equal, be treated with respect as to his or her person. This, however, in no way entails that such a person should never be given ideas that he or she can't *immediately* reflect upon or choose for themselves at *the moment*: the young child will be taught many things that only later she can process and the hypnotized subject

---

Hypnosis: Theory, Research and Practice, 1-20 (Oxford: Oxford University Press, 2008), 10.
10   http://hypnosisschool.org/hypnotic/hypnosis-school-code-of-ethics.php (accessed on February 11, 2011).

will be given suggestions during the session to which he consented that he will have no power to resist. Given this, how ought we to view the ethics of inception or the act of an extractor or dream navigator planting an idea in the mind of his unknowing, dreaming subject?

In the movie, we know the details of two cases of inception: the first between Cobb and his wife, Mal, and the second between Cobb and Fischer. Both situations are different but are the ethics?

In the case of Cobb and Mal, both knew they were sharing a dream. Nevertheless, because they were in their common dream for what felt like fifty years or so, Mal slowly started to loose touch with the real world and eventually came to the point where she thought the dream world was true reality. Cobb, however, didn't lose his grasp on reality, and, desperate to wake Mal up, planted an idea in her mind, namely, that "Your world is not real." Mal's mind – *with neither concession to the act of inception nor to the content of the act* – took to the idea and so agreed to "kill" herself in the dream, thus allowing her to wake up. However, unawares to Cobb, this idea had taken root like "a cancer" in Mal's waking mind as well, causing her to believe that the *real world* was "not real" and that the only escape is death. She, consequently, killed herself in the real world in addition to the dream world. Earlier on Ariadne told Cobb, "You're not responsible for the idea that destroyed her," but it's clear from what we know, he is. Nevertheless, is Cobb *morally* to blame? A bad end caused by an individual isn't the same as the individual being morally to blame for that bad end occurring.

Because Mal didn't consent, as a hypnotized subject does, to being given ideas against her will but for her benefit, we can't justify Cobb in this way. However, if Mal was, like a rationally undeveloped child, largely incapable of processing what is true or false, then for Cobb to have treated her in such a manner as to impose an idea on her doesn't seem morally objectionable. Mal clearly wasn't capable of processing what is true or false, and so for Cobb to have incepted her probably wasn't immoral. Yet this line of reasoning is incomplete.

I believe Cobb *is* morally to blame since he was negligent as to the effects of inception. Yes, it was terrible that Mal should, in her dream world, think it real, but *eventually* they both would have woken up; they couldn't have slept forever, even if in the dream world it felt like forever. Because of this and because Cobb didn't know what the effects of inception might be, he should have stayed his hand. He was reckless and his recklessness led to his wife's death, just as much as if, for example, he neglected to periodically check his natural gas fireplace for leaks and, unchecked, led to her death by carbon monoxide poisoning. Obviously, he's not as blameworthy as a man who intended to kill his wife, but negligence – failing to think of and perform an act one ought to think of and perform – is still a species of immorality.

The case of Cobb and Fischer is a bit different, but still points to Cobb having acted immorally. Cobb and his team were hired by Saito to incept Fischer – to give him the idea "I will break up my father's company" in order to prevent the birth of an energy monopoly or "superpower." Saito believed the end – preventing "total energy dominance" – justified the means – giving a person an idea against his will. And, just to be clear, inception *is* against Fischer's will since even though on the level of the dream Fischer will "give himself the idea," "obviously," we are told, "[it's] an idea that Robert [would] choose to reject" if he were *fully* aware of what was going on. Since Fischer neither consented to be incepted (as a hypnotized subject consents to being hypnotized) nor was incapable of rationally processing what was going on (as Mal and rationally undeveloped children are), there is little room to justify what Cobb and his team did. The world *may have been* spared an evil, but the cost of this hypothetical – treating a person as a mere means to an end – probably doesn't justify inception.

"YOU NEED TO LET THEM DECIDE FOR THEMSELVES"

After Cobb agreed to take the Fischer job, he went to France to visit his father-in-law, who had taught Cobb the ways of dream navigation and who Cobb hoped would introduce him to another skilled dream navigator or "architect." Knowing that Cobb, a fugitive, could only use his skills of dream navigation for illegal ends, the father-in-law plainly stated Cobb's intention, "You're here to corrupt one of my brightest and best." In a flash of moral clarity, Cobb replied, "You need to let them decide for themselves."

Although this statement agrees with what I've argued for herein about the ethics of idea-giving, particularly, that a rationally developed person's autonomy should usually be respected, Cobb, sadly, didn't heed his own words. In the case of Mal, he didn't let her decide for herself, though this wasn't in itself immoral since she was analogous to a rationally undeveloped child and needed to be forcibly given an idea; what made him immoral was his negligence. In the case of Fischer, Cobb again didn't let the other decide for himself since, despite what Fischer in his dream believed, the man didn't consent to having been incepted in the first place. Cobb, therefore, probably acted immorally throughout.

Chapter Three

"Evolution Isn't an Opinion, It's a Fact"? Evolution and the Ethics of Belief in *The Big Bang Theory*

In season three, episode one of *The Big Bang Theory*, Sheldon visits his mother, who happens to be a devout, though fundamentalist, Christian. Words and wit are exchanged, ending with a brief dialogue about evolution. Sheldon tells his mother, Mary Cooper, that "Evolution isn't an opinion, it's a fact," to which Mary replies, "And that's your opinion." Because terms aren't clarified, the audience is left with a false dilemma: either you believe in scientific facts or you believe in God; either you are rational or irrational.

Yet there is so much left unsaid here. First, how are the mother and son using the term "evolution"? Are they referring to the ancient earth thesis, whereby the universe, starting with the Big Bang, came into existence about 14 billion years ago and has been unfolding ever since? Are they referring to microevolution or changes within a species by way of genetic drift? Or are they talking about macroevolution or the common ancestry thesis, whereby all organisms are linked by a shared genealogy typically achieved by natural selection winnowing random genetic mutations? Second, are all these types of evolution really "facts," where a fact is (in science) a demonstrable concept or (in philosophy) a state of affairs reported by a true proposition? And third, is belief in God, as Mary seems to imply, incompatible with belief in any or all of these types of evolution? Moreover, we might add an extra question here that often arises in this type of exchange, namely, is there something *immoral* or *unjust* about failing to assess evidence, especially "facts," correctly? If Mary rejects a "fact," does she act immorally? If Sheldon makes obvious jumps in logic, does he act unjustly? It is these questions – concerning evolution, rationality and the ethics of belief – I want to examine herein.

WHEN IT'S OKAY TO WRESTLE BOBCATS FOR LICORICE

Everyone has a worldview or a collection of pre-scientific or pre-philosophical beliefs about the general contours of life. From the earliest ages, children are taught a number of things by their parents and insofar as their parents have proven to be the most reliable source for food, comfort and so on in their lives, children are rationally justified in accepting what they have been taught – be it that Jesus's birthday is on December 25 or that it's okay to wrestle bobcats for licorice.

However, as children get older, their cognitive faculties mature and provided that they have been encouraged all along to develop these faculties and exercise their free will, children will, and should, come to reflect critically upon what they have been taught not only by their parents but also by their school, state and society as a whole. This is to say that pre-philosophical beliefs ought to (a moral term) be reflected upon and rejected if the evidence – all things considered – is against it, neither asserted nor rejected if the evidence is nearly 50 / 50 for and against, or held – to the appropriate degree – based on the evidence, again, all things considered, being in favour of that belief. As John Locke says,

> He that believes without having any reason for believing may be in love with his own fancies, but neither seeks truth as he ought nor pays the obedience due his maker, who would have him use those discerning faculties he has given him, to keep him out of mistake and errour . . . doing his duty as a rational creature. . . . He that does otherwise transgresses against his own light and misuses those faculties which were given him to no other end but to search and follow the clearer evidence and greater probability.[1]

Thus, if justice means treating each as it ought to be treated, then treating each individual believer relative to his or her particular context, which is to say, relative to what he or she can and should know about the world, is the aim.

Importantly, there is nothing here that says a believer (of whatever sort) has a moral duty to pretend as if a belief from one part of his worldview doesn't have something to say about a belief from another part of his worldview nor is there anything here, as philosopher Alvin Plantinga has pointed out,[2] that demands

---

1 John Locke *Essay Concerning Human Understanding* 4.17.24.
2 "J. B. S. Haldane seems to think intellectual honesty requires him to be an atheist (given that he assumes God won't interfere with his experiments); as far as I can see, that's like thinking intellectual honesty requires me to deny the existence of my children, given that I assume they won't set my house on fire. There is an enormous difference between atheism and assuming that God won't interfere with my experiments. . . . God has created both us and our world, and created them in such a way that the former can know much about the latter. But this implies that God would not arbitrarily stand in the way of our coming to such knowledge – by, for example, capriciously spoiling our experiments. . . . Of course God's faithfulness and reliability along these lines doesn't mean that he never acts in ways outside of the normal course

that all truth-seekers and moral men adopt the position of methodological naturalism, which unreasonably requires all scientific and legal explanations to be explained solely in terms of "natural" phenomena, with no reference to divine or supernatural action or intervention. True, a naturalist like Leonard may explain things in terms of naturalism (that is, omitting reference to non-physical phenomena), but a Hindu, such as Raj, might not want to do this. Moreover, even if Hinduism as a whole can be shown to be improbable, it hardly follows that a lay or uneducated Hindu, who knows nothing of these arguments, would necessarily be unjustified or immoral in giving Hindu explanations of scientific phenomena; for that matter, even if metaphysical naturalism or materialism can be shown to be improbable, it would hardly follow that an uneducated naturalist or materialist would always be wrong to explain phenomena that exclude the supernatural. Nevertheless, we need to be aware that worldview beliefs aren't always held rationally and believers of whatever worldview can distort truth through insubordinate emotions and irrational desires.

Thus, while we can say in certain contexts that so-and-so "should know better" (with all its moral implications), it's not at all easy to judge when a person may be acting immorally or unjustly by assenting to, or dissenting from, a particular belief. We typically don't have enough information to judge this. However, for the sake of this chapter, let's assume that our two interlocutors, Mary and Sheldon, are familiar with the basic contours of Christianity and are rationally able to process basic biblical and scientific evidence pertaining to evolution.

"ALL THAT SCIENCE STUFF IS FROM JESUS"

Mary Cooper, who thinks "all that science stuff is from Jesus,"[3] is a Christian and as such there are typically three positions open to her in respect to evolution: young earth creationism, which accepts microevolution but denies the ancient earth and the common ancestry theses (Mary seems to favour this view[4]); old earth creationism, which accepts microevolution and the ancient earth thesis; and theistic evolution, which accepts all three types of evolution in their vigour. Sheldon, who seems to have rejected the Christianity of his youth (he doubts the rationality of prayer, saying, "My objections weren't based on difficulty [of praying],"[5] and says to his mom, "I don't really know

---

of things: It doesn't mean, for example, that miracles never occur." Alvin Plantinga, *Science and Religion: Are They Compatible?* (Oxford: Oxford University Press, 2011), 65.
3   *The Big Bang Theory* season 1, episode 4.
4   *The Big Bang Theory* season 5, episode 6.
5   *The Big Bang Theory* season 3, episode 1.

what Jesus thinks about"[6]), is likely a materialist or a metaphysical naturalist and as such there is really only one option open to him: unguided evolution, which asserts the truth of all three types of evolution but insists that a God who guides these processes is an unnecessary hypothesis. The debate between the Christian mother and the materialist son could, of course, extend to virtually everything, but to keep it in the realm of the evolution debate, two general themes are worth discussing: biblical themes (special revelation) and non-biblical ones (general revelation).

As for the biblical themes, Sheldon likely sees the Bible as nothing more than ancient fiction and would have very little to say on these matters; however, Mary takes biblical authority seriously and so it's rational for her to see what the Bible has to say on these matters (of course why it's rational for Mary to believe the Bible is authoritative in the first place is another matter, for another chapter).

Now on even the most literal account, there is nothing in the Bible that is opposed to microevolution and indeed much that would agree with it, such as the different races stemming from a common (human) ancestor; moreover, because it can be scientifically repeated or demonstrated, it's rightly called a "fact," and no one, not even Mary, would disagree with evolution so understood. However, the ancient earth and common ancestry theses are a different story. A superficial reading of the early chapters of Genesis indicates that God made the world in six days and there is certainly no hint in these chapters that man developed from ape, much less amoeba. But this, in itself, is uninteresting. Psalm 104:5 says, "the Earth can never be moved," but as Galileo demonstrated decisively – and, people tend to forget, all Christians happily conceded not long after – this verse doesn't need to be interpreted literally. Galileo says, "It being true that two truths cannot contradict one another, it is the function of expositors to seek out the true senses of scriptural texts. These will unquestionably accord with the physical conclusions which manifest sense and necessary demonstrations have previously made certain to us."[7] Can the early chapters of Genesis be reconciled with the old earth thesis? Can they be reconciled with the common ancestry thesis?

A typical old earth creationist would argue that the six days in Genesis refer to six extremely long ages in a gradual or progressive unfolding of creation: God, being outside of time, starts creation with the Big Bang ("Let there be light") which unfolds through the space-time void, eventually forming the

---

6   *The Big Bang Theory* season 2, episode 7.

7   Galileo Galilei, *Discoveries and Opinions of Galileo: Including The Starry Messenger (1610), The Letter to the Grand Duchess Christina (1615), Excerpts from Letters on Sunspots (1613), and The Assayer (1623)*, trans. Stillman Drake (New York: Anchor Books, 1990), 186.

primordial gas cloud that will become the Earth; God – working through secondary and primary causes – sees to it that the surface and atmospheric waters are separated, which then allows for life to flourish; subsequently, God causes inanimate matter to come to life, beginning with vegetation, which removes the carbon dioxide from the atmosphere, lowering the Earth's temperature, providing oxygen for future animals and clearing the sky so that the sun, moon and stars can now be seen (implying that these bodies weren't made on the third "day" but were rather visible on it); then, the Creator makes animal life to spring up: first smaller marine life, then the "big reptiles,"[8] then birds, and then, a "day" later, other land-based animals, culminating in man, who is made from "clay" (a physical body) and God's "breath" (a created rational soul or spirit: the "image of God").

This old earth creationist account takes Genesis's "days" loosely and does challenge some of the literal features of the Genesis story (such as when the sun, moon and stars were made), but since the Hebrew word for "day" is a looser term than it is in English and since all agree that Genesis has poetic elements (the flood story uses poetic chiasms, for instance), it's only a slightly less familiar read of the Bible than the purely literalist account given by young earth creationists. Additionally, the old earth creationist account has a far less stretched reading of the Bible than that of theistic evolutionists, who deny God any direct intervention in creation for billions of years, but then, oddly, allow Him to do all sorts of direct actions *after* man is made. A better reading of the first few chapters of Genesis and the Bible as a whole, then, would seem

---

8   In Genesis 1:21 we are told that God created *taninim gedolim*. *Gedolim* means "big" so we read this "the big *taninim*." Every English translation has a different word for this, but the singular form of this word *taneen* appears in Exodus 7 and gives us a clue to how this word should be translated. The argument goes like this: in Exodus 4:3, we were told that God commanded Moses to throw down his staff in front of the Burning Bush and it became a *nahash*, which is the Hebrew word for "snake." Nevertheless, in Exodus 7:10 when Moses throws down the same staff in front of Pharaoh, it became a *taneen*. Furthermore, in Exodus 7:15, God told Moses to go to Pharaoh at the water's edge with his staff that turned into a *nahash* and do another miracle. This means that in these verses in Exodus, *nahash* become *taneen* which became *nahash*. Moreover, since *taneen* must be a general category of animal (as is the case with all animals mentioned in the first chapters of Genesis), *nahash* – snake – must belong to the general category *taneen*. Thus, Genesis 1:21 ought to read, "And God created the big reptiles," which can easily be seen as referring to dinosaurs or what the (not so foolish) ancients universally called "dragons" (as in the water dragon Tiamet in *Enuma Elish*). Of course, even if we admit that some of the ancients knew about real dinosaurs or "dragons" (either by special revelation as in Genesis 1:21 or by other means), it hardly follows that human beings had to have co-existed alongside dinosaurs or "dragons" (indeed, the fossil records make this highly improbable).

to favour young or old earth creationism.

However, when we compare the biblical account of the age of the Earth with what we know from physics, astronomy and geology (and here Sheldon, Raj and Leonard speak with authority), the young earth creationist interpretation of Genesis's "days" looks highly improbable. Although there is a lot of scientific evidence here,[9] let's look at three examples, beginning with light.

When we look to the night sky, we can see objects that give every appearance of being many light-years away from us, suggesting that their light began to travel from them to us many years ago. Sirius, the star brightest from Earth, is twelve light-years away and so the light we see from it is twelve years old, and the Andromeda galaxy is two million light-years away suggesting that the light from it is two million years old. Since the most distant galaxies are over ten billion light-years away, it seems likely that, all things being equal, those galaxies, and hence the universe, is at least that old.

Second, consider Sheldon's much-loved Doppler Effect. Nearly everyone, including young earth creationists, agree that the universe is expanding from an original starting point. Consequently, we can measure the age of the universe by calculating how long it would take for a universe our size to get from zero to the present. For example, if Sheldon and the gang went on a road trip to northern California and drove precisely 50 miles an hour and went 100 miles in total, they would have traveled for precisely two hours. Likewise, by knowing the universe's rate of expansion (determined by the Doppler Effect or by bouncing radiation off of moving objects to determine their speed) and the average distance between galaxies (by comparing the actual brightness of a galaxy to its apparent brightness), we determine, all things being equal, that the universe is about 12-14 billion years old.

And third, consider the fossil record. There are many layers with no humanoid fossils in them, and only much later, when there are no longer any dinosaur fossils to be found, do humanoid fossils begin to appear. It seems reasonable to infer, therefore, that dinosaurs existed long before human beings and were extinct, all things being more or less uniform, millions of years before them.

Young earth creationists try to respond to this evidence with, by their own admission,[10] flimsy – possible but improbable – reasons: God created light

---

9   Globular cluster dating, sedimentary layers and radiometric dating also seem to support the ancient earth thesis.

10 Young earth creationists Paul Nelson and John Mark Reynolds write, "Recent creationists should humbly agree that their view is, at the moment, implausible on purely scientific grounds." Paul Nelson and John Mark Reynolds, "Young Earth Creationism," in *Three Views on Creation and Evolution*, ed. Stanley Gundry, J. P.

in transit such that it only *appears* to be billions of years old (just as the body of the newly created Adam only had the *appearance* of maturity), the universe expanded *way* more rapidly in the beginning than the best science tells us is possible, and dinosaur bones are heavier and therefore sunk below human bones.

Indeed, in order to explain this latter point, they argue for a global flood that destroyed "every living creature" on Earth that wasn't on Noah's ark.[11] Of course, while the global flood theory has some explanatory power (how certain marine fossils ended up on top of mountains, for example), young earth creationists probably demand too much of this little engine (to use a Sheldon metaphor). To postulate a global flood that destroyed all the land-based animals not on the ark would mean that after the flood (which presumably would have been responsible for breaking Pangaea into seven continents), animals such as koalas would have had to exit the ark and then, from Turkey, manage to walk and swim (!) unscathed to Australia. God, of course, could intervene such that these little guys make it to the Land Down Under (just as it's logically possible for Him to make light in transit and so on) but it doesn't seem particularly likely.

Moreover, a global flood isn't required on an orthodox reading of the Genesis text. Even though the flood is said to have covered "*all* the high mountains under the entire heavens,"[12] this hardly needs to be read literally, for young earth creationists surely don't take literally the fact that "*All* the countries [Scotland?] came to Egypt to buy grain from Joseph"[13] or that "*All* the kings of the Earth [Korean kings?] . . . sought Solomon to hear his wisdom."[14] The flood story could easily be read as a local (perhaps, Black Sea-based) flood that destroyed all human life save for those who were on the ark (this seems to be the purpose of God sending the flood, after all), and indeed, there is ample support from marine geology that just such a local flood occurred.[15] Thus, it's probably better to say with old earth creationists or theistic evolutionists that the animals on the ark were restricted to middle eastern animals or animals in the epicenter of the flood.

Nevertheless, young earth creationists have one thing going for them in respect to animals: an easy explanation of animal suffering. For them, all

---

Moreland and John Mark Reynolds, 39-102 (Grand Rapids, MI: Zondervan, 1999), 51.
11 Genesis 6:4.
12 Genesis 7:19.
13 Genesis 41:57.
14 2 Chronicles 9:23.
15 See William Ryan and Walter Pitman, *Noah's Flood: The New Scientific Evidence about the Event that Changed History* (New York: Simon & Schuster, 1998).

death, or at least animal and human death, is the result of man's fall: prior to man's disobedience, there was no animal death. Young earth creationists could even borrow a page from an ethicist like Peter Singer, arguing that higher animals seem to suffer pain, this pain – a baby zebra being torn apart by a lion, for example – is a bad thing (an ideal world, and certainly a world made by a good God, would not have such pain built into it); therefore, the common ancestry thesis, which would see God using natural selection to cull the unfit, is unlikely.

A theistic evolutionist like Francis Collins (the man who mapped the human genome) thinks that quantum uncertainty can account for free random mutations – so free, in fact, that even God doesn't determine or desire some of the creatures nature makes.[16] Animal pain, then, would be the result of nature producing destructive creatures who are opposed to God's will, such as the ichneumonidae (wasp) who lays its eggs inside a live caterpillar or even the cat that toys with the mouse before killing it. This is to say, that bad creatures arise from nature's freedom, just as evil people arise from man's freedom.

Old earth creationists typically think theistic evolutionists commit a category mistake when they talk about nature's "freedom" (apparent randomness) and man's freedom (the ability to act as a first cause). That is, while man's potential for evil is a good thing (even if the evil acts he commits aren't), nature's potential for evil serves no purpose. In other words, while it makes perfect sense why God would allow man to commit evil (if God stopped every evil choice, man wouldn't be free), it doesn't make a lot of sense why God would allow, and not intervene and stop, mindless nature from producing genuinely bent or corrupt creatures (if such weren't bent or corrupted by other free-willed creatures).

But young earth creationists also have problems. Old earth creationists typically point out the improbability of the young earth creationist's original assertion, namely, that there was no death before the Fall. To postulate that would be to explain away a deluge of evidence from palaeontology and geology.[17] To make sense of some of this, some old earth creationists, such as C. S. Lewis, suggest that death before the *human* fall is possible because Satan and a third of the heavenly hosts – free-willed creatures whose choices God respects

---

16 Francis Collins and Karl Giberson, *The Language of Science and Faith* (Downers Grove, IL: IVP, 2011), 130.

17 Of course, old earth creationists, who agree with young earth creationists that pre-fallen Adam couldn't die, also have to postulate some pretty mysterious mechanisms to explain how Adam, if he, for example, were to fall from a mountaintop, would survive (Raj, who loves these types of hypotheticals, might suggest that the sinless Adam's body was like that of Wolverine's, whose miraculous healing powers would prevent him from dying from such a height even if he could still experience some pain).

(just as He respects the choices of human serial killers) – corrupted nature before man even arrived on the planet; indeed, they point to the fact that it was likely Satan who possessed and corrupted the serpent which subsequently tempted Eve.[18] Thus, it would have been Satan, and not God, who encouraged (whatever this means exactly) carnivorous activities among the beasts, and all of this would have been still a "good" creation since a good creation requires, among other things, free willed angels. After corrupting the animals (for example, the dinosaurs, hence Satan's link with the "dragon"?), the corrupted animals would have, through microevolution, developed carnivorous teeth, claws, poisons and dispositions.

Yet if Lewis's solution doesn't fully satisfy, old earth creationists need only say that even if a clear *how* isn't readily available, we should at least assert four probable *thats:* (1) that there is good evidence to suggest that God is good (evidence for another chapter), (2) that His creation is good (thus, while quantum uncertainty is a fact, this hardly precludes God from intervening to design the best possible world[19]), (3) that pointless animal suffering, at least higher animal suffering, is bad,[20] and (4) that geological and paleontological evidence suggests that there was animal death before the Fall.

"SO STUBBORN"

When we turn specifically to non-biblical themes in respect to the evolution debate, Sheldon, our materialist, has more to say. Here the debate shifts from inter-Christian debates about evolution to pitting some types of Christianity

---

18 "The origin of animal suffering could be traced, by earlier generations, to the Fall of man – the whole world was infected by the uncreating rebellion of Adam. This is now impossible, for we have good reason to believe that animals existed long before men. Carnivorousness, with all that it entails, is older than humanity. . . . But the doctrine of Satan's existence and fall is not among the things we know to be untrue. . . . It seems, therefore, a reasonable supposition, that some mighty created power had already been at work for ill on the material universe, or the solar system, or, at least, the planet Earth, before man ever came on the scene." C. S. Lewis, *The Problem of Pain* in *C. S. Lewis: Selected Books* [Long Edition] (London: HarperCollins, 1999), 542.
19 "A mutation accruing to an organism is random just if neither the organism nor its environment contains a mechanism or process or organ that causes adaptive mutations to occur. But clearly a mutation could be both random in that sense and also intended and indeed caused by God." Alvin Plantinga, *Science and Religion: Are They Compatible?* 75.
20 General revelation and special revelation both denounce needless animal suffering, not just because to treat animals cruelly is to make ourselves cruel, but also because to do so does seem to wrong animals themselves. Nature is first and foremost for God's good pleasure (hence the mosquito), and only secondly for man's use.

against naturalism in respect to evolution. Though I don't want to commit the fallacy of selecting evidence, I do think that at least four topics are worth briefly examining.

The first topic is the Cambrian explosion, during which all the major body plans (phyla) of the animals appear in a span of merely five to ten million years. Young and old earth creationists both point to this incredible diversity and complexity within such a short period of time as strong evidence against hands-off (theistic) or unguided (naturalistic) evolution. They argue that based on what we see here, there are far too few transitions between major biological categories to fit what we'd expect if hands-off or unguided evolution were true. A few old earth creationists admit that logically speaking, God could use macroevolution to create, but even if so (and there is no strong reason to think He has done so), the Cambrian explosion makes it clear that God would also have to directly intervene in more particular acts of speciation.

Theistic and naturalist evolutionists universally admit there is a major problem here (Sheldon would likely feel compelled to join these even though we know him to be "so stubborn" he'd stay in his room "until the Rapture" in order not to have to apologize[21]); nevertheless, a desperate minority has gone so far as to reject Darwin by proposing a punctuated equilibrium evolutionary theory (where periods of equilibrium are punctuated by periods of rapid change) to account for the Cambrian explosion. The lack of a convincing mechanism to account for this speed fluctuation has resulted in few followers, however.

The second topic is closely related to the first, though this time on the molecular level. Darwin had said, "If it could be demonstrated that any complex organ existed which could not possibly have been formed by numerous, successive, slight modifications, my theory would absolutely break down."[22] Young and old earth creationists try to demonstrate this by pointing to the apparent "irreducible complexity" of molecular machines such as the cilia. A system is said to be irreducibly complex if it has a number of different components that work together to accomplish the task of the system and if you remove one of the components, the system no longer functions. Such a system is highly unlikely to be built piece-by-piece through the hands-off or unguided gradual process of macroevolution because the system has to be fully present for the thing to function. A mousetrap is the most common example: first, you need the flat wooden platform, then you need the metal hammer, next there is the spring, then the catch release, and finally, the metal bar that connects to the catch and holds the hammer. If you take away even one of these pieces, it doesn't become half as efficient as before but becomes totally useless: it can't

---

21 *The Big Bang Theory* season 1, episode 4.
22 Charles Darwin, *The Origin of Species* (New York: New York University Press, 1998), 154.

catch any mice.[23] Moreover, all five parts have to be put in precisely the right place in order for it to work, and while human intelligence can explain the mousetrap, hands-off or unguided evolution has a very hard time doing so since natural selection chooses systems that are already working – not ones that it hopes will work in the distant future.

Hands-off and unguided evolutionists typically reply to this type of argument by saying fewer components might well make something other than a mousetrap that is still useful; however, this might be true of a mousetrap (three of its components can make a handy syringe for Sheldon's luminous fish experiment), but this doesn't seem to be true for molecular machines. Thus, many hands-off and unguided evolutionists again bite the bullet of improbability, merely saying as Daniel Dennett does, "the inability to imagine how this is possible is not the same as proof that it is impossible."[24]

The third topic is broken DNA. Hands-off and unguided evolutionists both rightly point out that while young and old earth creationists are quick to highlight examples in nature that suggest goodness and intelligent design, they tend to ignore or understate the flaws in nature or dysteleology. For example, why do men have nipples? Why does the human jaw bone appear incomplete? Or, more strongly, why would a good God, who made the world in a hands-on manner, see to it that all primates – monkeys and men alike – have in them the same broken gene which prevents the production of the enzyme needed to produce vitamin C – that which is needed to prevent scurvy? "To claim that the human genome was created by God independently, rather than having descended from a common ancestor," Francis Collins writes, "means God inserted a broken piece of DNA into our genomes. This is not remotely plausible."[25]

In response, all young earth creationists and nearly all old earth creationists point to common design, rather than common ancestry, as the reason for the biological similarity between man and monkey (just as a painter can use the colour red in more than one painting). Moreover, both would explain the broken pieces of DNA as the result of the curse of the Fall, when God cursed everything under man's authority with elements of brokenness (increased pain in childbirth, less cooperative nature, cancer, etc.); thus, just as man (an inferior) rebelled against God (his superior), so too do those under man's authority (inferiors) rebel against man (a superior) as a result of God's just curse. Finally, both have something going for them (at least against theistic evolutionists) insofar as they believe in the historical Fall: they can be truer

---

23 Michael Behe, *Darwin's Black Box* (New York: Simon & Schuster, 1996), 110.
24 Daniel Dennett, *Science and Religion: Are They Compatible?* 75.
25 Collins and Giberson, *The Language of Science and Faith*, 43.

to the orthodox understanding of Jesus, the Second Adam,[26] who alone can represent all people and subordinate creation in order to restore, and indeed, improve, upon them and it.

The fourth and final topic is the apparent fine-tuning of the universe. When the twentieth century's most famous atheist, Anthony Flew, came to believe the universe had a Divine Creator, he cited scientific evidence for his conversion – not just the unexpected inability of naturalist scientists and philosophers to account for consciousness, the apparent contradiction between macroevolution and The Law of Limitation of Variation in Progeny, how DNA got programmed, the way animate life arose from inanimate matter and C. S. Lewis-Alvin Plantinga's "evolutionary argument against naturalism,"[27] but other things as well: "The laws of nature, life with its teleological organization, and the existence of the universe can only be explained in the light of an Intelligence that explains both its own existence and that of the world."[28] Young earth creationists, old earth creationists and theistic evolutionists alike all agree with Flew, pointing out that naturalists have no good explanation for (1) how the Big Bang started in the first place (God being outside of time and, by definition, the Unmoved Mover, can easily do this, whereas as mere matter can't), (2) how it is that scientific laws (not to mention moral laws) came to be (theists claim these laws were first ideas in God's mind and then were made binding on His creation, but naturalists really have no material account for these), and, my main point in this section, (3) how life on our planet is even possible given the extreme conditions after the Big Bang and the short time span of 14 billion years.

The evidence for this latter point is particularly impressive. Without hypothesizing an infinite number of *literal* parallel universes and Earths – stuff straight out of Sheldon's *Green Lantern* collection – it's virtually inconceivable to assert unguided evolution on this matter.[29] Consider, as an example, Stephen

---

26 1 Corinthians 15:45.
27 In a nutshell, the evolutionary argument against naturalism argues that where N is naturalism, E is macroevolution and R is the proposition that our cognitive faculties are reliable, (1) P (R / N & E) is low; (2) One who accepts N & E and also sees that (1) is true has a defeater for R; (3) This defeater can't be defeated; (4) One who has a defeater for R has a defeater for any belief he takes to be produced by his cognitive faculties, including N & E; therefore, (5) N & E is *self-defeating* and *can't rationally be accepted*. Plantinga, Science and Religion: Are They Compatible? 17. Cf. C. S. Lewis, *Miracles* (New York: HarperCollins, 1996).
28 Anthony Flew, *There Is a God: How the World's Most Notorious Atheist Changed His Mind* (New York: HarperOne, 2007), 155.
29 "The postulation of God is the postulation of *one* entity of a simple kind . . . . The postulation of the actual existence of an infinite number of worlds, between them exhausting all the logical possibilities . . . is to postulate complexity and non-

Hawking's statement that with enough time, eventually a group of monkeys hitting the keys on a typewriter will produce a sonnet.[30] Is this – and this is certainly more probable than to meet all the conditions that would need to be met in order for us to be here today – remotely probable? Let's say that Penny makes 500 grab bags, each of which holds the twenty-six letters of the English alphabet, the goal being to produce Leonard's favourite Shakespearean sonnet, which is 500 letters in length. Leonard is blindfolded and reaches into one bag and pulls out a letter. The likelihood that he will draw out an *s* for the first letter of the sonnet (which begins "Shall I compare thee to a summer's day") is 1 in 26. The likelihood that in the initial two draws from the first two bags he'll get an *s* and an *h* is 1 in 26 x 26, and so on for the first 500 letters. Ignoring space between words, the odds of getting the entire sonnet by chance is 26 multiplied by itself 500 times or 10^{700}. To appreciate the size of this number, consider that the entire known universe weighs around 10^{56} grams, that the basic particles in the universe is 10^{80}, and that the age of the universe is about 10^{18} seconds. If you were to convert the entire universe into microcomputers each weighing a billionth of a gram and you ran each a billion times a second nonstop from the beginning of time, you'd still need more than 10^{500} universes to get the sonnet.[31] The fact of our existence is highly improbable given unguided evolution.

"SOME OF IT MAKES SENSE, SOME OF IT IS CRAZY"

I began this chapter by talking about the ethics of belief, stating that it's very difficult, though not impossible, to say in certain contexts that rational failures may also be seen as moral failures. Christopher Hitchens has suggested that "religion should be treated with ridicule, hatred and contempt,"[32] and the unspoken suggestion by many is that a fundamentalist Christian like Mary *should* – not just an intellectual *should*, but a moral *should* – give up many of her beliefs that are held in the face of stronger evidence. I partially agree, but the knife cuts both ways.

On the one hand, if, for the sake of argument, we say that Mary is a passionate, informed young earth creationist, then it may be somewhat blameworthy, both intellectually and morally, for her to deny the ancient

---

prearranged coincidence of infinite dimensions beyond rational belief." Richard Swinburne, "Argument from the Fine-Tuning of the Universe," in *Physical Cosmology and Philosophy*, ed. J. Leslie (London: Macmillan, 1990), 172.
30 Stephen Hawking, *A Brief History of Time* (New York: Bantam Books, 1998), 123.
31 Gerald Schroeder, *God According to God: A Scientist Discovers We've Been Wrong about God All Along* (New York: HarperOne, 2009), 36.
32 Christopher Hitchens (University of Toronto lecture, 2009).

earth thesis. What Raj says of Hinduism, we might say of Mary's young earth creationism: "Some of it makes sense, some of it is crazy."[33]

On the other hand, if Mary's son Sheldon is in fact a determined metaphysical naturalist, espousing unguided macroevolution, he, too, can be blamed (and more so because he is "one of the great minds of the twenty-first century"[34]) for failing to see that unguided macroevolution is not only not a fact – it's not demonstrable – but is also improbable given the Cambrian explosion, molecular complexity, the fine-tuned nature of the universe, and other considerations such as the laws of nature and the nature of consciousness. Indeed, even if Sheldon were a theistic evolutionist, he wouldn't fare much better. Thus, Mary prays, "Oh Lord, thank you for this meal and help Sheldon get back on his rocker."[35] To this, I – a tentative old earth creationist – would say, "Amen."

---

33 *The Big Bang Theory* season 4, episode 16.
34 *The Big Bang Theory* season 1, episode 4.
35 *The Big Bang Theory* season 1, episode 4.

Chapter Four

"I Don't Think Those Rules Apply Anymore": Law and Theft in *The Walking Dead*

In season one, episode two of *The Walking Dead*, Andrea, a survivor of the zombie apocalypse, tells the hero, Rick Grimes, about her sister Amy's love of mermaids. Staring down at one embossed on a necklace in an abandoned store, Andrea asks Rick if he thinks it would "be considered looting" if she were to take the necklace, to which the former cop quickly replies, "I don't think those rules apply any more, do you?"

In this case, and in countless others, the old rules or laws are challenged because of radically altered circumstances. However, in both the TV series and the comic books, it's never very explicit what kind of rules or laws are being challenged. The question that needs asking is whether all laws are subject to change, or just some. To answer this question, I believe what is required is a clear distinction between the Natural Law or the universal moral law, and its extension or application, both in individual ethical matters and in laws of state or positive laws. Thus, distinguishing these two types of laws – the Natural Law and positive law – and seeing how they function in *The Walking Dead* universe, especially in regard to the case of stealing, is what I intend to do herein.

THE NATURAL LAW

Law itself or law in general is a kind of "rule or measure of acts" that either commands or forbids certain actions.[1] While not identical to law, justice (the command to treat each and everything as it ought to be treated) is that with which the law is most concerned. Although God (by any name true to His essence) isn't under any law, neither is He, according to Aquinas, above it. The Supreme Being is, in fact, identical to the Eternal Law, and this Law is revealed to the minds of all rational beings – humans and perhaps others – in the form of the Natural Law. The ancients (and not so ancients) called it by many other names – the Egyptians, *Ma'at*; the Hindus, *Rita*; the Iranians and

---

1 Thomas Aquinas *Summa Theologica* pt. 1-2, q. 90, art 1.

Zoroaster, *Asha*; Confucius, The Way of Heaven; Plato, Goodness; the Stoics, *Natura*; Kant, the Categorical Imperative – but all meant roughly the same thing by it: a divine or uncreated law that all people can know and obligates all who can know it.

Of course, this doesn't stop some from objecting to its existence, pointing out that there are those who seem neither to know it nor to acknowledge it. This objection can be dealt with by clarifying two things.

First, most – from Mencius to Descartes, from Moses to C. S. Lewis – agree that the Natural Law is understood in one's mind (a faculty in the soul or spirit[2]) and so some, such as very small children like Judith Grimes or the brain-damaged, aren't able, because of physical restrictions, to act fully rationally and hence wouldn't be able to show signs of moral discernment. This is not at all to deny that a fetus or a small baby like Judith, for example, isn't in all likelihood an actual rational soul, spirit or person: just because she can't demonstrate empirically observable signs of rationality, it hardly follows that she isn't a rational soul or spirit who has these. It may be the case that the body, or better, the brain, of the baby hasn't developed such that the rational soul or spirit can act through it; indeed, even toddlers need to understand the terminology before they can see the truth of certain moral propositions and to learn terminology requires time and study. An undeveloped or damaged brain, through which the mind or spirit works, could explain why some show no signs of having knowledge of the Natural Law.

Second, granted free will, it seems perfectly possible that a person could know what the right choice or course of action is, and still refuse to accept it or follow it. We see this all the time. The Governor, for example, appears to have denied the Natural Law, insisting that torturing women, such as Michonne, for fun is okay, yet it hardly follows from this that he is right for maintaining this belief.[3] He is, insofar as he thinks torturing women for fun morally acceptable, wrong, and it seems most probable that he is wrong because somewhere along the line, he simply didn't *want* to believe in the Law. He preferred a lesser thing (his opinion or base desires) over the greater thing (the Truth). Of course we can soften the Governor's blame to some degree by pointing out that the culture he was raised in (postmodern America) largely taught that ethics are relative (to the individual or the group), and thus he was something of a victim

---

2   Dr. Jenner is one of those who disagrees that the self is an immaterial soul or spirit. Pointing to the picture of the zombie virus taking over the brain of his dead wife, he tells Rick and the group: "Somewhere in all those ripples of life [the organic wiring, synapses in the brain] is *you*. . . . Then comes death. Everything you ever were or will be. Gone. . . . The frontal cortex – the *you* part – that doesn't come back. Just a shell driven by mindless instinct." *The Walking Dead* season 1, episode 6.
3   *The Walking Dead* vol. 1, #29.

of his culture; nevertheless, because he is a free, rational man, who was neither brain-washed nor indoctrinated to the point of having no free will at all, he is still morally blame-worthy for failing to heed the commands of the Natural Law even when it was muffled by the noise of false cultural opinions. In short, he didn't *want* the Truth enough.

Moving on from the mere existence of the Natural Law to its relation to human beings, we see that while all those who acknowledge the existence of the Natural Law insist that its precepts are binding in and of themselves, most elaborate on the connection between the Natural Law and man's destiny or purpose, especially in respect to man's happiness. *Rita*, for example, is upheld by the god Varuna, who sees to it that insofar as people act against *Rita*, they are punished, and insofar as they act with it, they are rewarded (this later developed into the more specific Hindu concepts of *dharma* and *karma*). Or again, in Christianity, God, who encompasses the Natural Law as part of Himself, is also the Creator or Designer of humanity, meaning that He designs humans to function according to a specific design plan which they, because of free will, can choose to act with or against. To act with the design plan is to function properly or *naturally* and to act against it is to function improperly or *unnaturally*, but in either case, acting in accordance with the Natural Law is part, though not the entirety, of what it means for a person to function properly or naturally, and insofar as a person functions properly or naturally he is said to be *happy*.

In a short interview about *The Walking Dead* TV series, Sarah Wayne Callies says of her character, Lori Grimes, "She sort of becomes one of the guardians of humanity, saying it's not enough to be alive, it's not enough to simply avoid being eaten. We have to retain our humanity; we have to retain the heart and rituals and soul that make us human."[4] A person who acknowledges the Natural Law (under one name or another), will agree that Lori has the right idea, but will add that as a "guardian of humanity," Lori needs to understand, perhaps above all, the principles of the Natural Law since to fail to do so is, as she says, to wander far from the path of humanity and thus, we could further add, far from the path of the happiness proper or natural to human beings.

Of course, it's one thing to talk about the Natural Law, and it's another to say what it looks like in detail and practice. While the practice part will be discussed in the next section, what is essential is that the Natural Law *itself* isn't about details so much as very general statements about what is natural for man, especially in respect to the general moral principles developing some particular aspect of justice or the notion of treating each thing or person as it ought to be treated. Although the principles themselves are self-evident as

---

4   Sarah Wayne Callies, "Extras," in *The Walking Dead* season 1, disc. 3 (AMC, 2011).

soon as the terms are understood (and thus there is no need for *argument* to prove their truth), it's helpful to look at a few of these principles, and to use examples from both world philosophy and *The Walking Dead* to illustrate.

One basic principle is that of general beneficence or the sacredness of life principle, which both forbids and commands. We see the principle generally forbidding the harm of others in the Norse saga *Volospá* when we read, "In Nástrond [the place of fiery punishment] I saw . . . murderers,"[5] and in Lao Tzu's *Tao Te Ching*, which states, "Since they do no harm to each other, virtue flows."[6] We see the principle generally commanding us to love all humanity in Cicero's "Men were made for the sake of men that they might do one another good,"[7] and in Jesus's Golden Rule: "Do to others what you would have others do to you."[8] In issue #82, Morgan alludes to this principle when he tells Carl, "We get so focused on getting what we need that we stop caring about other people. Maybe it's what we have to do to get by, but it takes away a piece of your soul every time." And when Glenn saves a tank-entrapped Rick and is later asked why he saved him, Glenn says, in keeping with this principle, "Call it a foolish and naive hope that if I'm ever that far up shit creek someone might do the same for me."[9]

Special beneficence or just preference for those closest to one's self is another principle. All things considered, a person acts well or justly to favour his or her family and friends over and against others. In *The Law Code of Manu* we are told, "Even weak husbands strive to guard their wives,"[10] and in *The Epic of Gilgamesh*, Gilgamesh is admired for his devotion to his friend Enkidu. Likewise, in issue #7 of the comic books, when Rick offers to let Tyresse and his daughter sleep in the RV with Rick and his family, Lori is upset with her husband for what she perceives to be him neglecting his moral duty to protect his family from this new potential threat, saying, "Don't be so trusting, Rick." Similarly, in season one, episode five, Morales says that he and his family won't go with the others to Fort Benning, explaining, "I gotta do what's best for *my* family."

Another principle is that of piety or proper respect for one's superiors – be it for one's god, ancestors, rulers, elders, parents and so on. Exodus 20:2-3 says, "I am God . . . do not have any other gods above me;" Plato asked Euthyphro, "Aren't you afraid that in taking your father into court you may turn out to

---

5   *Volospá* 38-39.
6   Lao Tzu *Tao Te Ching* 60.
7   Cicero *De Officiis* 1.4.
8   Matthew 7:12.
9   *The Walking Dead* season 1, episode 2.
10 *The Law Code of Manu* 9.6.

be committing an act of impiety yourself?"[11] and Confucius insisted, "The services of love and reverence to parents when alive, and those of grief and sorrow to them when dead: these completely discharge the fundamental duty of living men."[12] Guillermo, the custodian-turned-leader of an abandoned hospital, demonstrates a proper sensitivity to this principle staying behind to help the elderly when others "took off, just left them here to die."[13] It's even possible to see respect for the dead – respect, in a sense, for those that have gone before or elders in death – as a potential motive when Glenn checks a zombie-corpse's wallet for an organ donor card before they hack the zombie-corpse to bits and use its organs to mask their smell.[14]

Related to this, though in the downward direction, are general duties to posterity, nature, and those who are weaker or in lower positions. "Those who oppress the young and cheat them because of greed," the *Buddhist Scriptures* declare, "are themselves reborn *katapūtanas* [rotten bodied ghosts] to feed on birth-impurities,"[15] and the Egyptian *Teaching of Amenemope* says in all seriousness, "Laugh not at a blind man nor tease a dwarf."[16] Rick demonstrates this principle when he returns to, and puts out of her misery, the legless zombie-woman, telling her, "I'm sorry this happened to you,"[17] and does so again when he protects the zombie-bitten Jim from being outright killed, declaring, "Jim isn't a monster or some rabid dog. He's a sick, sick man."[18]

I could go on to mention many other principles such as "be brave" but the idea should be clear by now: the Natural Law and its justice reveal themselves in many general ways to all people. However, specificities surrounding or flowing out of the Natural Law, such as what secondary principles we can deduce from basic or primary ones and what to do when two or more principles conflict, are less clear, and I'll need another section or two to deal with these issues, especially insofar as they further extend to laws of state or positive laws. Additionally, because it's impossible to do justice to all that could be said about the Natural Law and positive law, I will, as I mentioned in the introduction, restrict myself to the topic of theft to see how this relates to the Natural Law and how it should, or shouldn't, be dealt with in the positive laws of state.

---

11 Plato *Euthyphro* 4a.
12 Confucius *Hsiao King* 18.
13 *The Walking Dead* season 1, episode 4.
14 *The Walking Dead* season 1, episode 2.
15 *Buddhist Scriptures*, ed. Donald Lopez Jr. (Toronto: Penguin, 2004), 11.
16 *The Teaching of Amenemope* 25.1-2.
17 *The Walking Dead* season 1, episode 1.
18 *The Walking Dead* season 1, episode 5.

WISDOM AND THEFT

When Andrea asks Rick if he thinks it would be okay if she were to take the mermaid necklace from the store in zombie-infested Atlanta, she can be seen as asking not only whether it would be illegal if she were to take the necklace but also, and more basically, if it would be immoral, unjust, and, in our sense, unnatural to do so.

Although some believe that "do not steal" is a general command of the Natural Law, this should probably be seen as a secondary or deduced principle. Prior to the command not to steal is the principle of general beneficence. When one person takes what belongs to another person without the other person's consent, the first person fails to treat the second person with proper beneficence, in effect treating the second person as if he or she weren't an equal. To make this clear, most of us wouldn't consider it stealing if a starving person (a superior) took food from a mere animal (an inferior).

In addition, what makes the command "do not steal" derived is that it's connected to two statements about human nature – statements which can, with minimal work, be grasped by a careful, truth-seeking person, and which give content to the basic moral principles. The first statement is that all human beings are rational souls or spirits and, in this respect, are equal (even if they are unequal in countless other respects such as positions of authority or in terms of ability, beauty and so on). And the second statement declares that human beings can – at least as things now stand – own things (for if all ownership were illusionary, then the word "steal" would lose all meaning).

What can be said, then, to Aristotle, for example, who denied the first statement, declaring most barbarians "natural slaves" and women "incomplete men" (both lacking the rationality of Greek men), or the cannibalistic "hunters" in *The Walking Dead* comics who see their quarry as less human than they?[19] Aristotle seems to have confused spiritual or soul value (the value of being a rational soul or spirit) with spiritual or rational function (the perceived inferior intelligence of non-Greeks and women), and hence was led astray, while the cannibalistic hunters appear to have taken the principle of general beneficence ("value life," including one's own life) and applied it *only* to themselves (to love themselves at all costs), which gave them false justification for hunting and killing other humans who would normally be preserved under such a principle.

In this regard, I should also add something central to Natural Law, namely, the notion of virtue. The virtuous person is he or she who gathers together all the relevant moral principles and factors in a particular case, and then discerns what the proper course of action is: in such cases, we no longer speak of "all things being equal" but rather "all things considered." This kind of discernment is what Aristotle calls "practical wisdom" or Kant "practical

---

19   *The Walking Dead* vol. 1, #61.

reason." It weighs, balances, and discerns. For example, when we meet the cannibalistic hunters in the comic books, there seems to be two derived principles or injunctions in conflict: "Preserve one's own life" and "Don't kill innocent people." The only way that the hunters can preserve their own lives is through killing, and eating, innocent people (such as their own children). What is the right or just thing to do in this situation – starving to death, which would ultimately conflict with the preservation injunction? Or killing an innocent person to eat them, which would conflict with the don't kill an innocent person injunction? Generally speaking, it seems that my right to life should only extend to the point where I don't take another innocent life in the process; thus, starving to death, in this case, is morally preferable to killing and eating innocent people (especially, one's own children since we also have the principle of special beneficence). Moral principles themselves may be easy to understand, but knowing how to apply them isn't always so.

As for the second statement – the statement about ownership – most animistic religions, for example, disagree with it, arguing that because all material things are inextricably tied to a given spirit, human beings can't own anything except, perhaps, for their own material bodies (for to claim to own "dead matter" is to take what belongs to another spirit). Moreover, the general mood of apocalyptic literature, and *The Walking Dead* in particular, is often that ownership and personal property are exaggerated concepts that are folly in the mouth of the furnace, or, in our case, the mouth of the zombie. While one might sympathize with the view that shows at times the vanity of worldly possessions (apocalyptic literature is great for idol-smashing), a view like the animistic one is problematic in a world of imperfect people since it's ripe for abuse, that is, for the strong to take an unfair or better portion of what might legitimately or naturally belong to the community of people. This is to say, first, that granted when human beings initially found themselves on Earth, none had an absolute claim to the Earth and so the goods of the Earth – laying aside for the moment animal rights and so on – properly belonged to the community of human beings under God. Yet, second, because imperfect people didn't, and don't, share communal goods justly, it was – and still is – up to human beings to decide how to share or divide up the goods, and an individual's share of the goods is what we call personal property. Thus, while personal property is a concept derived from a more basic concept, namely, the community of goods, it does seem legitimately derived.

All this, then, makes stealing morally prohibited. So what can be said about Andrea and the necklace? If she were to take it, would she be stealing – would she be acting unjustly, unnaturally? ==Because the original owner of the necklace== (not to mention any legitimate heir) ==is very likely dead or worse, the necklace can reasonably be thought to belong to no one now and so whoever==

were to take possession of the necklace now would have a legitimate claim on it, properly appealing to "the right of first claim."

But this is a fairly easy case. To test our theory further we could problematize the situation a bit: What if Andrea found, and claimed for herself, four units of food (where a unit is indivisible) and Rick, for example, found none? Moreover, what if Rick – let's say he is surrounded by zombies – had no reasonable means of finding and claiming his own food? If Rick were to take any of the food held by Andrea, would he be stealing? Although many interpretations are possible when we get down to applied or practical ethics, I would say that he wouldn't be stealing for the following reasons.

Since moral duties usually (but not always) imply corresponding moral rights, and since the principle of general beneficence makes it a duty to do good to human beings, a moral right to life – in the same general sense as the duty to preserve life – may reasonably be inferred. In other words, Rick, just as much as Andrea, has the same basic claim to food and survival, and so for Rick to take two units of food would be simply for him to appeal to the principle of general beneficence and the notion that equals should be treated as such – in an absolute sense, the food still belongs to the community and justice demands proper distribution, where proper distribution likely means equal distribution.

However, if Andrea had five units of food, then I think Rick *would* be stealing if he were to take three units since even though both Rick and Andrea equally have the right to food and survival, Andrea has the additional right of first claim (a right subordinate to the right of survival, but a right nonetheless) which would tip the scale in her favour if the survival of the two of them were in question. Of course, this reasoning only works *ceteris paribus* – all things being equal. If we were to factor in that Rick is a larger man than Andrea and probably needs more food to survive or if we were to factor in Rick's greater survival value to the group, then things might look a bit different. But such are the complexities of applying the Natural Law to particular situations.

POSITIVIZING THE NATURAL LAW

And things are no less complex when it comes to relating the Natural Law to the laws of state, that is, when constructing positive laws. Although it's universally agreed upon by those who acknowledge the Natural Law that the Natural Law is a foundational element in the construction of positive laws, it's not always agreed upon how much of the Natural Law needs to be factored in when making laws of state. Why make all murder (a prohibition derived from general beneficence) illegal, but not make it a crime to fail to be patriotic at all times, where patriotism is a command derived from the principle of just preference to those closest to one's self? Or again, why is it a crime to lie in court, but not a crime to lie to one's parents?

The answer resides in the difference between an individual and the state. While individuals are called to discern and enforce the Natural Law in all its particularities in respect to the scope of the self, the state – conceived of minimally – is merely charged with discerning and enforcing public justice. Thus, while a just individual will both privately and publicly love his country (even if he is, in both circumstances, also critical of it), the state will only be concerned with patriotism insofar as a failure to be patriotic would harm the public, such as in the case of treason. Ditto for lying to one's parents and lying in court.

Thus, because theft is not merely a private matter, but is also a public matter, most governments make it illegal. But what about the United States? Obviously before the zombie apocalypse, stealing was a crime, hence Andrea asked Rick if it "would be considered looting" if she were to take the mermaid necklace. But does the United States government still exist and have authority in *The Walking Dead* universe such that taking the necklace would be illegal?

Previously, I argued that if Andrea were to take the necklace, she probably wouldn't be acting immorally since the necklace likely belongs to no one. Nevertheless, what I assumed there is that there is also no government which, even if the original owner of the necklace were dead, might possibly require Andrea to surrender the necklace to them as the proper possession of the commonwealth. This, I should add, would almost certainly be the case of the Governor and his city or even the Community and its territory. If the government were still functioning, then its positive laws would also be functioning, and so stealing would still be illegal and thus if Andrea were simply to take the necklace (as opposed to using it for survival purposes), it's possible that she would still be acting illegally and, insofar as the Natural Law requires us to show piety to those above us – here, the laws of the land – Andrea might thus be considered immoral for taking the necklace.

However, at least thus far in *The Walking Dead* it seems clear that there is no longer a "United States of America" with its positive laws and legal authority. Rick, for example, doesn't stop the abusive Merle Dixon because Rick is a *cop*, but rather because he is a *good man*, saying, "All I am any more is a man looking for his wife and son."[20] It's precisely because the positive laws of state have broken down that some, such as Carol (who in issue #27 proposes a polygamous marriage between herself, Rick and Rick's wife, Lori, saying, "We don't have to follow the old rules, we can make new ones"), imagines that there is no longer any binding morality – morality being, as with the positive laws of state, merely a social construct. But the Natural Law and its principles are prior to the positive laws of the land and, as we have seen, are not merely the

---

20   *The Walking Dead* season 1, episode 2.

basis of just positive laws but are ever-binding to individuals. So, even when the laws of state are no more, the Laws of Nature still are. Theft is wrong, even if there is no government on Earth to enforce this command; however, in the case of Andrea and the necklace, it's likely that she isn't breaking any positive law nor, for that matter, any law of Nature.

THE REAL "ABOMINATIONS"

In issue #61 of the comics, Father Gabriel calls the zombies "abominations" and fully endorses their destruction. His language is biblical – the same language used to denounce those who violate the Natural Law, such as murderers, liars, thieves and so on. While it's true that zombies are unnatural in the sense of being "against God's design," Father Gabriel commits a category mistake by lumping "bad" things with "evil" things.

A bad thing is simply something that isn't functioning according to its general design plan (and here, we should add, that this term *general* is key), whereas an evil thing is, strictly speaking, a *free will* which chooses to act against what is natural or just. Cancer is bad, defaced paintings are bad, spilled whiskey is bad, but it would be odd to call cancer, defaced paintings and spilled whiskey evil. And the same is true for zombies: they are bad, but not evil; they are unnatural in one sense, but they aren't violating the moral principles of the Natural Law.

The Governor admires the zombies and says "they are no different" than humans insofar as "they want what they want."[21] But this says more about what happens to a human being who willingly ignores the Natural Law than it does about zombies and humans themselves, for a human being who willingly ignores the Natural Law reduces himself to the level of a zombie, where hunger, strength and the mood of the group rule supreme. To demonstrate our humanity, we need, as many in the *The Walking Dead* universe still recognize, the Natural Law and justice, not only to keep individuals *qua* individuals on the path to true happiness, but also to underpin positive laws which aid individuals *qua* nations as they strive for the same goal.

---

21 *The Walking Dead* vol. 1, #28.

Chapter Five

Do We All Need to Get Shot in the Head?
Regarding Henry, Rights and Ethical Transformation

Regarding Henry, J. J. Abrams's first solo attempt at writing a screenplay, is one of the most underrated films of the '90s. Not only does it feature Harrison Ford at his best (which already makes it worth the price of admission), but also – more importantly – it has a clear, powerful storyline concerning one of the most important philosophical topics of all: ethical transformation. Consequently, what I'd like to do in this chapter is to examine ethical transformation – especially the ethical transformation of Henry Turner, *Regarding Henry*'s protagonist – vis-à-vis philosopher Nicholas Wolterstorff's theory of justice and rights. Ultimately my goal is to answer the question poised in this chapter's title: Do we all need to get shot in the head (in order to become better, happier people)?

"YOU NEVER APOLOGIZE"

Henry Turner is a man who at the beginning of the movie seems to have it all: he's a successful Manhattan attorney with a beautiful family and all the worldly goods one could hope for. If pleasure were the same as happiness, Henry would be a happy man indeed. However, they aren't the same, and Henry isn't happy.

According to Abrams's screenplay, the chief source of Henry's unhappiness is his unethical behaviour. Henry's injustice extends to his wife, Sarah, whom he cheats on and to whom he "never apologize[s]," his daughter, Rachel, whom he neglects, and those on the opposite side of the legal bench, whose case he distorts. While few will disagree that these are in fact instances of injustice, most can't clearly articulate why. Thus, justice needs to be defined to get at the precise nature of Henry's immorality and subsequent misery.

In his book *Justice: Rights and Wrongs*, Nicholas Wolterstorff argues that justice is ultimately grounded in rights, wherein rights are normative social relationships or proper bonds between persons and things.¹ People have rights to certain goods, and justice means rendering to each his, her or its rights – treating each person or thing as he, she or it ought to be treated.² For instance, Sarah Turner has a *right to* the good of being apologized to when she has been wronged, and Henry acts unjustly when he denies her this.

We'll notice from this that Wolterstorff thinks that it's better to approach justice from the point of view of the recipient (rights) rather than from the point of view of the agent (duties and obligations) since "If one thinks exclusively in terms of obligations, and if, furthermore, one thinks of guilt as guilt for violating the moral law rather than guilt for wronging the other, then the person who has been wronged falls entirely out of view."³ This is a helpful observation (especially if we remember that he is not denying that there are obligations and a moral law as well).

Let's say that after cheating on his wife, Henry felt bad about it, but let's say that he felt bad because he violated the universal moral law which states that a person should, all things being equal, keep his promises (in this case, keep his marriage vows). While this sense of violating basic moral injunctions is extremely important, it's incomplete; something more needs to be said. For the sake of argument, let's agree with Wolterstorff that breaking the moral law by performing such acts as lying is to *wrong* God, who is the Lawgiver behind the moral law and who has the *right* to be obeyed by His creatures. Yet even here if Henry were to ask only God for forgiveness, he would – if this were all there is to it⁴ – still be acting imperfectly since he has wronged his wife and

---

1   Nicholas Wolterstorff, *Justice: Rights and Wrongs* (Princeton: Princeton University Press, 2008), 4.
2   Wolterstorff traces a version of this definition all the way back to the Old Testament, though such a definition also has its roots in Aristotle's proportionate equality, and, most clearly, in Augustine, who writes, "The righteous man is the man who values things as their true worth; he has ordered love, which prevents him from loving what is not to be loved, or not loving what is to be loved, from preferring what ought to be loved less from loving equally what ought to be loved either less or more, or from loving either less or more what ought to be loved equally." Augustine *On Christian Doctrine* 27.28. For both Augustine and Wolterstorff, God is the ground of ontology and axiology; it's God who created all things and it's His creational laws – the universal moral law being just one instance of which – reveals to the righteous man or the man of prudence how each thing ought to be treated.
3   Wolterstorff, *Justice*, 9. This is partly what C. S. Lewis means when he says of the universal moral law, "Only a Person can forgive." C. S. Lewis, *Mere Christianity*, in *C. S. Lewis: Selected Books* [Long Edition] (London: HarperCollins, 1999), 339.
4   Although he doesn't discuss it, Wolterstorff, as a Christian, must somehow deal with the dynamics of rights being violated by one person yet being made right by another. For instance, even if Christianity is correct in maintaining that God, in

justice demands that *her* rights be respected and upheld as well. In other words, in order to be just Henry must somehow make things right with not only God (whose rights as the Creator he has trampled on) but also his wife (whose right to having a faithful husband Henry has disregarded) and even, if we wished to push the case, his daughter (insofar as children have the right to being raised in a stable household).

While some may say this is all fine and well, others may want more clarification on the matter, namely, to know what *kind* of rights Henry has violated. Has he violated (leaving God aside for the moment) his wife's and his daughter's socially conferred rights or their natural rights? Socially conferred rights are rights that people have been given by society, for instance, my being free to give my students the grade they deserve has been conferred on me by my university. In contrast, natural rights are rights with which people are born. While all agree that there are socially conferred rights, not all agree that there are natural rights. Since I want to argue that Henry has violated the *natural rights* of his wife and daughter, we need to see why there must be natural rights.

Wolterstorff argues for natural rights by distinguishing objective obligations, which are obligations that hold in general, such as "do not lie," from subjective obligations, which are obligations attached to a subject or person, such as "Henry should not lie to his wife." Wolterstorff then argues that all who accept that there are objective obligations (those who don't he has nothing to say to) will also accept that there are subjective obligations since obligations aren't given in a void. Following this, Wolterstorff introduces his "principle of correlatives," which states that "If Y belongs to the sort of entity that can have rights, then X has an obligation towards Y to do or refrain from doing A if and only if Y has a right against X to X's doing or refraining from doing A."[5] For instance, if Sarah is the sort of entity that can have rights (and presumably, as a human being, she is), then Henry has an obligation towards her to refrain from lying to her if and only if Sarah has a right against Henry to Henry's refraining from lying to her. What this means, of course, is that if Henry's subjective obligation not to lie to Sarah is *natural* (which Wolterstorff

---

Jesus, can forgive people for violating *His* right to be obeyed, what can be said of the person who has been wronged by an impenitent other? Is injustice thus ever-enduring? In some sense, yes. If we concede that God's omnipotence means the power to do all that is logically possible, then we admit that God can't do nonsense, including the nonsensical idea that He could right all wrongs even the wrongs committed by impenitent created beings against other created beings. Yet while God can probably only right some wrongs, not all wrongs, those who are with Him will not lack for happiness, for He is Happiness and all the wrongs committed against us by impenitent others will have no deep impact on our happiness.

5   Wolterstorff, *Justice*, 34.

takes it to be), then the correlative subjective right, namely, Sarah having the right not to be lied to by Henry, is also *natural*.

So, Henry Turner begins the movie as a deeply unjust man – a man who doesn't respect the natural rights of others, a man who doesn't treat each as they ought to be treated. Nevertheless, it still remains to be seen why this makes Henry miserable, which is to say it still remains to be seen how happiness is connected to justice.

"STARTING FROM SCRATCH"

One evening Henry runs out to a convenience store to buy some cigarettes but in the process interrupts a robbery, resulting in his getting shot. One bullet enters his chest, which causes internal bleeding, and another pierces his frontal lobe, which controls some rudimentary behaviour. Combined, this causes anoxia or a lack of oxygen to the brain, resulting in brain damage. Henry survives but experiences total memory loss. However, with the help of his physical therapist, Bradley, and his family, Sarah and Rachel, Henry starts to recover physically. But that's not all. Henry, we are told, "is in some ways . . . starting from scratch," meaning that Henry's being shot in the head affords him the opportunity to look at ethical situations from a proper perspective and choose, without the chains of vice holding him down, to do what is right. And this is what we see happen in three cases.

First, Henry starts to spend time with his daughter, which is to say that he respects her right to enjoy quality time with her father. Both Henry and Rachel, moreover, *like* spending time with each other, which suggests that there is some connection between happiness and justice. The final scene in the movie, when Henry essentially rescues Rachel from the boarding school she hates, says it all.

Second, Henry discovers that the malpractice suit he won in defending a crooked hospital against an elderly plaintiff is unjust since the plaintiff did in fact warn the hospital of the problem and so had a right to compensation. After turning his back on his own firm for the sake of justice, Henry is told by the plaintiff, "I like you much better now."

And third, Henry is shocked to discover both that Sarah had cheated on him and that he had also cheated on her. Nevertheless, now free from the strangle hold of vice, Henry sees that such behaviour is unjust and so apologizes to his wife, who reciprocates. This leads to a renewed marriage.

Abrams's point in all this is to show that ethical transformation towards justice leads to happiness. Nevertheless, it's not clear from Abrams's screenplay what exactly happiness is, nor whether the desire for happiness is prior to the desire for justice or whether the desire for justice is prior to the desire for happiness. Both of these questions need to be answered.

Above All Things

"I DON'T LIKE WHO I WAS"

Happiness is a difficult word to define, but the ancients weren't so far off when they spoke of it as "flourishing." A happy life was a "flourishing life" – a life wherein one realizes one's true self and, at least in the case of Aristotle, actively enjoys certain physical or worldly pleasures as well. Because one's true self is a rational soul, spirit or person, one is most one's self when one acts, among other things, rationally. And because reason teaches us that we ought to obey the universal moral law and cultivate virtue, the happy person is he who is moral and just (plus, in the case of Aristotle, also enjoys certain pleasures of the body as well). Already on this model it's easy to see why Henry becomes happier as he becomes more just – why he speaks truly when he says, "I don't like who I was." Nevertheless, Wolterstorff thinks that such an account of happiness – even the Aristotelian account, which would make Henry's renewed health and beautiful family genuine factors in his happiness – is incomplete.[6] Why?

To begin with, rights are what philosophers call "states of affairs," which in English grammar typically take the form of infinitives or gerunds, such as "Sarah's right *not to be* lied to" or "Rachel's *receiving* quality time with her dad." More specifically, rights are states of affairs of which a person is a constituent. For example, Sarah doesn't have a right to the *sun setting*. But she may have a right *to be free to watch the sunset*. Additionally, not all states of affairs of which a person is a constituent are legitimate rights. For instance, Sarah doesn't have the right *to be happy*. But she does have the right *to be free to pursue, and possess a legitimate means to achieve, happiness*.[7]

To go deeper, it needs to be stressed that rights are not purely individualistic. Consider Henry's treatment of his wife. By cheating on, and lying to, her, Henry violates Sarah's right to be told the truth and have a faithful husband. Yet as I suggested earlier, when Henry violates Sarah's rights, their marriage becomes unstable. This instability, in turn, affects Rachel, who has the right to enjoy a stable family and respectable parents. Henry's injustice toward one, indirectly affects the other. Truly no man is an island.

Wolterstorff, as I said, thinks the ancients' understanding of happiness is incomplete. We can now start to see why. When Henry was shot by the robber, the robber didn't just violate Henry's rights; he also violated the rights of Sarah and Rachel as well in that he deprived them of a husband and father and all that those offices entail. Sarah can't be perfectly happy if her *husband* is injured by another. But that's not all. When Henry's lawyer friends slander him *behind his back* (that is, without Henry having *any* knowledge of it), Henry

---

6 Wolterstorff, *Justice*, 136.
7 See C. S. Lewis, "We Have No 'Right to Happiness,'" in *C. S. Lewis: Essay Collection & Other Short Pieces*, ed. Lesley Walmsley (London: HarperCollins, 2000), 388-392.

has been *wronged* (even if he hasn't been *hurt*) since he has the right *to not be slandered* period. Or again, if Henry and Sarah hadn't reconciled, then they would have wronged their future (unborn) grandchildren, whose rights *to have a stable extended family* would have been violated.

Thus, because the ancient (so-called *eudaimonian*) conceptions of happiness are strongly agent-centered, they fail, or so Wolterstorff argues, to account for many of the recipient aspects of happiness.[8] We should say, then, that happiness entails not only being a virtuous person – which is the most important aspect of happiness – and possessing certain worldly goods, such as health, money and so on but also enjoying the goods to which one has right to, which is to say being treated as one ought to be treated.

If all this is required in order to be happy, then who could ever be happy? It's true we can't speak of any person being perfectly happy since every person has, at the very least, been slandered unapologetically once in his or her life.[9] Nevertheless, we can state the obvious truth, namely, that the closer one comes to being perfect and enjoying the goods that constitute happiness, the happier he or she will become. Thus, since Henry manages to reform his character, he has achieved the most important aspect of happiness. Indeed, even though he suffers financial problems as a result of quitting his job at the law firm and endures ridicule by his former colleagues, Henry is still happier than when he was immoral but rich and well-liked by his peers. In this way, getting shot in the head was a bad thing (a violation of his right not to be shot) but it resulted in a greater good: a more moral life.

ON BUYING PUPPIES

Before we can conclude, there remains an important question that has been

---

8   Wolterstorff, *Justice*, 176.
9   How can God be the perfection of Happiness if He can be wronged by others? Many theologians think God is impassible (can't be affected by anything outside Himself) because they imagine that only if God is impassible can He be perfect. However, biblical evidence is against this doctrine. For example, the Bible makes it clear that God created man because He *desired* man's love and friendship, and God, moreover, gets *angry* at man for not obeying His commands. While verses that talk about God's "hands" for example are clear instances of anthropomorphism (depicting God as a man), I don't think the verses that talk about God's emotions and desires are so. Man, as spirit or substance, has the essential property "being emotional" or "having desires," and my guess is that this is part of what it means to be made in the image of God – that God Himself has the essential property "having desires." Of course, this doesn't help explain in what sense God is the perfection of Happiness if He can be wronged and therefore lack in happiness. I think the best we can do here is to chalk it up to mystery – neither to deny that God is perfect Happiness nor that He has emotions and desires.

raised but not answered: is the desire for justice – the desire to treat each as they ought to be treated – prior to the desire for happiness – that is, the desire to be a certain kind of person and enjoy the goods to which he has a right – or vice versa?

Those who say that the desire for justice should be prior often consider those who think the desire for happiness prior to be somehow *selfish* or *egotistical*. Conversely, those who think the desire for happiness is prior often consider those who think the desire for justice prior are cold, robotic and, frankly, inhuman.

Although Wolterstorff doesn't err in equating selfishness and self-interest, he also doesn't provide a clear solution to this problem. Thus, I suggest we take a page from C. S. Lewis, who develops the critical distinction between selfishness and self-interest.

For Lewis, selfishness is a form of injustice: it's an instance of taking or desiring to take what doesn't belong to one's self, which, of course, entails violating the rights of others. Nonetheless, it doesn't follow from this that unselfishness is a virtue: simply to deny oneself goods and pleasures that one may have a *legitimate, natural right to* is only good in *certain* circumstances, such as if Henry gave up his right to eat his lunch so that Rachel could eat; such unselfishness is not good in *all* circumstances. To defend one's rights, to desire that one's rights be respected and thus to desire one's own happiness is hardly selfish or unjust *in and of itself*.[10] For instance, if Sarah married Henry simply for his money, we could say that Sarah would be selfish or unjust since she wouldn't be treating Henry as he ought to be treated, namely, as an entity that is more than a means to money. However, it's hardly selfish or unjust of Sarah to make financial stability *one* of the considerations in her decision to marry Henry since it's proper that a husband take care of his wife and having money is one of the ways he can achieve this.

Because happiness has to do with both what one does (especially the performance of one's obligations to the development of a virtuous character) and what one receives (especially, though not exclusively, one's rights safeguarded), it seems odd to speak about the desire for justice and the desire for one's own happiness as being totally different things. The desire for justice is *part of* the desire for happiness. For example, Henry is shown to have a *desire* to make Rachel happy, a desire that ultimately leads him to buy her a puppy. However this desire to treat Rachel justly – that is, to respect her rights to be loved by her father – is, of course, on one level connected with Henry's own desire to be happy since he can't be happy without being just. My sense is that language is the problem here. If we say Henry shows love to his daughter out of a sense

---

10   C. S. Lewis, "The Weight of Glory," in *C. S. Lewis: Essay Collection & Other Short Pieces*, ed. Lesley Walmsley (London: HarperCollins, 2000), 99.

of justice, then we applaud; but if we say he does it out of a desire for his own happiness, we pause. This, however, just goes to show that we ==still falsely think that to desire our own happiness is always selfish, rather than properly self-interested.== Perhaps this is unavoidable. More than a few of the greatest philosophers and religious leaders understand man to be broken-but-good, meaning that man naturally unnaturally so-to-speak desires not proper self-interest (and hence justice) but rather selfishness (and hence injustice). Because of this, Abrams is perhaps wise, for by not revealing which desire motivates Henry's acts of justice, everyone can see the obvious and all-important truth, which is that justice and happiness are inextricably linked.

"IT WAS A TEST.... I HAD TO FIND MY LIFE"

After discovering his wife cheated on him, Henry, in a moment of confusion, seeks out the company of his physical therapist, Bradley, who tells Henry a story of how he, Bradley, had his dreams of being a football player crushed by a bad knee injury. He goes on to tell Henry how he used this bad situation for ethical transformation, saying, "It was a test.... I had to find my life." This, we know, Bradley did, for he became a brilliant physical therapist and, by doing his job justly (that is, well), he also found a lot of happiness. Bradley's story, of course, foreshadows Henry's own story of ethical transformation – of being shot in the head only to become a better man, which is also to say, a happier man, for it.

So, at last we come to the question asked at the beginning of this chapter: Do we all need to get shot in the head (in order to become better, happier people)? In a perfect world – in a world where love of justice is strong enough and is indeed seen as one with the proper love of self – then the answer is certainly no. But we don't live in such a world; in our broken-but-good world, where legitimate self-interest usually becomes selfishness, most of us would probably do well to be shot, as Henry was, in the head.

Chapter Six

"I'm the King; That's What I Do": King Neptune and the Duties of Kingship

Near the beginning of *The SpongeBob SquarePants Movie*, King Neptune is about to execute the royal crown polisher for simply doing his job. When asked by his daughter, Mindy, why he has "to be so mean," Neptune replies, "I'm the king; that's what I do." But is this really so? Do kings really have to be cruel and ruthless? How are they distinguishable from tyrants? Indeed, what should a king be like – what is his character and what are his duties? In this chapter, using King Neptune as my example, I will answer these questions and others with the help of Dante and his classic treatise on kingship, *De Monarchia* (*On Monarchy*).

EXECUTING POLES AND OTHER WRONG ACTS

Dante begins *De Monarchia* by claiming, "All men whose higher nature has endowed them with a love of *truth* obviously have the greatest interest in working for posterity."[1] What's important to notice here is that he assumes from the very outset the existence of truth, which was obvious to our forefathers but not as obvious to us nowadays. For Dante, truth is an objective quality. It's really out there and, in some measure, can be discerned by the human mind. For instance, we say the propositions "1 + 1 = 2" or "It's always wrong to torture a child for fun" are *true*, not because they're merely our subjective opinions, but because these opinions, which presumably are held for the right reasons, have a rightness or correspondence with deeper reality. This reality, for Dante, is first God Himself (thus, 1 + 1 = 2 is primarily an idea in the Divine Mind and it's true because it's grounded in the divine, unchanging nature) and second God's creational or natural laws (God issues commands, based on His unchanging nature and ideas, and these commands, such as "it's always wrong to torture a child for fun," require obedience in creatures). We could even say truth is a kind of justice – it's the quality that obtains when we treat each thing or person as it ought to be treated. So, when King Neptune tries to execute a pole he

---

1 Dante *De Monarchia* 1.1.

happened to bump into, his behaviour isn't right; it doesn't correspond with how people should act; it isn't *just* because treating each thing as it ought to be treated means not holding things responsible for actions that they didn't do.[2]

"BEHAVIOUR BEFITTING A KING"

And speaking of God and justice, this leads to a few more assumptions Dante held.

To begin with, kingship is primarily a matter of God's choice or election.[3] On a Dantean reading, King Neptune, though a god (lower case "g"), would still have been created by God (capital "G"). In this way, Dante would likely argue that King Neptune, just like Augustus Caesar, was "ordained by nature for rule,"[4] while others, such as Patrick and Plankton, were not. Of course, this isn't to say that Patrick and Plankton were made for no purpose – far from it – but it's only to say that Neptune was made to rule, while the other sea creatures were made for other tasks, such as comedy or invention. This, in fact, perhaps makes Neptune partially right for imprisoning his negligent son, Triton, since it's at least true that the boy needed to "learn to embrace his destiny."[5] Moreover, we could even see the female fish's exclamation upon hearing that King Neptune will be eating at the Krusty Krab "I'm a huge fan of the royal family. I just love everything they do" as demonstrating people's God-given love of hierarchy. In other words, respect for the royal family is evidence, albeit weak evidence, that kingship is God-ordained and therefore good in and of itself.

However, nowadays many might see this blatant theory of hierarchy as inherently *unjust*. But here we must be careful. Justice, we recall, means treating each thing or person as it, he or she ought to be treated – that is, according to their unique natures. But God Himself made the natures of all created things and so justice means treating a king as a king, comedy as comedy, and so on. In other words, those who think it unfair that God made Neptune king are actually the ones who are promoting unfair or unjust behaviour because they want to treat a king as if he weren't one. This is why in the Bible David didn't kill King Saul, an evil ruler by all accounts, saying that it isn't right "to raise a hand against the LORD's anointed."[6]

Nevertheless, Dante isn't oblivious to the fragment of truth in this objection. That's why he labours to show, with some dubious reasoning, that

---

2 *The SpongeBob SquarePants Movie*, directed by Stephen Hillenburg (Nickelodeon Movies, 2004).
3 Dante *De Monarchia* 3.16.
4 Dante *De Monarchia* 2.6.
5 *SpongeBob SquarePants* season 6, episode 26.
6 1 Samuel 24:6.

those who God chooses to rule will demonstrate, in their actions, that they were supposed to rule. Using the Romans as his example, Dante argues (1) kings and emperors should rule for the good of all people, (2) the Roman emperors ruled, at least better than anyone else, for the good of all people, (3) therefore, the Romans were God's political elect.[7] Leaving aside the most questionable proposition – (3), the conclusion to the syllogism – Dante, who's following Plato and Aristotle here, seems correct in maintaining that kings or political rulers ought to be servants of the people: they ought to be thinking of the good of all those below them. In other words, if a king wants to live up to his name and nature and not simply be a tyrant, he must act justly and part of doing so means serving his people. He mustn't be indifferent to servitude; hence, Queen Amphitrite is correct when she says to the mopey Neptune, "Surely this isn't the behaviour befitting a king – hiding in bed for days on end, doing nothing but watching daytime television!"[8] Indeed, Neptune should be an active servant of his people; thus, Princess Mindy is right when she asks her Dad, "Where is your love and compassion?"[9]

Nevertheless, serving the people is only one part of what it means for a king to act justly or according to his nature. The other part, that which must be paired with service, is the assertion of strength and authority. A king, in other words, must be able to judge his people and make important decisions that will affect, sometimes unpleasantly, those below him. In this way, Neptune isn't wrong for referring to the people of Bikini Bottom as "my . . . flock," nor for seeing the need for some "smiting."[10]

"YOU WON'T BE KING UNTIL YOU LEARN TO . . ."

Of course, to talk about serving people and exercising strength is to talk very narrowly about the duties of kingship, and, indeed, it's to get ahead of the ball. To be a proper or just king, one must first be a proper or just person.

Men, gods and talking sponges all have one important thing in common: they are rational souls, spirits or persons; they have been created, so Dante would say, with intellect, free will, desires and so on. They act justly or properly, therefore, when, in this bare sense, they act according to their nature, which is to say, among other things, when they act rationally.[11] Following a Christian appropriation of Plato and Aristotle, Dante believed that the first thing a rational soul or person realizes when he acts rationally is that people

---

7   Dante *De Monarchia* 2.5.
8   *SpongeBob SquarePants* season 6, episode 26.
9   *The SpongeBob SquarePants Movie*.
10 *SpongeBob SquarePants* season 6, episode 26.
11 Dante *De Monarchia* 1.3.

are made for happiness.[12] And even though many – perhaps most – people will be mistaken about *what* constitutes their happiness (due to limited knowledge and sin), all in fact want happiness, which, for rational souls, is the realization of one's true self. However, because God created all things, one's true self can only be realized by finding it in God the Creator. Therefore, the more rational a person is the more he will seek out God, and what he discovers along the way – on the way to God – is that if he wants to draw close to God, he needs to act justly, for God is the source of all Justice. Indeed, if he wants to be in perfect fellowship with God, thus discovering his true nature and destiny, he needs to have a nature that is like God's, for no injustice can enter into the presence that is the burning holiness of God (even Spongebob knew that only if he became an immortal could he live in Atlantis as Neptune's fry cook[13]). Thus, acquiring – in large part by God's grace – a virtuous character is necessary in order to be a properly functioning person.

As a typical medieval thinker, Dante believed that a virtuous character will be made up of at least seven virtues, four cardinal (prudence, courage, temperance, and justice) and three theological (faith, hope and love). Needless to say, a king worthy of his name will possess these to a very high degree and certainly more than the average person.

Prudence, the first virtue, is practical, but not pragmatic, wisdom. A king must understand God's laws relevant to political life and all that is relevant to politics and be aware of how to apply his knowledge to particular problems that arise. In this way, he is supremely practical, but isn't pragmatic since pragmatism, denying or leaving aside any question of objective truth, asserts only what works. Plankton is the most pragmatic one in Bikini Bottom, for he will do whatever it takes to acquire the recipe for the Krabby Patty. A prudent ruler, therefore, will always endeavour to find ways to achieve the goals of politics, namely, to secure the rights, freedom and security of the people, but never at the cost of violating God's natural, moral laws. As a wise man, the king will remember that he is below God and responsible to God for the well-being of the people underneath him. Because he is wise, he understands that he must be a servant-leader; he knows when to be generous and when to be firm. In "The Clash of Triton," Neptune shows *some* understanding of the need for this balance (thus, he tells Triton, "Son, I understand if you want to keep me locked up in this cage, but . . . release these others for they are innocent"); however, for the most part, Neptune is imprudent, typically seeing "smiting" as the solution to every political problem.[14]

Courage is the virtue that controls the passionate part of the soul. It's

---

12   Dante *De Monarchia* 1.4.
13   *SpongeBob SquarePants* season 1, episode 19.
14   *SpongeBob SquarePants* season 6, episode 26.

what *moves* people to act in the face of fear or laziness. This virtue is vital for people, but especially for rulers, since a good, but cowardly, politician will never be able to act upon his convictions. Dante quotes approvingly a passage from the *Aeneid* where Aeneas, the father of the Romans, is told, "You are to impose the ways of peace, sparing those who submit and being inexorable to the proud."[15] In other words, kings must be courageous; they must be unafraid of establishing the common good. Triton, Neptune's hippy son, began as a prince who cared about the people, going so far as to discover a cure for "all mortal diseases;" nevertheless, Neptune, with passion denounced him, saying, "How many times do I have to tell you? We are gods – we don't have diseases nor do we care whether or not the mortals contract them!"[16] On the one hand, Neptune has courage to enforce his political convictions, but sadly they are misguided ones: he has courage but little prudence. On the other hand, Triton has some prudence (his priorities of service to his people shows wisdom), but has no courage to stand up for what is right: he has prudence but no courage. Needless to say, a king worthy of his name must have both virtues.

Temperance is the virtue of self-control. It's the habit in the soul that, following the guidance of wisdom, uses the passionate part of the soul to control the appetitive part. In plainer language, temperance is the strength of will that not only resists temptation (as courage does) but goes further and pacifies the hungers of the appetite (for food, drink, sex, power and so on) to such a degree that there is harmony within the soul. The truly self-controlled man is one at peace with himself; the truly self-controlled king is at peace with himself and so can, with no ambition for power or money or fame, dedicate himself to his political office. Neither Neptune nor his son, Triton, appear to be at peace with themselves – both are whimsical and temperamental – and so could hardly be free from the temptations that arise with kingship. Were Mindy Neptune's son, and not his daughter, she would make a superior ruler since she shows herself to level-headed and slow to anger.

Justice we have already discussed, though I should add that all virtues are such because they demonstrate justice. For example, the wise man is he who knows many true things and is aware of how to apply these truths to particular situations; he knows what a thing is and what to do with that thing; he treats, with his mind, each thing as it ought to be treated. Or again, the courageous woman is she who knows when to act and when not to and then does the proper action; she acts, with her passion, the way she ought to in each particular situation. And finally, the man of temperance demonstrates a harmony within his soul; his soul functions as it ought to, namely, as an internal harmony. Thus, we can see that justice touches all aspects of life, the political

---

15 Dante *De Monarchia* 2.7. Cf. Virgil *Aeneid* 6.847.
16 *SpongeBob SquarePants* season 6, episode 26.

life not the least of which. Consequently, a king must be just and fair, acting properly in each situation and treating all things and persons as they ought to be treated; this requires wisdom, courage and temperance. When Neptune punishes SpongeBob for Patrick's hostile words ("Your friend's arrogance will cost *you* dearly!"[17]), he acts unjustly since Patrick alone should be punished for his disrespectful behaviour. Moreover, when Neptune initially fails to keep his promise to make the one who can draw the golden spatula his royal fry cook, he is, as SpongeBob says, "a liar," which is to say, an unjust person, since justice requires that promises, all things being equal, be upheld.

Those are the four cardinal virtues, but what about the theological ones? Dante, as I've said, was a Christian political thinker and as such thought that the king is primarily chosen by God. Accordingly, the king – at least with the advent of Christ – should be a Christian one, and that means, among other things, that he should demonstrate faith, hope and love both as a person and as a king.

As a virtue, faith has to do with both being aware of God's existence and something of His nature, and loving that of which we are aware. This isn't blind belief or loyalty – far from it. It's *knowledge* that God communicates to people, and it's *love* that flows from this knowledge. It's trusting, in the face of irrational desires, in a God who we have good reason to believe exists and is good. This virtue, of course, is vital to kingship since ignorance of God and His ways will always lead to poor practical political solutions. For example, if Neptune were aware of God and something of His nature, he'd know that since God is the Just King, he, too, ought to be a just king. Faith, in other words, would give Neptune both knowledge about how he ought to act as one under God's authority, and confidence to do so.

Hope must be distinguished from a *wish*. Hope is the rational desire to find one's true self in the presence of one's Creator; it's the desire for True Happiness, for God, who is a *real* person. A wish is something that a person wants but can't actually get: in its worst form it's a kind of wish-fulfillment or neurosis. When we say, "I wish I could jump to the moon" or "I wish I were you," we assert things that are impossibilities for man: *I can't really jump to the moon* and *I can't really be you.* However, when we say, "I hope to see you at the party" or "I hope to see you in Heaven," we know that it's a *real* possibility that I could see you at the party or that I could see you in Heaven: I could, if things worked out, *really* see you there. By faith – rational knowledge of God's existence – people can know that God exists, and thus it's a rational or real possibility to find one's true self in God. Hope is the rational desire for this real possibility. All people, but especially kings, need this virtue since without the desire to find one's true self – without a desire for the truth of the matter

---

17 *SpongeBob SquarePants* season 1, episode 19.

– a person will fall into the temptation to create oneself, to do whatever one likes, ignoring the deeper reality behind things. Dante again praises Aeneas because he sought "the divine pleasure by waging a single combat;"[18] in other words, King Aeneas had his eyes set on the heavens and thus, because his priorities were correct, got the Earth thrown in. King Neptune, on the other hand, never sets his eyes above, nor inclines his heart to, anything but his own private concerns (attending house parties[19] and so on), and so understandably is a wayward ruler.

Love or *agape* is the perfection of the moral law or justice in that while law and justice have to do with treating each thing as it ought to be treated, love has to do with going beyond this, with treating each thing with *more* consideration – in a positive sense – than is required. Love, in Shakespeare's wonderful phrase, "seasons justice."[20] For example, if a king were slandered by one of his subjects, he would have, by law and justice, the right to punish the criminal. However, out of love, the king might choose to take the injustice upon himself so-to-speak, and, provided the criminal repented, forgive him and no longer hold him accountable for his crime. This would be the virtue of love. Needless to say, it's quite foreign to Neptune.

"YOURS IS SUPERIOR; THEREFORE, I CONCEDE TO YOU"?

Using King Neptune as my example and Dante as my guide, I discussed the character and duties of a king. What we saw is that, first and foremost, a king must be a good or virtuous (mer)man. For this reason, he needs to acquire at least seven virtues: prudence, courage, temperance, justice, faith, hope and love. After this, the king must be aware of what it specifically means to be king, namely, being aware of the specifics of the public square. Although King Neptune and his son, Triton, each possess some of the virtues, neither have enough to be considered good persons and neither have enough knowledge of politics to be, in a specific sense, good rulers. Should they, then, be deposed? Should Neptune follow SpongeBob around and serve as his lackey since SpongeBob makes "superior" patties?[21] Dante would probably say no, calling for Neptune's reform instead; however, each of us must answer this question in our own way.

---

18 Dante *De Monarchia* 2.10.
19 *SpongeBob SquarePants* season 3, episode 11.
20 William Shakespeare *Measure for Measure* 4.1.
21 *SpongeBob SquarePants* season 1, episode 19.

CHAPTER SEVEN

"NO OTHER GODS BEFORE ME": GOD, ONTOLOGY AND ETHICS IN *THE AVENGERS*

When Asgard, the home of the Norse gods, fell from the sky and landed in Oklahoma, one Christian pastor nearby began his Sunday sermon by asking, "Small-g gods? Big-G? Are the Asgardians 'gods'? And if they are, well, where does that leave my God?"[1]

Though I feel for this pastor and his disrupted equilibrium, it's clear that in the Marvel Universe, of which the Avengers and Thor are a part, God – capital "G" – exists. Dr. Strange learns about Him from the massive but not all-powerful cosmic being Eternity, who says, "I and my brother, Death, comprise all your reality! Neither he nor I am God, for God rules all realities!"[2] Thanos, even when he acquired the Heart of the Universe and bested the Living Tribunal (God's right-hand man), was naggingly aware of the Supreme Deity weaving the Titan's mischief for some higher purpose: "Was this my moment of triumph," he asked himself, "or but a facet of another's grand plan?"[3] And finally, the Fantastic Four and Spider-Man – all of whom have been Avengers at one time or another[4] – have personally met Him: the Fantastic Four by entering Heaven itself,[5] and Spider-Man when God appeared as a homeless stranger to comfort the weary Web-Slinger.[6]

So God exists . . . but how do we reconcile this with the plurality of beings in the Marvel Universe, and, more particularly, with the diversity found in the Avengers – diversity that includes a god like Thor? Moreover, how should we understand this in light of Exodus 20:3, which commands, "You shall have no other gods before me"? In this chapter, I will try to articulate how God

---

1   *The Mighty Thor* #1 (June 2011).
2   *Dr. Strange* vol. 1, #13 (April 1976).
3   *Marvel Universe: The End* #6 (August 2003).
4   The Thing became an Avenger in *The West Coast Avengers* vol. 2, #9 (June 1986), Mister Fantastic and Invisible Woman in *The Avengers* vol. 1, #300 (February 1989), the Human Torch in *The West Coast Avengers* #50 (November 1989), and Spider-Man in *The Avengers* vol. 1, #329 (February 1991).
5   *The Fantastic Four* vol. 1, #511 (May 2004).
6   *The Sensational Spider-Man* #40 (September 2007).

stands in relation to the Marvel Universe – the universe which includes all the possible worlds (realities, dimensions and times) in which the Avengers belong. Although this will start as an exercise in ontology (a defense, as we shall see, of the plurality of diverse beings), it will end with an ethical argument, namely, that though the Avengers are many and diverse, they are unified in their love of the Good, which, I will suggest, is actually a love for God seen through a glass darkly.

AVENGERS DISASSAMBLED

In the Marvel great chain of being, God is at the top – He's the first tier being – and though He can be spoken of and to, He is of a different category than all other beings. He is the Creator; everything else is creation. It's telling that in three instances that God is depicted – one in *Dr. Strange*,[7] one in *The Fantastic Four*[8] and another, as the Fulcrum, in *The Eternals*[9] – He is depicted as either Stan Lee or Jack Kirby, the literal creators of the Marvel Universe.

In addition to being the Creator, God "is all-powerful and all-knowing. He is the very essence of what holds reality in its place."[10] As such, God "sets the stage" for the drama of creation to play out.[11] However, though God is clearly transcendent and of a different category than all other Marvel beings, He is also immanent, interested and invested in what goes on in the realities He creates: "The play is your lives," He tells the former Avengers the Thing, Invisible Woman, Mister Fantastic and the Human Torch, "Your adventures become our exploration."[12] Just as an author has intentions as he writes, so too does God have intentions – perfect intentions – in His creation; He tells Spider-Man, "We all have a purpose, Peter. We all have a role to play."[13] And if the nature of God still seems ambiguous, He is clearly meant to be likened to the Judeo-Christian God, possibly alluding to Jesus even when He tells the heroic but suffering Peter Parker, "And, you know, if it's any consolation, I've asked a lot more from people much closer to me than you."[14] Indeed, "His only weapon," the Watcher tells the Invisible Woman, "is love!"[15]

Below God in the Marvel great chain of being – and switching categories from Creator to creature – is the Living Tribunal. Although likely second to

---

7 See *Strange Tales* #157-163 (June-December 1967).
8 *The Fantastic Four* vol. 1, #511 (May 2004).
9 *The Eternals* #9 (May 2009).
10 *The Eternals* #9 (May 2009).
11 *The Fantastic Four* vol. 1, #511 (May 2004).
12 *The Fantastic Four* vol. 1, #511 (May 2004).
13 *The Sensational Spider-Man* #40 (September 2007).
14 *The Sensational Spider-Man* #40 (September 2007).
15 *The Fantastic Four* vol. 1, #72 (March 1968).

God in authority (and third to God in power, after the wielder of the Heart of the Universe), the Living Tribunal is a mysterious figure of the Ezekiel 1 sort: like the "Living Creatures" of Ezekiel 1:6, each of whom have four faces, the Living Tribunal has four faces (three and a "void"[16]), and like the Living Creatures, who adore God in His throne room, the Living Tribunal is "the representative of The-One-Who-Is-Above-All"[17] (another name for God and one which should not be confused with the prime Celestial The One Above All,[18] who is a mere Celestial – a servant of the Fulcrum). The Living Tribunal's "task is to sit in judgment of events on the far end of the cosmic scale,"[19] and each of his three visible faces represents a mode of his righteous judgment: necessity, equity and vengeance. Each face can be likened to an angel in the Bible who pours out judgement in the name of The Most High,[20] and it's perhaps not unimportant that the Living Tribunal's face of necessity paraphrases Jesus ("Do unto others as you would have others do unto you") when he tells the She-Hulk, "Necessity is the Cosmic mirror which reminds us to always judge others as we would have ourselves judged."[21]

Below the Living Tribunal in terms of might, though not in terms of order of creation, is the wearer of the Infinity Gauntlet. Though the Gauntlet is sometimes spoken of as "the Mantle of Supremacy"[22] and its wearer sometimes claims to be God in terms of power and knowledge,[23] the power of the Gauntlet is power only over one reality, not all realities. Indeed, the Living Tribunal (not to mention God) can nullify the Gauntlet's power at will, but rarely does so because it's an important piece in the free will drama called creation.[24]

Following God (the first tier being) and the Living Tribunal (the second tier being) are a group of primordials called the cosmic beings or astral deities of the universe. These include the Celestials, Lord Chaos and Master Order, the Stranger, the Watcher, Galactus, Love and Hate, Kronos, Eternity,[25] and, most recently, the Chaos King (it's not very clear how he differs from Lord Chaos).[26] Most of the cosmic beings are beyond, and in some measure, cause,

---

16 *Silver Surfer* vol. 3, #31 (December 1989).
17 *The Infinity War* #2 (July 1992).
18 *Thor* vol. 1, #287 (September 1979).
19 *The Infinity War* #3 (August 1992).
20 Exodus 12, 2 Samuel 24:16, 1 Corinthians 10:10, Hebrews 11:28, and Revelation 9:11.
21 *She-Hulk* vol. 2, #12 (November 2006).
22 *The Infinity War* #2 (July 1992).
23 *The Infinity Gauntlet* #1 (July 1991) and *The Infinity War* #6 (November 1992).
24 See *The Infinity War* #4 (September 1992).
25 *The Infinity Gauntlet* #3 (September 1991).
26 *Chaos War* #1 (December 2010).

the physical fluctuations of the Big Crunch (the collapse of the multiverses) and the subsequent Big Bang (the explosion of the multiverses into a plethora of dimensions, universes and worlds), yet none of these beings are absolutely indestructible or eternal in the strict sense of the word: all suffer defeat at one time or another.

Below the cosmic beings are the fourth tier beings, the elders of the universe, who include the Collector, the Grandmaster, Chthon, Gaea (Mother Earth), and possibly Death. If Death is in fact an elder and not a cosmic being (the new literature suggests this, but not the old[27]), then one possible way to relate the elders to the cosmic beings is to take a page from Hesiod's *Theogony*, which suggests that there are four primordial gods (Chaos, Gaia, Tartaros and Eros), who in turn gave birth to all other beings. Chaos, for example, gave birth to Nyx (Night), who in turn gave birth to Thanatos (Death).[28] I believe something like this is also true in the Marvel Universe, for when the Avengers Hercules and Thor ask Eternity why he helped them fight Thanos and Death but won't help them fight the Chaos King, Eternity replies: "Thanos merely wanted to kill everything. The Chaos King is the Darkness and Chaos that existed before existence itself. He is an anti-god, the void against which I am defined. He and I walk hand in hand. If I fight him, I fight myself."[29] Of course, this only helps clarify to some extent the positions of the Chaos King (Chaos) and Love (Eros or the force that pulls things together[30]), and not Gaea (Gaia), who is a primordial goddess in Greek mythology and merely an elder in the Marvel Universe (even if, confusingly, in the Marvel Universe she and her fellow elders wield the Power Primordial). Nevertheless, both Gaia and Gaea spring out of Chaos: as an equal in the mythology or as a subordinate in the Marvel Universe. How, of course, Greek polytheism relates to Judeo-Christian monotheism is an important matter, but I put this aside for the moment.

Now in Greek mythology Gaia is supposed to have given birth to Uranus, together with whom she gave birth to the titans or giants. The titan Kronos, Hesiod further reports, is the father of the gods, the chief of whom is the Olympian Zeus.[31] As with the relation between the cosmic beings and the

---

27 In the old literature, Death is often depicted as Eternity's opposite, which would make him or her a cosmic being. However, during the Chaos War, the Chaos King is depicted as Eternity's true opposite and Death is a clear subordinate. See *Captain Marvel* vol. 1, #27 (July 1973) for the old and *Chaos War* #2 (January 2011) for the new.
28 Hesiod *Theogony* 116, 123 and 759.
29 *Chaos War* #2 (January 2011).
30 Empedocles, *The Poem of Empedocles*, in *Selections from Early Greek Philosophy*, 4th edition, ed. Milton Nahm (New York: Appleton-Century-Crofts, 1964), 114.
31 Hesiod *Theogony* 137 and 412.

elders, the relation between the elders and the sky fathers can't be perfectly understood within the framework of Greek mythology and polytheism. For example, in the Marvel Universe, Kronos is one of the cosmic beings (a superior being) but in Greek mythology is a titan (an inferior being – one below the four primordials though still above the gods). Nevertheless, Greek mythology certainly has some explanatory power. In the mythology, Gaia, for instance, is the mother or grandmother of the gods, including the sky father, Zeus, and in the Marvel Universe, Gaea is said to be the mother of all the sky fathers – not just Zeus, but also Osiris, Odin and others. She tells Hercules, "I was the first to form out of chaos. I birthed the gods themselves. I am the true fount of creation . . . the source of all that the gods can do and have done."[32] Additionally, insofar as the sky fathers Osiris and Odin are depicted in the Marvel Universe as subordinate beings, this largely agrees with both Egyptian mythology (where Osiris appears to have been one of the children of Ra, who himself, though uncreated, sprang from the watery-void, Nun[33]) and Norse mythology (where Odin is the child of the giants, who are the product of the cow Audumla, who in turn is the offspring of the two primordial elements, Fire and Ice[34]).

Of course, all this talk about tiers of beings only explains some things such as longevity and lineage. We who have been influenced by Greek philosophy and Judeo-Christian theology might rightly maintain that that which is oldest is that which is strongest, wisest and most indestructible – Plato believes this to be true of the Forms and Judeo-Christians of God – but for us to project this onto Greek and Norse polytheism would be anachronistic. In both of these cases (not to mention in the case of their root source, Mesopotamian mythology[35]), the late-coming sky fathers – Zeus and Odin – were able to defeat their respective fathers (the giants) and claim supremacy even while the primordials lingered, or so we have been made to believe, in the background.

In the Marvel Universe, too, lesser beings, such as Thanos (an Olympian god modified by the Celestials[36]), can wield the Infinity Gauntlet, which in turn can defeat Eternity, and Hercules the sky father is able to best the Chaos King. Thus, in respect to created things in the Marvel Universe, order of existence is one thing that separates the cosmic beings, elders and sky fathers

---

32 *Chaos War* #4 (March 2011).
33 Cf. Douglas Brewer and Emily Teeter, *Egypt and the Egyptians*, 2nd edition (Cambridge: Cambridge University Press, 2007), 98.
34 *The Prose Edda* 2.4-6. Also see *The Poetic Edda* 1.3 and 1.18.
35 In Mesopotamian mythology the second tier god Ea kills his first tier father – the primordial Apsu – and Ea's son, the third tier god Marduk, slays the first tier primordial goddess, Tiamet, to become the king of the gods. *Enuma Elish* 1.4, 1.69 and 4.104.
36 *Thanos* vol. 1, #1 (December 2003).

even if not much else, absolutely speaking, does.

We should expect, then, that when we turn to look at the differences between Avengers – for my purposes, I'll discuss Thor, the Hulk, the Wasp and Black Widow – that differences between them will rarely be absolute differences. So what makes them somewhat varied? I begin with Thor.

Gaea gave birth to the sky father Odin, who is the supreme god of the Asgardians, and together (Gaea in the guise of Jord and Odin as himself) they gave birth to Thor.[37] In all likelihood, Odin claims the title of sky father and the powers that go with that office because he was directly, without the aid of a lower father, birthed by Gaea, an elder, whereas Thor is a lower god (a sixth tier being we could say) because his blood was diluted by having a sky father for a parent and not just an elder.

Most of the gods, including Thor's Asgardians, live in dimensions different from that of human beings, although through greater knowledge and magical powers, they are able to intervene in the human dimension more easily than humans can in the gods': Thor can generate a portal between the Asgardian dimension and the Midgardian (earthly) dimension just by waving his hammer, whereas a mere superhuman like the Hulk or a mere human like the Black Widow can't do so. Of course, the key phrase is "more easily" since a superhuman and human *can* enter the divine realms or dimensions by "mere" human means such as the magic of Dr. Strange or the very advanced technology of Reed Richards and Stark Enterprises.[38]

The gods' greater magical ability also seems to give them greater resistance to the magical attacks of beings relative to their own stature. For example, although Lord Nightmare, who is a being roughly on par with the gods, was able to take control of "those with mortal minds," a god such as Thor remained unaffected.[39] Of course, this greater magical ability should not be mistaken for greater knowledge since the ability to do something isn't the same as the ability to *explain* how one did it. For example, few would argue that, on the whole (a key phrase), a Henry Pym or Bruce Banner is smarter or more knowledgeable than a Thor or Hercules; indeed, whereas both Pym and Banner can explain how to manipulate extradimensional space (as Pym does with his Pym Particles and Banner does when he transforms into the massive Hulk), Thor, though he manipulates the dimensions every time he teleports, can't really explain how he does so.

As with their magical ability, the gods' strength generally exceeds that of mortals, even superhuman ones. When Skaar, son of the Hulk, asks, "Gods? So what? We've fought every monster and demon," the She-Hulk quickly

---

37 *Thor* vol. 1, #300 (October 1980).
38 *The Avengers: Earth's Mightiest Heroes* season 1, episode 24.
39 *Chaos War* #2 (January 2011).

replies, "You don't understand. Gods are a bit different."[40] And indeed, they are. "Among mortals," Hera tells the Hulk, "you may be the strongest one there is but Father Zeus could vaporize you with a thought," and although Zeus doesn't do so, he does soundly defeat the Hulk, chaining him up like Prometheus for vultures to pick at him. In fact, even though Loki magically possesses the Hulk in order to turn him against Thor, saying, "Only you brought near defeat to the mighty Thor,"[41] Thor, and not the Hulk, can lift the magical hammer Mjolnir, and Thor, not the Hulk, emerges victorious: as the Wasp says of herself and fellow Avengers, "Thor, we already know you are the strongest."[42]

Of course as with most everything in this graded but not rigidly fixed universe, these kinds of statements are general, not unqualified. Consider two things. First, strength is an unclear term. Does it mean mere physical might or does it include, even leaving magic aside, other non-physical abilities? Graviton's power over gravity, for instance, is sufficient to defeat Thor and so he rightly asks, "Do you think I would surrender because of your supposed godhood? Perhaps I too am a god."[43] Second, even if, for the most part, gods are physically stronger than superhumans (seventh tier beings, we could say), a single god, such as Hercules, can be physically defeated by a group of lesser (superhuman) beings, which is what happens when Mr. Hyde, Goliath and the Wrecking Crew beat him within an inch of his life.[44]

And this raises the important question of what it means to be an immortal anyway. In philosophy, we typically say an *eternal* thing is that which is "outside" of time, having no beginning and no end; an *immortal* thing is that which has a beginning in time but no end; and a *mortal* thing is that which has a beginning and end in time. In the Marvel Universe, only God is eternal. Because all other beings are creatures (that is, are created by God), all other beings are either mortal or immortal. But because all creatures, save for Thanos and Adam Warlock, have died,[45] it seems very likely that all creatures can die, and indeed, it's certainly within God's power to permanently extinguish any of His creatures, including Thanos and Adam Warlock. Thus, strictly speaking, everything in the Marvel Universe is mortal. Nevertheless, there is another sense in which not just the cosmic beings, elders, sky fathers and gods but also superhumans, aliens and humans as well can be thought of as immortal, or,

---

40 *The Incredible Hulks* vol. 1, #622 (February 2011).
41 *Hulk vs. Thor*, directed by Sam Liu (Marvel Animation, 2009).
42 *The Avengers* vol. 1, #220 (June 1982).
43 *The Avengers* vol. 1, #159 (May 1977). Also see *The Avengers: Earth's Mightiest Heroes* season 1, episode 7.
44 *The Avengers* vol. 1, #274 (December 1986).
45 *Marvel Universe: The End* #6 (August 2003).

in the words of Thor, "ever defying *the eternal sleep*."[46] The sky fathers Odin and Zeus, for example, have died multiple times but they, as naked souls, continued to endure, albeit in different forms, in their respective underworlds alongside, importantly, the naked souls of mere superhumans and humans who have perished. All creatures are able to die, yet all (by God's decree to be sure) are able to endure as well; indeed, it's not unusual in the Marvel Universe for cosmic beings, elders, gods and humans alike to be resurrected or reincarnated again (whatever this looks like exactly).[47] Thus, when the gods are called "immortal" we should just take it to mean they can't die from old age or diseases,[48] not that their physical (?) bodies can't perish. Thus, to use the term "immortal" as a synonym for "god" is imprecise, and it is made more so by, among other things, the fact that a superhuman mutant like Wolverine is also unlikely to die of old age and disease.[49] But I digress.

The Hulk, the Wasp and Black Widow are all ontologically on lower levels than the god Thor, though this is mostly in respect to lineage and age and only to a lesser extent in respect to natural immunities and abilities. All four, of course, were made by God via His servants Eternity[50] and Gaea and in this respect are equals, but human beings, we are told, were given the finishing touches by the sub-sub-sub-subcreator Odin ("Some whisper that he made the first man"[51]), which, if true, would mean that while Thor, as the son of Odin, was *begotten* by Odin (who, I hasten to add, was of course himself ultimately created by God), the Hulk, the Wasp and Black Widow were in a more strict sense *created* (or touched up) by Odin.

But just as not all gods were created equal in respect to ontological status, power and so on (I don't say worth), so too is it with humans. The Celestials, we are also told, long ago arrived on Earth and experimented with the human ancestors (the ones Odin made?), producing, in addition to the superpowered Eternals and Deviants, humans with the mutant X-Gene, which either endows these superhumans with powers upon birth (as in the case of the Ultimate Wasp) or gives them latent powers which need to be unlocked by such things as radiation (as in the case of the Hulk).[52]

---

46   *The Avengers* vol. 1, #277 (March 1987).
47   For example, see *Thor* vol. 3, #1 (September 2007).
48   *The Avengers* vol. 1, #48-50 (January-March 1968).
49   *Wolverine and Hercules in: Myths, Monsters and Mutants* #1 (March 2011).
50   Eternity says, "I am Adam Qadmon, the archetypal man, and in my bosom grew mortals, each on their various worlds! At first they were only algae in their great mother seas . . . simple souls . . . but over the eons, I advanced them . . . from one cell to two, to many . . . to man!" *Dr. Strange* vol. 1, #13 (April 1976).
51   *Thor* vol. 2, #83 (October 2004).
52   *Thor* vol. 1, #287 (September 1979).

Mutations often appear very random and so it's unusual, though not impossible, for two mutants to share the exact same powers. Accordingly, because the longevity formula that the Black Widow drank likely would give *any* human great longevity (her very ordinary partner also drank the formula and also got increased longevity), she should not be seen as a mutant with latent powers needing to be awakened by the formula.[53] The same is true of the Earth-616 Wasp (the Wasp of the regular *Avengers* universe), who was not alone in drinking Pym Particles and developing the ability to manipulate extradimensional space.[54] These two are both human. The Ultimate Wasp, however, is born with mutant powers,[55] and the Hulk, as we know, was born with latent mutant powers. In terms of ontology, then, the Ultimate Wasp and Hulk (despite seeing his mutation as a "disease"[56]) would likely be seventh tier beings (homo sapiens superiors), while the Earth-616 Wasp and Black Widow would be eighth tier beings (homo sapiens). In respect to knowledge, power and immortality, the same things that I have said about the cosmic beings, elders, sky fathers and gods could be said of superhumans and humans: generally the higher beings are stronger, more knowledgeable and longer living, but all of this is, again, generally speaking.

So how does one make sense of all these beings, including other gods, given the existence of one supreme God in the Marvel Universe? Doesn't God – the Judeo-Christian God, who is clearly the model here – say, "You shall have no other gods before me"?

The term "god" (lower case "g") is used in the Bible to describe not only non-existent deities represented in statues (such as Dagon in 1 Samuel 5:4), but also rebellious created angels (such as Satan) and even, importantly, human beings; Psalm 82:6 reads, "I said, 'you are gods;' you are all sons of the Most High" – a passage quoted and elaborated on in John 10:34, "Jesus answered them, 'Has it not been written in your law, 'I said, you are gods'? If he called them 'gods,' to whom the word of God came (and Scripture cannot be broken), do you say of Him, whom the Father sanctified and sent into the world, 'You are blaspheming,' because I said, 'I am the Son of God'?" Thus, we can gather that the existence of other "gods" – rational created beings, it seems – is perfectly compatible with Judeo-Christianity as it is with the Marvel Universe.[57] Indeed, we should expect that if God is the Creator (essentially,

---

53 *Black Widow: Deadly Origin* #1 (November 2009) and #3 (January 2010).
54 *Tales to Astonish* vol. 1, #55 (May 1964).
55 *Ultimates* vol. 1, #6 (July 2003).
56 *The Avengers* vol. 3, #74 (January 2004).
57 Jesus's admitting that humans are "gods" (that is, rational souls, spirits or persons) shouldn't be taken to mean that Jesus Himself is only a "god" in this sense. Jesus isn't just a "god" (a human being) but is also "God" (hence, "I am the Way, the Truth and the Life . . .").

that is), then it's actually probable that He would create more than just humans and angels (two types of "gods"). To say the Bible doesn't mention rational beings other than angels and humans and therefore such beings don't exist is to commit the fallacy of the argument from silence: true, we don't know if other "gods" (created aliens of all sorts) exist or not, but given the existence of God, such are likely, and we should delight in this probability.[58] Nevertheless, while the diversity of the Marvel Universe may give us a hint as to what Heaven is like, Heaven will not be made up of any and all. If God is the Good – and we know from both the Bible and Marvel comics that He is – then the ethics of His creatures matter, and this is what I want to explore next.

AVENGERS, ASSEMBLE!

In the Marvel Universe, as in our own, ontological status – that which generally goes hand in hand with order of creation, longevity, power, knowledge, etc. – is no measure of moral goodness. Our universe has Satan and the Marvel, Mephisto: both are extremely old, powerful beings that happen to be very bad. But this isn't just true of the devils. When wearing the Infinity Gauntlet, Adam Warlock foolishly imagines that a proper supreme being must not permit "good and evil to cloud his judgment,"[59] and even his "good" aspect, the Goddess, is nothing of the sort, imagining that goodness is something that can be forced, rather than wooed.[60] Indeed, Galactus and the Celestials massacre millions in the worlds they destroy; the goddess Hera shows her immorality when she tells

---

58 In the Marvel Universe, as in our own, some misguided Christians view such ontological diversity in a negative light. Consider three examples. First, in *The Avengers* vol. 1, #171 (May 1978), Thor walks through a Christian nunnery and begins to feel a bit "uncomfortable," finally explaining to his companion, "E'en my father, Mighty Odin, who is called all-powerful, doth lay no claim to supreme divinity . . . and yet, t'would seem that many mark my very existence as an affront to this edifice!" Second, in *The Avengers* vol. 3, #28 (May 2000), Lupe / Silverclaw, who is the daughter of the goddess Peliali, tells the Avengers that the Christian missionaries that raised her tried to make her disbelieve (rather than properly understand in light of greater revelation) all the old stories and ways and were "nervous about my powers, which they considered ungodly." And finally, in *House of M* #8 (November 2005), shortly after most mutants on Earth lost their powers, Rev. William Ryker foolishly says in respect to the remaining mutants, "[This has been] foretold in Scripture for years now, and now the cleansing has finally begun. The abomination of humanity that was 'mutantkind' is now seen to be what it always was . . . a disease of our own decadence and indulgences. God's will has been done, and now it is up to man to finish His work [that is, kill the remaining mutants]."
59 *The Infinity War* #2 (July 1992).
60 *The Infinity Crusade* #3 (August 1993).

the Hulk, "An oath to a monster means nothing;"[61] and Eternity himself is at odds with God, the Supreme Being and the Supreme Good, when he tells Dr. Strange, "I am above such petty emotions as gratitude!"[62] Power and privilege rarely, it seems, translate into right actions.

So how has evil come to be? Hints are sown throughout the Marvel Universe – hints in keeping with a basic Judeo-Christian account. In *The Fantastic Four* vol. 1, #511, God tells the Four that they are His "collaborators," saying, "You're no one's puppets. . . . Nobody can do your living for you," and in *The Sensational Spider-Man* #40, when Peter asks God why he has been given his powers, God replies by showing Peter the scores of people he has saved along the way, saying, "They are some of the point, Peter." God creates because He loves to create, to be sure, but He creates rational beings, spirits or persons ("gods" of all sorts) for communion with Him – for them to commune with the Good – and to spread Goodness to others: "'Love the LORD your God with all your heart and with all your soul and with all your strength and with all your mind,'" Jesus tells us, "and 'Love your neighbour as yourself.'"[63] Because good and evil only have meaning insofar as a person is free, God has given all His "gods" free will to choose between Good or evil, God or anything else that comes above God the Good: the true meaning, then, of "You shall have no other gods before me" is not to deny the existence of other gods, but rather to love everything properly, God and Goodness above all else. Evil creatures, then, are simply those who value or elevate anything else above God the Good and His moral laws. The wise understand this, thus the Watcher tells the Dreaming Celestial, "The pulse that seemed to be completely random at first, but now registers with every cycle? That is what humans call a conscience. It's what recognizes and differentiates good from evil. It took me even longer to realize that the best thing to do was simply heed it."[64]

Though diverse and not particularly powerful in the grand scheme of things, the Avengers – here I'll limit myself to Thor, the Hulk, the Wasp and Black Widow again – also understand this.

To begin with, the god: Thor understands that the difference between right and wrong is important and so he tells "the slayer of the gods," Devak, "I have long agreed that some gods are malevolent and dangerous. But your inability to discern between good and evil makes you equally as dangerous."[65] And though "not exactly humble"[66] and at times brash ("Dropping a nuke on

---

61   *The Incredible Hulks* vol. 1, #622 (February 2011).
62   *Dr. Strange* vol. 1, #13 (April 1976).
63   Luke 10:27.
64   *The Eternals* #9 (May 2009).
65   *Thor* vol. 2, #78 (July 2004).
66   *The Avengers* vol. 1, #220 (June 1982).

a problem isn't the Avengers' way, Thor."[67]), the God of Thunder loves the good. He can't abide Kang the Conqueror attacking the Wasp and others who are weaker ("Villain wouldst thou strike at women and babes?"[68]); he "spit[s] upon [the] unholy judgement" of the cosmic Celestials;[69] he is hospitable to a fault ("A stranger in need of the Avengers' help," he says as he opens the door to the villain Wonder Man[70]); he sides with the right even when it costs him personally (he abandoned his 9th century Viking followers after several of them butchered innocents in a Christian monastery[71]); and he fights "in the name of justice,"[72] pledging, "those who practice evil shall be cast down beneath our heels!"[73] However, more than this, he, as a true hero, understands that justice is perfected or completed by love: indeed, by *agape* or sacrificial love, the supreme love, the love which the Bible claims is one of God's names.[74] Thor, as a lover of the good, loves justice (treating each as it ought to be treated) and mercy (going beyond, in a positive way, the commands of justice), saying, "I shall not falter in my resolve to protect this planet and save its people!"[75] And so he does, even when faced with the terrible ethical dilemma of having to kill an innocent (the human-time-bomb Wasp) to show this love.[76]

The Hulk, Black Widow and the Wasp are also dedicated to the good.

The Silver Surfer knows that "Bruce Banner," the Hulk's human side, "would die to give others life."[77] And the Hulk himself, though certainly not without flaws,[78] feels the same way when it comes down to it – here, saving Thor from the Collector ("He fought to free me from the Elder's control," Thor says, "No matter how he is attacked . . . the Hulk remains a hero"[79]) and there, sacrificing himself to Zeus to spare his family ("Here you are asking for miracles, offering yourself as a sacrifice," Hera mocks him, "Dying for other

---

67 *The Avengers* vol. 3, #63 (March 2003).
68 *The Avengers* vol. 2, #2 (January 1997).
69 *Thor* vol. 1, #300 (October 1980).
70 *The Avengers* vol. 2, #7 (June 1997).
71 *The Marvel Encyclopedia*, 2nd edition (New York: DK, 2009), 336.
72 *Thor* vol. 1, #388 (February 1988).
73 *Thor* vol. 1, #300 (October 1980).
74 1 John 4:8.
75 *Thor* vol. 1, #388 (February 1988). Also see the 2011 live-action *Thor* movie, where Thor, as a Christ-type tells Loki, "These people are innocent. Taking their lives will gain you nothing. So take mine and end this." And then, dying, we hear the words, "It is over," echoing the words of the dying, sacrificial Jesus, "It is finished" (John 19:30).
76 *Secret Invasion* #8 (January 2009).
77 *The Avengers* vol. 2, #12 (October 1997).
78 The events of *World War Hulk* and certainly *Hulk: The End* make this clear.
79 *The Avengers: Earth's Mightiest Heroes* vol. 1, #3 (March 2011).

people's sins"[80]).

Natasha Romanova, the first Black Widow, is also flawed – she is deeply cynical[81] and has killed more than her fair share – yet she came around to become a lover of what's right: "You have to see you're being manipulated," she tells Yelena Belova (the second Black Widow), "You have to do the right thing;" "I agree," she tells Daredevil, "Hunting down the Punisher is the right thing to do;" "I've decided," she informs the Winter Solider, "working with you to honor Captain America's memory. . . . It's the right thing to do;" and to her long-time colleague Ivan, she states plainly, "You say I pick sides. I pick good guys. I pick kindness and mercy."[82]

Finally the Wasp, because of her lesser abilities, is often afraid. Yet precisely because of this, she is perhaps the most impressive hero of all, for she never fails to help those in need despite the great danger to herself. Thus, Captain America solemnly states, "[She is] the bravest person I know,"[83] and Henry Pym does likewise, saying, "Janet van Dyne was the very essence of heroism, of duty. . . . All over the world, she was a symbol of selfless humanity."[84]

Every one of these heroes – all of the Avengers, I would dare to generalize – love the Good, and since the Good is an aspect, or essential property, of God, they can be said to love God either clearly or through a glass darkly.

Above: *The Avengers: Earth's Mightiest Heroes.*

---

80   *The Incredible Hulks* vol. 1, #622 (February 2011).
81   *The Avengers* vol. 1, #351 (August 1992).
82   *Black Widow: Deadly Origin* #4 (February 2010).
83   *The Avengers: Earth's Mightiest Heroes* vol. 1, #3 (March 2011).
84   *The Avengers* vol. 3, #20 (September 1999).

GOOD GODS

In one particular *Avengers* comic, Duane Freeman, the representative of the American government to the Avengers, tried to pressure Iron Man into accepting more minorities into the team, to which Iron Man replied, "We don't recruit for skin color. The Avengers aren't about equal representation – the squads are too small for that. We're about getting the job done – and that's it. We've had minority members for years – from black and Hispanic heroes to gypsies and mythological gods. We'd never exclude anyone – anyone – because of their race."[85]

And something similar is true of God, both in the Marvel Universe and our own. The Creator is pleased to accept not only human beings, but also any and all free-willed creatures – "gods" – He has made; yet He accepts them under one condition: they must love Him . . . they must, that is, love the Good. In this way, the Avengers are a model for us all, for though they are diverse, they are unified – unified in their love of Goodness Himself.

---

85 *The Avengers* vol. 3, #27 (April 2000).

CHAPTER EIGHT

"THE POWER TO GO BEYOND GOD'S BOUNDARIES"? *HULK*, HUMAN NATURE AND SOME ETHICAL CONCERNS THEREOF

"We live in an upside down world," remarks director Ang Lee, "biblically, we lost Paradise."[1] This comment, I believe, is central to Lee's vision for his 2003 movie *Hulk*, based on the Marvel comic book series *The Incredible Hulk*. In past films, Lee demonstrated an array of philosophical approaches, but in this movie, the philosophical themes and concepts are religious ones, especially Judeo-Christian ones. For example, when Bruce Banner (a.k.a. the Hulk) blows up a frog during a lab test, his long-time love, Betty Ross, jokes that now they know who they can turn to when a "plague [of] frogs start falling from the sky." The allusion to the ten biblical plagues is clear, as is the implication that Bruce is a kind of Moses figure who, on the side of the spiritual and the age-old normative, will be a future hero. Further allusions to, not to mention direct statements about, Bruce being like the biblical Isaac and being "predestined" to a certain life path are sown throughout, yet all in service to the general theme of losing paradise.

What is "paradise" in this movie such that it can be lost? Probably drawing on the general ethos of Taoist and Mahayana Buddhist sympathies with the natural world, but fleshing these out in more Judeo-Christian terms, Lee seems to suggest that "paradise" is the state of peace or harmony that exists when the laws of nature are discerned and respected. The heroes are those who obey objective natural laws, especially those pertaining to what is natural to humanity, and the villains are those who, in the words of Banner's father, David, aspire for the "power to go beyond God's boundaries!" In the movie, Lee makes it clear that the villains are the metaphysical materialists, who reduce human nature and personal identity to mere bundles of matter and then treat them accordingly, while the heroes are those who recognize that human nature is an immaterial essence and treat it as such. In strict metaphysical terms, the vision of human nature and natural laws in *Hulk* is also at odds with most Chinese conceptions of human nature and natural laws,

---

1   Ang Lee, "Commentary on *Hulk*," in *Hulk*, disc 1, directed by Ang Lee (Universal, 2003).

but this, I believe is accidental to Lee's purpose in the film. What I shall argue, then, is that *Hulk* can be seen as a polemic against materialistic reductionism of human nature and ethics, and that this polemic takes place vis-à-vis the preferred vision of human nature and natural ethics which is, very roughly, Judeo-Christian.² Lee, of course, isn't himself a Jew or Christian, but Stan Lee, the creator of the Hulk, is Jewish with Christian sympathies, and it makes sense that insofar as Lee wanted to stay true to Stan the Man's vision, that these conceptions of human nature and ethics would be apparent in the film.³ Is Bruce Banner identical to the Hulk? If so, how? Can genetic engineering affect human nature? How does ethical behaviour shape personal identity? Is all genetic modification of human nature unnatural? These questions, and other ethical ones having to do with human nature in *Hulk*, will be explored throughout.

MATERIALIST MONSTERS

Hulk begins with David Banner,⁴ Bruce Banner's father, working in his military lab on an experiment having to do with genetic improvement. We read notes like "Regeneration is immortality," which is highly suggestive that David is a metaphysical materialist, who believes that man is nothing but a bundle of matter or a collection of accidental properties. We infer this since if David believed that a human being is a rational soul, spirit or person, which is an indivisible substance with essential properties (an essence), then he would very likely believe that human beings possess a kind of immortality already (one independent of bodily existence), and hence wouldn't likely be so obsessed with genetic immortality.

But besides being a metaphysical materialist obsessed with bodily immortality, David is also – not coincidentally, the movie seems to suggest – a bad man. When the military properly forbids him to experiment on human subjects, he defies them and experiments on himself. In addition to the immorality of disobeying a direct order for no good reason, David is a

---

2   Judeo-Christian conceptions of human nature and ethics, of course, owe a great deal to Greek philosophy, in particular, Aristotle, who was the first to speak philosophically about substances, properties, accidents and essences.
3   Lee apparently loves Western superhero comics, especially Stan Lee's Marvel heroes. Thus, even in *The Ice Storm*, Stan Lee's *Fantastic Four* play an important metaphorical role in the film, and in *Hulk* Ang Lee says plainly, "I'm a translator of that comic world." Ang Lee, "The Unique Style of Editing Hulk," in *Hulk*, disc 2, directed by Ang Lee (Universal, 2003). In the Marvel universe, the chain of being starts with a Judeo-Christian-like God, followed by a host of lesser entities, including The Living Tribunal, the primordials, the elders, sky fathers, lower gods, and so on.
4   In the comic books it's Brian Banner, not David Banner.

bad man because he fails, after having injected himself with an experimental drug, to take precautions to prevent his wife, Edith, from getting pregnant, ultimately resulting in her conceiving a child with altered DNA (I take it that, all things being equal, it's immoral, and not "genetic discrimination," for a person intentionally to try to conceive when the risk of the child having a serious defect is high). Furthermore, when the military discovers that David experimented on himself, they shut him down, and in a fit of rage (take note), he kills Edith while trying to dispose of his experiment, his son, Bruce.

Later on, when David is finally released from prison, he kidnaps Betty Ross, Bruce's girlfriend, and expresses his extreme annoyance that she wants to "cure [Bruce], fix him." To David the materialist, social Darwinism, the ethics endorsing "survival of the fittest," is most logical. Thus, he sees the powerful but out-of-control Hulk to be the true person, and Bruce to be "a weak little speck of human trash." In his Hulk state – internally, a state of foggy rationality – Bruce actually agrees, calling his normal state "a puny human." That David agrees with the fairly dull-witted Hulk is important since both largely act subhuman rather than super-human, all the while imagining it the other way around. Thus, Ang Lee tellingly admits, "Sometimes I think the father is the real Hulk." That is, the materialist is the monster.

David's argument, then, assumes, in true materialistic fashion, that there is no natural, proper, essential or "designed" pattern for how things – the world around him and his own person – should be, and so there is really no reason for him not to do as he pleases. And since what pleases him is to experiment on himself and his child, there is no reason for him not to do so; thus, he says, "It's the only path to the truth that give men the power to go beyond God's boundaries!" David obviously doesn't believe in a literal God, but rather uses God as a metaphor for the notion of indivisible essences and the proper functioning of such. Moreover, since unchanging wholes and the proper functioning of such wholes have a normative or ethical dimension which forbids man from doing *whatever* he likes, David rails against this ethical dimension as well, speaking with admiration for "a hero of the kind that walked the Earth long before the pale religions of civilization infected humanity's soul!" Savage, amoral "heroes" of the social Darwinist kind is what David the metaphysical materialist clamours for.

But David isn't the only metaphysical materialist monster in the movie. Major Glenn Talbot, a former solider now working in the private sector, is the other materialist in the movie and, not coincidentally again, is also the secondary villain. Talbot has a keen interest in the genetic experiments that Bruce and Betty are working on, but while Bruce and Betty want to use their experiments to find cures to benefit humanity, Talbot wants to privatize their research and use it for military purposes, ultimately, to make money. This is the first suggestion that he is a villain. Later on he becomes clearly so when he's not opposed to killing Bruce in order to get his sample of the Hulk DNA: "I'm going to carve off a piece of the real you," he says. Talbot's social Darwinian ethics ("I'm stronger, so I can take what I like") suggests he's a metaphysical materialist since he appears willing to reduce Bruce / Hulk to his DNA (a part of his physical make up), rather than seeing him as a rational soul, spirit or indivisible essence with inherent personhood and inherent rights. Bruce / Hulk is matter to be exploited.

SOUL AND BODY

Against the metaphysical materialists are those who respect "God's boundaries" of stable essences and natural laws. Bruce and Betty are the foremost proponents.

We know that Bruce was born with an altered genetic code that boosts his immune system. Thus, when his experiment with gamma-infused nanomeds (nanobots that help repair the body from the inside) goes wrong, he (risking his life to save his assistant's) miraculously survives. However, the experiment-gone-wrong further alters his bio-chemistry. Does Bruce's altered DNA mean that he is no longer himself?

To begin with, it's the metaphysical materialists – the villains in Lee's movie – who imagine that one's personal identity is one's DNA (on account of DNA being bio-chemistry, which is, in turn, matter). Against them the movie makes it clear that if a person were identical to his DNA, then any alteration to his DNA would imply the literal loss of self, which is implausible and certainly not true of our hero, Bruce.

To elaborate, consider gene therapy. We are all born with "junk DNA," much of which disposes us to an array of diseases, in particular, cancer. Now if we were able to remove the junk DNA or even fix the junk DNA (discover a drug to cure cancer), then we would, in fact, be curing not the same person, but creating a new one. The drug wouldn't save "me," but would in fact kill "me" and create a new man. Moreover, imagine that in the course of this treatment "I" suffered traumatic brain damage such that "I" lost many or most of my memories. If "I" am identical to my memories *qua* bio-chemistry (organized by my DNA), then in losing memories, "I" would, again, literally cease to be "me." The improbability of this is expressed in our ordinary language, "I forgot something" *not* "I died." As we shall see, when Bruce's DNA is radically altered (not once, but twice), he is still clearly shown to be himself.

True to the spirit of the early comics,[5] Ang Lee makes it no secret that although Bruce's body has undergone an alteration, it's still *his* body and *he* is

---

5 In *The Incredible Hulk* vol. 1, #3 (1962), we are told that the Hulk "isn't really just an inhuman monster to be destroyed. . . . He's Bruce Banner!"

still *himself.* But what holds the unity of the body together through change, and what constitutes Bruce's personal identity? The answer to both of these questions is the human soul or spirit as roughly conceived in Judeo-Christian terms.

When Bruce becomes the Hulk, Betty, who knows Bruce "better than anyone," immediately recognizes the green monster to be Bruce vis-à-vis his eyes or "the widow to the soul." Or again, when Bruce-as-the-Hulk later goes on a rampage, Betty tries to calm him down and this conversation ensues:

Bruce: "You found me."

Betty: "You weren't hard to find."

Bruce: "Yes, I was."

Betty could see, where others could not, the truth of the matter, namely, as she later explicitly says, that Bruce-as-the-Hulk is "a human being." She can recognize the indivisible soul or spirit inside the green monster, and we, the audience, were meant to see this as well. In his director commentary, Lee says his obsession with CGI in the movie (including being the principle actor in the Hulk motion capture suit!) wasn't so much to make a spectacular smash-fest, but rather was "to unify" that which was previously separated. This is to say that while in the comic books and TV show the Hulk always looked radically different than Bruce, in *Hulk*, Lee intentionally tried to let Bruce's soul or spirit shine through the green body by mapping Eric Bana's eyes and facial features onto the CGI Hulk: "The challenge was could I make Bruce Banner and the Hulk one person, instead of like in the comics or TV series where there are two actors or two different entities."[6]

Lee's brilliant and unique effort to show the unity of Bruce through CGI is a strong metaphysical comment on the nature of the soul and spirit, and is consistent with the general Judeo-Christian theme throughout, namely, that the human soul or spirit is best conceived as a substance with both essential and accidental properties.

Central to this is the notion that some essential properties in the human substance are non-degreed, meaning they are either 100% present or 100% not. The essential property "being human," "having the ultimate capacity for rationality," "having the ultimate capacity for language," and so on are such properties and if these properties aren't present, the substance isn't a human substance or soul.

---

6 Ang Lee, "Evolution of the Hulk," in *Hulk*, disc 2, directed by Ang Lee (Universal, 2003). In addition, we are told that Lee was chosen to the direct the movie because what comes through in all his films is "the humanity," and here, the humanity of the Hulk.

Of course, based on the behaviour of Bruce-as-the-Hulk, it might not seem as though the Hulk has all of these; indeed, he himself even spoke of "that mindless Hulk," and certainly, if taken literally, being mindless would disqualify the Hulk from being human. However, this language is rhetorical, rather than metaphysical, and, more importantly, this confusion stems from a misunderstanding between ultimate capacities and lower capacities.

The human person – in our case, Bruce – is a soul or spirit. This means, among other things, he can still be himself or a human person without a body (the ancient Chinese just as much as Jews and Christians talk about the possibility of such "disembodied ghosts"). Because Bruce's Hulk body, brain and bio-chemistry are different than his human body, brain and bio-chemistry, Bruce – as a soul – can't (or at least not optimally) actualize his ultimate capacity for rationality, language and free will in his Hulk body. His Hulk body, in other words, doesn't have the lower capacity that Bruce's human body does for rationality, language and free will. Nevertheless, the absence or near absence of demonstrable, empirical evidence of these ultimate capacities doesn't at all mean that such ultimate capacities are absent. All it means is that the lower capacity – or bodily capacity – isn't there.

To clarify, take a human fetus, an infant, a mentally handicapped person or one who is brain dead. If we have reason to believe that the soul or spirit is that which animates the body (we will discuss this in a moment), then the beating heart of a human fetus makes it extremely likely that a human soul or spirit is present. However, the fetus can't demonstrate its ultimate capacity for rationality, language and so on because its lower capacities aren't developed yet; nevertheless, insofar as it's a human soul, it must necessarily possess these ultimate capacities in a non-degreed way. If we think the fetus is ensouled, then it is 100% human, not 40% or even 99%.[7] Ditto for the infant who can't demonstrate much or any rationality early on, the mentally handicapped person and the brain dead. The same reason that Talbot is immoral for wanting to kill the Hulk (it's not a human person) is the same reason it's likely immoral, all things being equal, to engage in abortion, infanticide and eugenics.

Now in the course of this, I've assumed that the soul doesn't merely have a body in the same way that a captain "has" a ship. Judaism and Christianity (and Chinese religion in its own way) has long insisted that the soul's connection to the body is more intimate than this, and this intimacy is what Lee tries to demonstrate through the soul-in-the-body CGI depiction of Bruce-in-the-

---

7   As a side note, this is why the Christian creeds declare Jesus *fully* God and *fully* man, since it's a logical contradiction for Jesus to be "half man" or "possessing half a human soul." Of course, while this statement (like the one declaring God "three persons in one substance") isn't a logical contradiction, it also isn't very clear as to its meaning.

Hulk. The general idea is this: the soul is prior to the body, to be sure, but it also gives rise to, and guides, the development of the body via the body's DNA. The ultimate capacity for the soul to develop or form a body with both general human features (arms, legs, etc.) and also specific ones (facial features, fingerprints, etc.) means that it's likely that even if the material the soul has to work with has been altered, the body's form will still both be humanoid and demonstrate unique features determined by the particular soul's "this-ness" or the essential property that differentiates one human soul from another. This is why Christianity depicts our new bodies in Heaven as ones still *visibly* similar to our current ones, why the Hebrews (and Chinese) tend to depict human ghosts as observably similar to their embodied forms, and why the Hulk is both humanoid and has Bruce's facial features.

In terms of controlling the formed body, the soul and its faculties direct the brain, which in turn controls the actions of the body. The soul affects the body, but, crucially, the body also affects the soul. When DNA is altered, bio-chemistry changes, including the bio-chemistry in the brain (scientists have only recently discovered that our actions literally alter our brains). The result is that the soul can no longer move the body as it previously could, but must now move it in accordance with the new biological makeup (its different lower capacities). The body and soul are intimately related (as Jews, Christians and the ancient Chinese insist), but not, as with the materialists, reducible to each other.

THE HULK EVENT

So what exactly *is* "the Hulk"? Lee has called *Hulk* a "psycho-drama,"[8] which suggests that it's primarily about the *psuche* or soul and its faculties, such as the conscious mind, the subconscious mind, free will, memory and emotions. "The Hulk," of course, can refer to the large, green skinned body that Bruce takes on, but in terms of psychology and metaphysics, it's best thought of as an "event," such as a flash of lighting, the dropping of a ball, or an explosion of anger.

When Betty first encounters Bruce-as-the-Hulk she hypothesizes that Bruce's "anger is triggering the nanomeds," which in turn changes Bruce's human body into the Hulk. In other words, the Hulk is an event triggered by rage. But this is still just Hulk 101, and Lee would take us further.

Discussing his movie *Crouching Tiger, Hidden Dragon*, Lee says that "crouching tigers" and "hidden dragons" have to do with what lies below the surface, in particular the hidden "passions, emotions, desires – the dragons

---

8   Ang Lee, "The Incredible Ang Lee," in *Hulk*, disc 2, directed by Ang Lee (Universal, 2003).

hidden inside all of us."[9] In his commentary on *Hulk*, Lee says that a common theme in all of his movies, and especially *Hulk*, is that of repression or what the human spirit holds back or "hides;" to say that we have "dragons hidden inside all of us" is, in more particular terms, a way of saying "we all have a Hulk inside us."[10]

The Hulk event, then, is an event triggered by anger, but not only anger flowing from conscious understanding (which we will return to), but also from subconscious – repressed – thoughts and memories, which Lee especially identifies with "anxiety" and "fear" (and in Bruce's case, the anxiety of having watched his father murder his mother). Thus, it's not accidental that our first glimpse of the Hulk is while Bruce is dreaming (an uncontrollable, often fear-inducing event), and that the Hulk is also first introduced to the external world by stepping from the shadows (often associated with fear of the unknown) into the light. Bruce describes the Hulk event as "being born or coming up for air" or as "a vivid dream ... [of] rage, power and freedom," to which he adds, "And you know what scares me the most? When it happens, when it comes over me, when I totally lose control ... I like it."

Bruce likes losing control vis-à-vis irrational fear, not because he knows that this is proper, right or good, but rather because he likes the numbing feeling that rage brings about. Strong hate often overcomes strong fear.

But this is the perverse, subconscious Hulk event (known, in the comics, as "The Devil Hulk"[11]). The hate, anger or rage that drowns out the anxiety brought on by repressed memories is no long-term or healthy solution to the problem. What is repressed must be brought to light and dealt with or else all sorts of disorders, including multiple personality disorders, can result; unexorcised ghosts hinder the natural harmony of the soul, body and external world and so mustn't be allowed to manifest in irrational spurts of anger.[12] Unbridled power is what David Banner dreams of, but he is, we recall, the villain.

If fifty years of the incredible Hulk has taught us one thing, it's that the solution isn't to label all anger bad, but rather to recognize that anger is good in and of itself, and must be naturally or properly manifested, which is to say

---

9   Ang Lee, et al., *Crouching Tiger, Hidden Dragon: A Portrait of the Ang Lee Film Including the Complete Screenplay* (New York: Newmarket, 2001), 76.
10 Lee, "Commentary on *Hulk*." This idea is also very true to the comic books, where in a dream-like sequence Hulk tells Bruce, "Hulk is your own dark thoughts, your own anger, your rage!" *The Incredible Hulk* vol. 2, #315 (1986).
11 Tom DeFalco and Matthew Manning, *Hulk: The Incredible Guide* (Toronto: DK, 2008), 129.
12 In *The Incredible Hulk* vol. 2, #377 (1990), we are told that Bruce suffers from a multiple personality disorder, but in this very issue, his personality is unified through the work of the psychiatrist to the super-heroes, Dr. Samson.

manifested in the service of rational deliberation aimed at truth. This is no easy task for human beings, much less one with the Hulk's bio-chemistry; however, it can be done.[13] For example, when the three genetically altered dogs attack Betty, Bruce-as-the-Hulk knows that he has a moral duty to protect the weak and, with this rational, moral consideration in mind, summons his anger to fuel his body to proper action, namely, to defend the weak. He does this again when he prevents the F-22 from crashing into a crowd of people on the Golden Gate Bridge. These acts are the actualization of the human essential property "to have the ultimate capacity to act morally" and so we can say that by acting morally and heroically, Bruce-as-the-Hulk becomes a more actualized human person. The Hulk body might be harder to control than the human body and so moral praise and blame will be a bit different;[14] however, the way they need to be controlled is the same, namely, with the higher faculties in the soul controlling the lower ones.

A PARABLE ABOUT PARADISE

I've said that Bruce and Betty are those who respect "God's boundaries" of stable essences and natural laws, while metaphysical materialists like David Banner and Glenn Talbot are those who don't. I've argued that Bruce and Betty correctly understand human nature to be a substance with a number of essential properties and that giving these properties full consideration, and acting in accordance with them (in particular, the ultimate capacity for morality) is natural and right. It's natural and right to consider the Hulk a person and treat him as such, and its unnatural and immoral not to; it's natural and right for Bruce to try and protect Betty from the dogs (especially since he himself was in no danger of dying), and it would be unnatural or immoral if he hadn't. The materialists are the real monsters in *Hulk* since they have an unnatural conception of human nature and, based on this unnatural conception, treat humans unnaturally.

What I've assumed throughout, however, is that part of what's natural to humans is to have the ultimate capacity not just for rational thought in general, but scientific thought in particular. It's natural for humans to want to study the

---

13   For the first two hundred and seventy issues of *The Incredible Hulk*, Bruce-as-the-Hulk couldn't rationally cause himself to become the Hulk, even though as the Hulk he did have enough rational control to occasionally do heroic deeds; however, in *The Incredible Hulk* vol. 2, #272 (June 1982), Bruce was able to improve on this to the point where he could even rationally cause his transformation into the Hulk. Needless to say, this is the ideal way to control anger. However, when new writers took over *The Incredible Hulk*, this was undone to some extent.

14   "I should have known that Bruce Banner isn't always responsible for what the Hulk says and does," says Bruce's pal Rick Jones. *The Incredible Hulk* vol. 1, #6 (1963).

physical world, and it's natural, all things being equal, for them to want to test, experiment and discover. Our heroes, Bruce and Betty, not to mention Ang Lee's own wife, a microbiologist, understand this well.

Nevertheless, as with most aspects of life, there are tremendous complexities involved in this. For example, gene therapy, which has to do with restoring a broken original state, seems natural enough, but is it also natural to experiment with genes that aren't obviously broken? Even if we have some conception of what is natural to the human body, do we understand this perfectly? Could our bodies, at one time in the past – perhaps in Paradise – have been like the Hulk's in that they could grow larger and heal faster? Is our current "normal" really natural or is it still somewhat unnatural? What are the precise limits of human nature and the human body, such that if crossed, they would no longer be themselves?

Lee's proposal in *Hulk* is that "we lost Paradise" by defying "God's boundaries" of real wholes and stable natural laws, which, while not always obvious to us (hence the aforementioned questions), nevertheless need to be sought out as best we can. If we don't do this, we will be like Adam and Eve, who rebelled against God's natural laws, or the metaphysical materialists in *Hulk*, who manipulate human nature in ways that are unnatural and unjust, seeing Bruce as an animal to be experimented on, not a human person, a soul, with inherent rights, dignity and worth beyond any animal.

Chapter Nine

Superman: From *Anti-Christ* to Christ-Type

Although the Roman poet Lucian was probably the first to speak of a "super-man" or *hyperanthropos*, the term was popularized and entered the English language from the writings of the German philologist and philosopher Friedrich Nietzsche, who spoke of an *übermensch*. For Nietzsche, this word was a positive one, denoting a man whose ethics were "beyond good and evil," a man who had the "courage" to reject traditional morality in order to forge his own unrestricted destiny. Yet, English speakers who first encountered the word "super-man" were largely Judeo-Christians, who for the most part believed in a universal moral law, which meant that for them, the Nietzschean word "super-man" was unqualifiedly negative. But something happened between then and now that has rehabilitated the word "super-man," not as a recovery of the Nietzschean sense, but rather of the diametrically opposed sense, a Judeo-Christian sense. That thing – that event – was the advent of DC Comics's Superman, who, I will show, was created quite intentionally to subvert Nietzsche's *übermensch*.

To substantiate this, I will argue that the rehabilitation of the word "super-man" was intentional, yet what resulted was far more than the original authors dreamt of. The super-man in the works of Nietzsche and the first *Super-Man* short story is a literal antichrist, yet he becomes, through gradual changes over the years, nothing less than a Christ-type par excellence. Thus, what started out subjective became the herald of what is objective; what began with power directed to amoral self-actualization became power directed toward the betterment of others; what was once the mad prophet decrying the death of God is now the greatest modern symbol of Immanuel, God-With-Us.

ÜBERMENSCH AS ANTICHRIST

Friedrich Nietzsche espoused a particular form of moral relativism, asserting four key things.

First, he rightly accepted the fact of cultural relativism, namely that different cultures often reach different moral conclusions. This claim is, as I said, a fact and is asserted by people as diverse as Plato, Lao Tzu, Thomas Aquinas and the Buddha. However, Nietzsche coupled this objective fact with a more dubious argument. He thought the greatest German philosopher, Immanuel Kant, didn't go far enough in his theorizing insofar as Kant still dogmatically asserted the existence of certain objective truths, in particular, logical truths (the Law of Contradiction), mathematical truths (1 + 1 = 2) and moral truths ("It's always wrong to torture a child for fun"). Leaping logic in a single bound, Nietzsche oddly argued that cultural diversity and dogmatic assertions for objectivity prove that there is no objectivity, in particular no universal moral law or objective norms that all cultures can know.

Second, accepting the Judeo-Christian argument linking the universal moral law and God (that is, the argument that shows God is identical to the Good), Nietzsche went on to proclaim the non-existence of The Almighty, which for him became the cornerstone of his philosophy: "beyond question the major premise of Nietzsche's philosophy is atheism."[1]

Third, Nietzsche thought the loss of God would result in global madness because the death of Deity is connected to the death of objective norms, stable aesthetic values, proper emotional responses to such norms and values, and, last but not least, human dignity (since this would mean man is no longer made in the image of God). Nietzsche's philosophy is often called "nihilism" because it preaches the need to wake up to the fact of such barren nothingness.

And fourth, only the person who realizes that norms and values are nothing but human constructs is able, though by no means guaranteed to, become a new, superior type of man, the *übermensch* or super-man. That is, because Nietzsche believed living in any kind of illusion is objectively bad (we might agree but this is ironic for a denouncer of objective morality), he thought the super-man needs an unwavering desire to be free from the "social construct" that is objective morality, in particular, Judeo-Christian morality. Furthermore, accepting the near universal claim that people desire happiness but insisting, controversially, that happiness actually means "power," Nietzsche thought the "super-man," no less than a mere man, would have a will to, or desire for, power, yet the super-man would distinguish himself from a mere man by desiring power in a way that is free from all moral and social constraints. In short, he wouldn't worry about what others say is "good" or "bad" but would, by his own genius and creativity, construct his own norms in order to create for himself a persona of his choosing. The super-man would thus revile such "non-Aryan" (that is, Judeo-Christian rather than Germanic pagan[2]) virtues

---

1   George Morgan, *What Nietzsche Means* (Cambridge, Mass.: Harvard University Press, 1941), 36.
2   Friedrich Nietzsche *Twilight of the Idols* 7.4.

as pity and mercy, since pity would distract the super-man from his own goals of self-actualization. True, the super-man thrives on conflict and challenge; however, the super-man won't thrive, as the Judeo-Christian tradition has maintained, by the challenge of helping the pitiable or anonymous weak since the sense of power that the super-man would get from helping the weak is power that is dependent on conforming to society's arbitrary moral standards and thus is to take part in an illusion. To most of society, then, the super-man will be a kind of antichrist (the title of one of Nietzsche's books), not insofar as his primary goal is to hurt and deceive others (the weak think thus) but rather insofar as he hurts others "without thinking" – as a byproduct or the inevitable result of self-creation: "the truly powerful are not concerned with others but act out of fullness and an overflow."[3] We can see, then, that Jesus, for example, is far from Nietzsche's super-man ideal, for though the Christ strove under challenge, He lacked clarity about the proper purpose of such striving: Jesus was, in the words of Nietzsche, "a case of delayed . . . puberty."[4]

SUPER-MAN AS LEX LUTHOR

During World War I, "Feelings ran high both in Germany, where [Nietzsche's] *Zarathustra* was pushed to new sales records as a 'must' for the soldier's knapsack, and in England and the United States, where Nietzsche began to be considered as the apostle of German ruthlessness and barbarism. . . . During those war years, the 'superman' began to be associated with the German nation."[5] This feeling in America was intensified during World War II with "the advent of Hitler and the Nazis' brazen adaption of Nietzsche."[6] So, while Nietzsche himself was surprisingly neither a proponent of German nationalism nor a racist (he calls himself an "anti-anti-Semite"[7]), the English speaking world, though especially those in America, tended to see him as the unofficial philosopher of the Nazis.

In 1933, when Hitler – himself fuelled by a slight misunderstanding of Nietzsche's super-man – started to dream of world domination, American Jewish cartoonists Jerry Siegel and Joe Shuster wrote a short story for *Science Fiction* #3 called "The Reign of the Super-Man." The use of the word "Super-Man" was a clear allusion to Nietzsche, though it depicted Nietzsche's super-man as a bald megalomaniac bent on global conquest. Super-Man, in short,

---

3   Walter Kaufmann, *Nietzsche: Philosopher, Psychologist, Antichrist*, 4th edition (Princeton: Princeton University Press, 1974), 194.
4   Friedrich Nietzsche *The Anti-Christ* 32.
5   Kaufmann, *Nietzsche: Philosopher, Psychologist, Antichrist*, 8.
6   Kaufmann, *Nietzsche: Philosopher, Psychologist, Antichrist*, 9.
7   Friedrich Nietzsche, Letter #430 in Kaufmann, *Nietzsche: Philosopher, Psychologist, Antichrist*, 44.

started out as a proto-Lex Luthor, and Lex Luthor was what Siegel and Shuster thought Nietzsche and Hitler were all about; indeed, by making Super-Man a villain, Siegel and Shuster clearly intended to subvert Nietzsche's savage super-man.

This understanding, of course, only gets Nietzsche partially right, for though Nietzsche's super-man does indeed crave power and is in fact willing to sacrifice whatever it takes to achieve power, the power he craves is more for self-actualization and absolute freedom of will than it is for world domination (even if world domination could arguably be an expression or entailment of these). Nietzsche's super-man, in other words, is more nuanced than Hitler or Siegel and Shuster's Super-Man, yet all three share the same distaste, even hatred, for Judeo-Christian morality, in particular, pity, mercy and self-sacrificial love.

JESUS WITHOUT THE CHRIST

In 1938, five years after his debut yet still during wartime, the Super-Man became Superman. In *Action Comics* vol. 1, #1, Superman was re-envisioned as nearly the opposite of the Nietzschean, antichrist Super-Man. Rather than let a perfectly good word like "superman" be associated with Nietzsche, Hitler and Lex Luthor, it was intentionally redeemed, though it remained subversive. While still strong and determined like the Nietzschean Super-Man, Superman became a hero of the Judeo-Christian sort: he accepted the principles of the universal moral law, in particular, concern for the weak, without question and never failed to act in accordance with these laws. Moreover, even if Siegel and Shuster intentionally made some parallels between Superman and Moses, such as them both being sent away from their parents only for them to become great heroes,[8] the parallels between Superman and another Jew – a more famous Jew – are much more striking.[9]

Jesus, who Siegel and Shuster must have taken special pride in calling a Jew and who Christians believe is the Son of, and indeed one with, Elohim or God the Father, was, at least on the level of myth and morality, the figure behind the creation of Superman.[10] Some of this was very intentional and

---

8   Howard Jacobson, "Up, Up and Oy Vey," *The Times*, March 5, 2005.
9   I'm not the first person to have noticed these parallels. For instance, see Stephen Skelton, *The Gospel According to the World's Greatest Hero* (Eugene, OR: Harvest House, 2006) and John Wesley White, *The Man from Krypton: The Gospel According to Superman* (Minneapolis, MN: Bethany Fellowship, 1978).
10   Jesus isn't the only famous biblical hero to be alluded to, or make an appearance in, Superman comics. Shazam! has the wisdom of King Solomon and the biblical Samson is an on-again-off-again friend of the Man of Steel. See *Superman's Pal, Jimmy Olson* #16 (October 1956) and *All-Star Superman* #3 (May 2006). Additionally,

explicit. For instance, in *Superman Comics* #1 The Man of Steel's adoptive mother, Martha Kent, was originally named *Mary*, and his adoptive father, named in a later issue, is Jonathan *Joseph* Kent. Though this allusion would later become obscured by changing "Mary" to "Martha" (or, rather, by introducing the concept of multiverses), the allusion to the Holy Family – who, we should nevertheless remember, are constantly depicted as church-going Christians[11] – reappears again with a vengeance in *Smallville*, when Martha, reworking St. John's "not that we loved God but that He loved us,"[12] says of young Kal-El, "We didn't find him; he found us."[13]

However, some of the connections between Superman and Jesus were only loosely made. Consider two examples, both having to do with names.

First, "Clark" in "Clark Kent" means "cleric" or "priest" and "Kent" is a form of the Hebrew word *kana*, which, in its *k-n-t* form, appears in the Bible, meaning "I have found a son." Thus, "Clark Kent" could mean "I have found a son, a priest," which could very well be an allusion to Jesus, who is called the True Priest. Yet even more strikingly, another derivation of the word *kana* is the Greek word *krista* or our English word "Christ." For those who think this is a stretch (I was one of them), we'd do well to remember that the word "Krypton" is from the Greek word "*kryptos*" or "hidden" – Krypton, Superman's home planet, being "hidden" from us on Earth. Thus it seems that either way "Clark Kent" was far from an arbitrary name, being intended to denote a priest or a saviour.

Second, some years later, Superman's real name was revealed to be "Kal-El" and his biological father, Jor-El. "*El*" is the Hebrew word meaning "(of) God" (such as in *El*ohim), which makes it clear that with this name as well there is a strong connection – both mythically, in terms of being a divine figure and morally, in terms of acting righteously – between God and Superman. Indeed, even years later when the Hebrew word "*el*" is explained to be actually a Kryptonian word, the divine connotations aren't completely lost, for if the Kryptonian "El" means "child" and "Kal" means "star," then "Kal-El," like Jesus, whose birth was heralded by the Star of Bethlehem, is also a "starchild."[14]

Yet if we return to the Hebrew word, we should note, in fairness,

---

the demons Satan, Beliala and Beelzebub are mentioned as real characters in the DC universe, and Superman encounters villains named Gog and Magog, Cain and Abel, and Sodom and Gomorrah, not to mention a former priest-turned-monster named Pilate. Even in *Smallville*, Darkseid is identified as "Lucifer." *Smallville* season 10, episode 21.
11 *Action Comics* vol. 1, #848 (May 2007).
12 1 John 4:10.
13 *Smallville* season 1, episode 1.
14 *Superman's Pal, Jimmy Olson* #121 (July 1969).

that "*el*" need not imply identity with God (as in *El*ohim) but could simply suggest service to God and His righteousness (as in the helper angel Gabri*el*). Moreover, that Superman was initially depicted performing local acts of justice, such as stopping wife beaters, gangsters and so on, and often in a very rough, non-idealized way, suggests that Superman was at this stage more like an angel (in later comics he is called "an angel sent straight from Heaven"[15]) or Jesus the healer and priest than a cosmic Christ. Thus, though both Jesus's and Superman's local acts of healing and heroics should be seen as representative of their pure hearts and devotion to even the lowliest (and in this sense philosopher Umberto Eco is wrong for thinking these are a "waste of means"), such acts, *at least by themselves*, aren't the acts of a mythical hero.[16] Consequently, although already both a direct challenge to Nietzsche's ideal and an important step in semantic change, Superman was only a partial Christ-type when he was re-envisioned in the 1930s.

MORAL ILLUMINATION

A short while later two new elements were added to the Superman mythology that further distinguished him as a Christ-type.

The first had to do with Superman's powers. Although Superman's powers were first explained to be the result of advanced Kryptonian evolution, they were later understood to be caused by the Earth's yellow sun. This had nothing to do with science or the evolution vs. creationism debates of the time. Rather, it had to do with substituting a poor myth for a more potent one. Superman's reliance on the yellow sun had nuances of Christ's reliance on God the Father, who's metaphorically, and cross-religiously, I should add, spoken of as the Sun. Indeed, there aren't many better metaphors for Truth and Justice than the Sun, which means that the Superman myth, here, takes a sharp turn upward toward a profound, irreducible, timeless fact about Reality. Plato, Carl Jung, Joseph Campbell and C. S. Lewis would all applaud.

The second had to do with Superman's absolute code against killing. During the early years of superheroes, there was a tremendous amount of social pressure to censor comics. One of the results was that DC Comics instituted a code that prevented any of its heroes from killing, and, in true Platonic fashion, made it mandatory that good always triumphs over evil (where good and evil were understood from the universal moral perspective, which is in keeping with Judeo-Christian concepts of Truth and Justice). Of course from the point of view of DC Comics, this was just good business, but from the point of view of comic book lovers, the result was a deepened sense that superheroes are

---

15 *Superman* vol. 1, #657 (February 2007).
16 Umberto Eco, "The Myth of Superman," in *The Role of the Reader: Explorations in the Semiotics of Text* (N.P.: First Midland, 1984), 123.

moral absolutists.

Of course, there are enormous problems for those who think that killing is absolutely wrong. What if a person was about to murder your child and you had the choice to kill the would-be murderer or let your child be killed? What would you do then? More importantly, what is the right thing to do? While most of us agree with the universal moral principle "Do no harm," we tend to take it as an objective truth, rather than an absolute one. That is, if there is a greater moral command than "Don't kill a would-be murderer," such as "Save an innocent from being murdered," then killing is not only justified, but the right thing to do.

While Superman does occasionally tackle some tough moral scenarios having to do with his code against killing, most of the scenarios are relatively easy compared to the one I just mentioned. For example, when Superman actually did execute some homicidal criminals from the Phantom Zone, he quickly came to the conclusion that because he had the strength not to kill them, he was wrong for doing so.[17] Though the capital punishment issue isn't straightforward, we could, without much trouble, agree with him here. Or again, in one episode of *The Justice League*, Superman is faced with the choice of killing Mongul's henchman Prega or keeping his own chains on and then being beaten to a pulp; Superman keeps them on until the fight is declared over, at which point he easily breaks them and says, quoting Jesus, to Prega, who asked why he didn't break them earlier, "It's called 'turning the other cheek.'"[18] Though this situation also isn't easy, probably the best of us would admire Superman for sticking to a non-killing version of Jesus's apparent personal pacifism.[19] Or finally, on another occasion, Superman was being mind-controlled by Maxwell Lord such that the *only* way the Man of Steel could be freed was for Lord to die. Wonder Woman, out of a sense of justice, killed Lord and set Superman free, but far from being grateful, Superman said on a later occasion, "Only the weak succumb to brutality."[20] Personally, I think Wonder Woman acted rightly, but Superman could also be seen as right in his anger insofar as Wonder Woman should have known that he would rather have been a slave than see Lord's neck broken. While not an easy case, it's easy compared to, say, a situation where Superman would have to kill a would-be murderer to save Lois, or even if he had the choice to either shoot down the airplanes heading for the World Trade Center (killing all aboard) or letting the planes hit (killing all on board and those in the buildings). Not yet faced

---

17 *Superman* vol. 2, #28 (February 1989).
18 *The Justice League* season 1, episode 12.
19 I say "apparent" since I'm not convinced that Jesus espoused pacifism in even this narrow sense.
20 *Kingdom Come* #3. Cf. *The Adventures of Superman* vol. 1, #642 (September 2005).

with such a choice (and probably never to do so), Superman remains adamant that killing sentient creatures is murder, plain and simple, though I hasten to add in his defense that most killings would, in fact, probably be murder for *him* since he does have the power to do otherwise, while we human beings usually don't.

Thus, if taken as a strict philosophical position, an absolute code against killing is hard to maintain, not to mention, admire. Yet because Superman's inflexibility came to be seen more generally as a symbol of moral integrity – a sign that Superman is willing to do whatever he can to keep all moral commands simultaneously rather than weigh one against another – he became a kind of moral ideal . . . as Christ was and is.[21] Thus, it's not his actual belief that killing is wrong that made him a Christ-type, so much as his unshakable moral convictions and refusal to compromise what he believes is right. "The world changed," Magog tells Superman, "but you wouldn't."[22]

Consequently, Superman's absolute devotion to the universal moral law and Judeo-Christian morality stands in stark contrast to Nietzschean power morality. Nietzsche says, "If you have such a boring and ugly object in yourself, by all means do think more of others than of yourself."[23] But Superman agrees with an old lady who says, "Some of true faith know in their heart the simple difference between helpin' others or just helpin' themselves."[24] Where Nietzsche sees sacrificial love as a weakness because it conforms to social standards, Superman, offering up his very soul to the demon Satanus in exchange for the souls of Metropolites,[25] sees sacrificial love as strength insofar as such conforms to the Highest Law. Nietzsche's super-man thinks himself brave for rejecting notions like forgiveness, but is thus aligned with the villain Lex Luthor, who, Superman says, "doesn't have the *courage* to change" because he can't overlook an insult.[26] Nietzsche might agree with the phrasing of *The Essential Superman Encyclopedia* when it says, "Enemies preyed upon [Superman's] moral code, turning it into a weakness;"[27] yet love is only a weakness if one thinks that true strength or happiness means, as Nietzsche would have it, caring only, or primarily, about one's self. As a result, Nietzsche's thoughts are shown to be like Bizarro's, which are dark and counterintuitive, and the Skeptic's, which

---

21 Similarly, Leo Braudy says that Superman "comes the closest to embodying Plato's idea of the Good." Leo Braudy, "The Mythology of Superman," in *You Will Believe: The Cinematic Saga of Superman* (Warner Bros, 2006).
22 *Kingdom Come* #2.
23 Friedrich Nietzsche *The Dawn* 131.
24 *Action Comics* vol. 1, #849 (July 2007).
25 *Action Comics* vol. 1, #832 (October 2005).
26 *Action Comics* vol. 1, #900 (June 2011).
27 Robert Greenberger and Martin Pasko, *The Essential Superman Encyclopedia* (New York: Del Rey, 2010), 405.

doubt the readily discernable,[28] but Superman's are shown to be illuminated by the heavenly rays of Truth and Justice.

KRYPTO, COMET AND A STEP BACKWARDS

Of course, to see Superman as a Christ-type does require a bit of picking and choosing. There are certainly elements along the way that don't help my argument, though these elements mostly have to do with mythical resonance.

Krypto the Superdog, Comet the Superhorse and Streaky the Supercat are three such instances. These, not to mention Supergirl, Superboy and the Kandorians, tend to diminish Superman's most mythical title, "The Last Son of Krypton." This title has great mythical weight not only because, as I said, the word "*kryptos*" is the Greek word for "hidden" or "secret" but mostly because the word "last" coveys the sense of uniqueness and wonder – wonder of some ancient mystery hidden, only to be hinted at or revealed in this one final person. Jesus is *the* Son of God, not *a* son of God: He is the connection to the great hidden mystery that is God, Our Origin. If there were more than one Jesus – more than one messiah who could bridge the way between God and man – then His importance would be reduced, and with it, His gravitas. The same is true of Superman. Krypto, Comet and Streaky might help sell comics, but only at the cost of tarnishing the myth of Superman.

Thankfully, myth is such that certain hostile elements can be ignored, not out of some fallacious selection of evidence, but rather because the elements hostile to the myth don't rightly belong to the myth in the first place. That is, the potency of a myth is directly correlated to how it reflects some higher, mysterious fact about God or Reality. Thus, since Superman is more a Christ-type insofar as he is the Last Son, the Superman myth – as a myth, not a fictitious history – is best shorn of its other "Super" elements.

Above: The Only Son and the Last Son in *Superman: Peace on Earth*.

---

28 *World's Finest Comics* #11 (Fall 1942).

ABOVE ALL THINGS

TRINITARIAN MOVIE MYTHOS

While the Superman comics during the '50s, '60s and '70s often had little in the way of *numinous* or mythical and moral *gravitas*, the first two Superman movies – *Superman: The Movie* (1978) and *Superman II* (1981) – played important roles in furthering The Man of Tomorrow's role as a Christ-type.

In these movies Superman is no longer merely Jesus the healer, priest and moral exemplar, but is now clearly depicted as a Son-of-God-type. In *Superman: The Movie*, Jor-El is a God-figure sending his only begotten son to become the saviour of a world: "Even though you've been raised as a human being, you're not one of them," he tells his son, "They can be a great people, Kal-El, if they wish to be. They only lack the light to show the way. For this reason, above all, their capacity for good, I have sent them you, my only son."

And such connections in the movie don't stop there: both Jesus and Superman were raised incognito on Earth, both began their mission at the age of thirty, both try – at least for a while – to hide their identities, both assume self-imposed servitude, and, among a myriad of other examples,[29] both fulfill prophecies; for instance, in *Superman II*, when Jor-El restores Superman's powers, and by doing so, exhausts his own, we are told, "The Kryptonian prophecy will at last be fulfilled: the son becomes the father and the father becomes the son" – Superman embraces the vision of his father and his father fills his son, Superman, with the power to achieve his vision. Here we have the first, though not the last, example of Trinitarian symbolism in the Superman myth.

DEATH AND RETURN

Superman is an *American* myth. This is important in its own way (as philosopher A. C. Grayling has pointed out[30]), but it's not important as *myth per se*. All the great myths, insofar as they are great, reflect universal, timeless aspects of Reality. The Americana, in other words, is peripheral to the myth itself.

In *Superman II*, The Man of Steel stills fights for "Truth, Justice and the *American Way*," but he also takes the first step beyond this toward becoming a world saviour: when General Zod and his lackeys uproot and discard both the American and Soviet flags planted on the Moon, it's a symbol of Zod threatening the entire planet. Consequently, Superman can no longer remain a domestic hero, but now must become an international, indeed, a cosmic, hero as well.

---

29 See Anton Kozlovic, "Superman as Christ-Figure: The American Pop Culture Movie Messiah," *Journal of Religion and Film* 6, no. 1 (April 2002).
30 A. C. Grayling, "The Philosophy of Superman: A Short Course," *The Spectator*, July 8, 2006.

This cosmic idea had been growing throughout the '80s, '90s and beyond, such that in *The Brightest Day* #15, Superman declares that he fights for "Truth, Justice and the Universal Way" and in *Action Comics* vol. 1, #900, Superman even renounces his U. S. citizenship, not because he doesn't love America, but because he, quite properly, loves the values particular to America less than he loves the values universally shared.

At the box office, the 2006 movie *Superman Returns* follows, and expands on, this trend, dropping the "American way" part of the phrase. In this movie, Superman is stripped of his cultural particularities (which may have had something to do with the movie's poor domestic box office gross), yet becomes, in the words of its director, Bryan Singer, "The Jesus Christ of Superheroes"[31] (which may have had something to do with the movie's better-than-expected international – that is, universal – box office gross).[32]

In this movie, parallels between Superman and Christ are everywhere, though six in particular are worth mentioning: (1) the movie begins with Superman saving a shuttle named Genesis; (2) later, from a God's eye perspective of the world, Superman tells the disenchanted Lois Lane, who denies hearing anything from up there, "[You hear nothing, but] I hear everything. You wrote that the world doesn't need a saviour, but everyday I hear people crying out for one;" (3) afterwards, when the giant globe on the Daily Planet is loosened by an earthquake, Superman catches it, symbolically representing the burden of the world on his shoulders; (4) a short while later Superman lands on a Kryptonite-poisoned landmass, whereupon he is beaten, scourged, humiliated and finally stabbed in the manner of the impassioned Jesus; (5) after that, he is pushed into the water – a typical symbol of passage to the underworld – only to emerge, be revitalized by the Sun, and then return to destroy the landmass; and (6) finally, after heaving the landmass into space, Superman falls from the sky in a crucifixion position, flat-lines in a hospital on Earth, but in the end returns from the dead. Because of all this wonderfully executed Christian symbolism, this movie is without a doubt the greatest expression of Superman as Christ.

Nevertheless, it wasn't, as I said before, as if Singer was unaware of the other Christian symbolism that had developed around The Man of Steel since the time of *Superman II*. Consider three cases.

First, in arguably the best Superman mini-series, *Kingdom Come*,

---

31 Bryan Singer, quoted in "The Spiritual Side of *Superman Returns*" by Stephen Skelton, *SuperHeroHype.com*, December 4, 2006, http://www.superherohype.com/news/featuresnews.php?id=4972 (accessed on February 19, 2010).

32 Bryan Singer, quoted in "4:11 with Bryan Singer" by Daniel Epstein, *Newsarama.com*, July 30, 2006, http://forum.newsarama.com/showthread.php?t=78755 (accessed on February 19, 2010).

Superman, like Jesus, is depicted as departing the world of man – taking hope with him – only to return, in a "second coming," to restore justice and order. Indeed, in a later, connected story, the Man of Steel even asks the Reverend Norman McCay, "Couldn't you tell me how you see my journey fulfilling biblical prophecy? Could I be part of Revelation?"[33]

Second, in *Superman* vol. 2, #24 (June 2004), Superman's priest friend and pseudo-confessor, Father Daniel Leone, is transformed into the monster Pilate, appropriately named since he thus becomes unintentionally opposed to Superman the Christ-type.

And third, in *Smallville*, Clark Kent is shown in a crucifix position in a cornfield,[34] and revealed, in a particularly powerful episode, to be everlasting.[35] In subsequent episodes, he would also be spoken of as a "saviour,"[36] have his blood used to save countless people,[37] and would be pitted against Doomsday, a biblically-named villain representing the final enemy.[38]

Of course, Doomsday was himself taken from an even earlier stage in Superman's history. In 1992, in an event that sold more than six million comics, DC had Superman die at the hands of the monster Doomsday. Reminiscent of Michelangelo's *Pietà*, Lois / Mary, holds the dying Superman / Jesus in her arms and says of Doomsday / Death, "You stopped him. You saved us all!"[39] In keeping with the Christ story, which talks about countless antichrists rising in Jesus's absence, Superman's death makes room for a number of false supermans to claim his identity and commit all sorts of evil in his good name. However, empty coffin and all, Superman comes back to life in time to defeat the anti-Superman, Hank Henshaw, and restore hope to the world once again.

CHRIST OR CHRIST-TYPE?

Nowadays The Man of Tomorrow has become such a Christ-type, that Superman literature, movies and TV series regularly make allusions, both comical and serious, to Superman being a god. Thus, in *Lois & Clark: A Superman Novel* we read,

> The *cell phone* rang.
> "God." Lois got it out and unfolded it, hoping for Clark.[40]

---

33 *JSA: Kingdom Come Special; Superman* #1 (January 2009).
34 *Smallville* season 1, episode 1.
35 *Smallville* season 3, episode 12.
36 *Smallville* season 9, episode 11.
37 *Smallville* season 9, episode 3.
38 *Smallville* season 8, episode 18.
39 Roger Stern, *The Death and Life of Superman: A Novel* (New York: Bantam, 1993), 130.
40 C. J. Cherryh, *Lois & Clark: A Superman Novel* (Rocklin, CA: Prima, 1996), 23.

Or again, in *The Essential Superman Encyclopedia*, the Man of Steel, in true God-like fashion, is even spoken of as a necessary being, "Superman's greatest significance was that he may well have been the one truly indispensible figure in all Creation – which perhaps explains why, in all the myriad parallel dimensions, there was always some form of Superman."[41]

It's not surprising, then, that some people have confused Superman as a Christ-type with Superman as an idol, or even, in a strange twist, Superman as an antichrist. Thus, when *Superman: The Movie* first came out, Richard Donner, the director, said that he received numerous threats – presumably from Christians – for making obvious connections between Superman and Jesus.[42] Such Christians perhaps meant well insofar as they wanted to prevent Superman from becoming a secular *replacement* for Christ – something that admittedly is a possibility;[43] however, it would be better to emphasize the way things were intended to be, namely, that the more Superman becomes like Christ, the more Christ is revealed: the copy, as Plato says, ought to point to its Original, rather than the copy becoming falsely mistaken for the Original.

And Superman himself agrees. While Gog says, "Worship me,"[44] and Lex Luthor asserts, "They will worship me as a god,"[45] Superman constantly denies his literal deity, breaking up cults dedicated to his worship,[46] wrestling with his own inner demons (in *Superman* #666, no less), and, in *Superman: Godfall*, by stating plainly to Lyla and the Kandorians: "I'm not God. . . . I'm just a man." Indeed, Superman would even agree with Nietzsche that people shouldn't put "blind faith" in him since such weakens individual dignity and resolve (though Superman wouldn't have a problem with people trusting in him for good reason and, of course, for accepting help when they can't save themselves).[47] Perhaps the right balance between seeing Superman as a Christ-type that enables, rather than a god-tyrant that stifles, is in *Superman: Peace on Earth*, which powerfully depicts Superman side-by-side with the Christ the Redeemer statue in Rio de Janeiro while at the same time making it clear that

---

41 Greenberger and Pasko, *The Essential Superman Encyclopedia*, 399.
42 *The Making of Superman: The Movie and Superman II* (USA Home Video, 1980).
43 John Lawrence sees Superman and other superheroes as "secular counterparts of religious leaders." John Lawrence, "The Mythology of Superman," in *You Will Believe: The Cinematic Saga of Superman* (Warner Bros, 2006). And Christopher Knowles believes that "superheroes have come to *fill* the role in our modern society that the gods and demigods provided to the ancients." Christopher Knowles, *Our Gods Wear Spandex: The Secret History of Comic Book Heroes* (San Francisco: Weiser Books, 2007), xv.
44 *JSA: Kingdom Come Special; The Kingdom* #1 (January 2009).
45 *Action Comics* vol. 1, #900 (June 2011).
46 *Superman / Batman: Worship*.
47 *Superman: The Last Family of Krypton* #3 (December 2010).

Superman's mission is not to usurp Christ but to be a Christ-like inspiration to people; thus, he says of world hunger, "It's not my place to dictate policy for humankind. But perhaps the sight of me fighting hunger on a global scale would inspire others to take action in their own way."

SEDUCTION OF THE INNOCENT?

In the 1950s, Fredric Wertham wrote a famous book, *The Seduction of the Innocent: The Influence of Comic Books on Today's Youth*, which argued that comic books and superheroes are unhealthy and dangerous. In his own way, Nietzsche would agree, for since he thought Judeo-Christian morality was toxic, and since comic books, in particular, Superman comics, are permeated with such, Superman comics would be toxic and dangerous as well. At best, the Man of Steel and his fans would be like Jesus and his: "a case of delayed ... puberty."

But it was this attitude toward Judeo-Christian morality, along with biblical motifs and stories, that prompted a strong response from Jerry Siegel and Joe Shuster, who intentionally set out to subvert Nietzsche's antichrist super-man, first by making Super-Man a villain, and then, second, by making him a Judeo-Christian hero of the first order. And this subversion continued over the decades to such a point that Superman has now become the greatest modern Christ-type and an inspiration to all but the Nietzsches, Hitlers, Luthors and Werthams of the world.

Chapter Ten

"Do You Believe You Will Meet Them Again?"
Gladiator, Gender and Marriage in the Next Life

Ridley Scott's *Gladiator* brilliantly depicts authentic masculinity, raising important gender-related questions along the way. The hero, Maximus, is strong, leader-like and benevolent. Indeed, part of what makes Maximus so attractive as a man is his devotion to his wife and family. Even when his wife and son are burned and crucified, Maximus hopes that one day he will be reunited with them, not as strangers, but as a family: "My wife and son are waiting for me," he tells his friend Juba. And so they are. When Maximus himself finally dies, we see him moving between the worlds toward those he loved so dearly.

As beautiful as this is, some Christians aren't moved by this. For them, Maximus not knowing of Jesus *per se* is enough to make this whole situation ridiculous, not only because they maintain that you must know of Jesus in His bearded, Galilean form in order to be saved by His death, but equally importantly, because Jesus, they say, denies that there is marriage in the next life: "When the dead rise, they will neither marry nor be given in marriage; they will be like the angels."[1] While I leave the epistemological and metaphysical considerations of salvation for another time, I do think this Christian objection to marriage in the next life is weak, springing from not only inattention to precise wording, but, more importantly, a poor understanding of gender and sex. Subsequently, in this chapter I will formulate an orthodox Christian theory of gender and sex and then use these findings to answer Maximus's question, "Do you believe you'll meet [your family] again – after you die?"

GENDER AS AN ESSENTIAL PROPERTY

That Plato is a brilliant philosopher I do not deny. That his view of the world was superior to the pagan priests of his day I also do not deny. What I deny, however, is that his view of gender was correct and superior to his polytheistic interlocutors. For the polytheists, the gods were gendered spirits or rational

---

1 Matthew 12:25.

souls. For Plato, gender is probably a social construct, meaning that spirits or rational souls – and certainly God Himself – is genderless. For Plato, rationality is all that matters, but for the polytheists, gender was also important. *Gods* and *goddesses* alike were worshipped by all polytheists, including Maximus.

But which side of this debate does orthodox Christianity come down on? Is God gendered or not? Are the gods – angels and demons – gendered or not? I begin with God.

Univocity means "in one voice" and those who think we can say some things univocally about God are those who think that when we say God is "*Agape*," we attribute to Him precisely what we mean by this: God is Self-Sacrifice, Benevolence. We can, of course, make mistakes in our understanding of this and any word (we might, for example, mistake the word "*agape*" for "a grape," and then wrongly imagine God to be purple and juicy), but in theory, we can understand what this word means and can really know, and say, something literally true of God. Yes, most of our language about God will be analogy, metaphor or simile, but, as Duns Scotus long ago pointed out, all analogy presupposes some univocity;[2] for instance, if we use the simile "God is like the Sun," we don't mean God is literally a giant ball of burning gas, but we do mean, among other things, that God, like the Sun, is *literally* "life-sustaining." And now the point.

Most orthodox Christians admit (consciously or unconsciously) that we can speak with some univocity in respect to God. For example, when we call God "Omnipotence," we mean He is literally so: He can do all that is logically possible. While some Christian feminists agree that we can speak about God univocally, all deny that gender terms applied to God are literally true: Father, King, God, husband, she-bear and so on are metaphors, the literal truth behind them being something like "powerful," "leader-like," or "caring."

To make their case against God being gendered, Christian feminists typically argue thus:

> All gendered words about God are social constructs.
> "God," "King," and "Father" are gendered words used to describe God.
> Therefore, "God," "King," and "Father" are social constructs.

Moreover, usually from a source that isn't biblical (for the ancient Christian feminists, it was Plato-inspired Gnosticism), modern Christian feminists typically assert that spirits are neutered, and thus reason:

> God is a spirit.
> No spirit is gendered.
> Therefore, God isn't gendered.

---

2   Duns Scotus *Ordinatio* pt. 1, d. 8, q. 4, n. 17.

In response, I'd insist that some of the gendered terms used of God are literally, univocally true. Words like Father, King and God – words depicting prime Masculinity – are "title-names"[3] or words literally true of God, while others like husband and bridegroom are metaphors based on God being literally masculine. Thus, while Miroslav Volf thinks gender "stems exclusively from the creaturely realm,"[4] C. S. Lewis is correct here when he says, "Gender is a more fundamental reality than sex."[5]

In metaphysical terms, the argument goes something like this. First, Scripture makes it clear that God is a "Spirit," which for the creeds is "a substance" ("Three persons in one substance") or an indivisible whole with a number of essential properties (qualities or attributes that are *necessarily* part of that substance). Second, based on a number of clear biblical claims, including God's own self-disclosure (such as in the Lord's Prayer), we have good reason to think that God has the essential property "being masculine" (or, more precisely, "being Masculinity"). And third, because I take it to be incoherent to talk about a person – indeed, the Person – as being *essentially* both masculine and feminine, and because all feminine language in the Bible used to describe God can easily be seen as accidental or metaphorical (for example, "being like a hen" or "being like a she-bear"), we have no reason to think God also has the essential property "being feminine." Indeed, when God is compared to a hen or she-bear these statements aren't literally true, but, as with all similes and metaphors, have a literal truth, namely that God, like a hen or she-bear, deeply cares for His children (or has the essential property "being deeply concerned with His creation"). Mary Daley thinks that although God is genderless, we should still consistently use "bisexual imagery" for the "Father-Mother God;"[6] but C. S. Lewis strongly disagrees,

> Suppose the reformer stops saying that a good woman may be like God and begins saying that God is like a good woman. Suppose he says that we might just as well pray to 'Our Mother which art in Heaven' as to 'Our Father.' Suppose he suggests that the Incarnation might just as well have taken a female as a male form, and the Second Person of

---

3   John Cooper, *Our Father in Heaven: Christian Faith and Inclusive Language for God* (Grand Rapids, MI: Baker Books, 1998), 284.
4   Miroslav Volf, *Exclusion & Embrace: A Theological Exploration of Identity, Otherness, and Reconciliation* (Nashville: Abingdon Press, 1996), 170.
5   C. S. Lewis, *Perelandra*, in *The Cosmic Trilogy* by C. S. Lewis, 145-348 (London: Pan Books, 1990), 327-328.
6   Mary Daly, "After the Death of God the Father: Women's Liberation and the Transformation of Christian Consciousness," in *Woman Spirit Rising: A Feminist Reader in Religion*, ed. Carol Christ and Judith Plaskow, 53-62 (San Francisco: HarperSanFrancisco, 1992), 59.

the Trinity be as well called the Daughter as the Son. Suppose, finally, that the mystical marriage were reversed, that the Church were the Bridegroom and Christ the Bride.

Now it is surely the case that if all these supposals were ever carried into effect we should be embarked on a different religion. Goddesses have, of course, been worshipped: many religions have had priestesses. But they are religions quite different in character from Christianity. Common sense, disregarding the discomfort, or even the horror, which the idea of turning all our theological language into the feminine gender arouses in most Christians, will ask 'Why not?' Since God is in fact not a biological being and has no sex, what can it matter whether we say *He* or *She*, *Father* or *Mother*, *Son* or *Daughter*?

But Christians think that God Himself has taught us how to speak of Him. To say that it does not matter is to say either that all the masculine imagery is not inspired, is merely human in origin, or else that, though inspired, it is quite arbitrary and unessential. And this is surely intolerable: or, if tolerable, it is an argument not in favour of Christian priestesses but against Christianity. It is also surely based on a shallow view of imagery.[7]

Nevertheless, some will object: if God made females, He must be the originator of this idea, and doesn't this suggest He is, if we must attribute gender to God at all, equally feminine? Not at all. To be sure, God is the originator of females and the feminine, but He is so not by "being" but by "possessing the idea of." In other words, while He has the essential property "being Masculinity," He has the essential property "possessing the idea of femininity." To clarify, we can say that while God has the essential property "possessing the idea of a horse" or "possessing the idea of rain," He isn't a horse or rain. He is God – and not Goddess – but He, of course, made all things that are feminine from His eternal idea of femininity, which, I hasten to add, is a very beautiful idea indeed.

GENDERED CREATED SPIRITS

If God – the Spirit, Soul, Person or original Substance – is essentially masculine, then it seems likely that those created in His image – other spirits, persons or rational souls – would also be essentially gendered. Although the Bible doesn't say explicitly that angelic beings – polytheism's gods and goddesses – are made in His image, we can infer this through other essential properties they possess which seem to belong exclusively to spirits or rational souls: among other things, angels have the ultimate capacity for free will (hence, Paul refers to

---

7   C. S. Lewis, "Priestesses in the Church?" in *C. S. Lewis: Essay Collection & Other Short Pieces*, ed. Lesley Walmsley (London: HarperCollins, 2000), 400-401.

the "elect angels"[8]), and they have the ultimate capacity for rationality (hence, Satan, Gabriel and others challenge, calculate, argue, tempt, pass on messages, etc.). But do we have biblical evidence for created spirits – specifically, angels – being gendered? I think yes.

In the Bible the angels or demons mentioned by name are masculine, which in itself makes it very likely that they are gendered. Some have objected to this, however, saying that because there is no Hebrew neuter term, the masculine was used instead. But this is unconvincing for many reasons, none more than the fact that even though in Greek there is a neuter term, none of the proper names of angels are in the neuter.[9]

So that the angels are depicted gendered is beyond question. But are all angels *masculine*? Are there only "gods" and no "goddesses"? The Hebrew and Greek words for the general class "angel" always refer to them in the masculine, but this, in itself, is uninteresting. Human beings in their general class are also classified in the masculine ("man"). Not to get ahead of myself here, but insofar as masculinity contains within itself the notion of authority, it's quite proper and just to use the masculine to cover both the masculine and feminine. Moreover, even if the Bible didn't mention any feminine angels, it would hardly follow that none exist (the Bible doesn't mention computers either). Nevertheless, I do think we have some concrete evidence for feminine angels. In Zechariah 5:9, we read, "Then I looked up – and there before me were two women with the wind in their wings!" Almost certainly this verse doesn't refer to human women since humans don't have wings. However, angels do. And because it's not at all clear what these winged women would be metaphors of if we were to read this verse purely metaphorically, it seems likely that this verse is depicting actual feminine angels. But, even if this reading is wrong, it seems very probable that angels, like God, are gendered spirits, and so without getting ahead of myself here again, we can say with high probability that whatever else Jesus means when He says we'll "be like the angels" in the next life, He is not denying us gendered properties.[10]

---

8   1 Timothy 5:21.

9   This is just one example of many, but in Matthew 25:41 we read, "*hetoimasmenon to Diabolo kai tois angelois autou*" ("having prepared for the Devil and *his* angels"). The word "Devil" (*Diabolo*) is masculine in the Greek and so is the possessive pronoun "his" (*authou*). The chauvinistic attitudes of some in the Middle Ages prompted a few, like Michelangelo, for example, to depict the Devil as feminine, and this tradition has trickled down to our modern age where we can still see, for example, Mel Gibson envisioning Satan in this way in his excellent but imprecise movie *The Passion of the Christ*.

10 Many agree with me here, including John Frame, "Men and Women in the Image of God," in *Recovering Biblical Manhood and Woman*, ed. John Piper and Wayne Grudem, 225-232 (Wheaton, IL: Crossway, 1991), 232.

So, from the Uncreated Spirit (God) and the created angelic spirits (angels or "gods"), we finally arrive at created human spirits (man). Nowadays many well-meaning Christians might object to me referring to human beings as spirits, seeing this as the specter of Plato or something worse. But this isn't an orthodox objection. Orthodoxy has usually maintained that the biblical understanding of a human being is that of a spirit, person or rational soul, which has a body.[11] We *are* souls and we *have* (most of the time) bodies. Of course, as I'll argue in a moment, the connection between the soul and body is extremely tight, but for my purposes here, their distinction needs to be noted.

If God and angels – the two other spirits that we know of – are essentially gendered, then it seems likely that humans would be as well. This argument can be further strengthened not only by biblical evidence (those who do appear after death, such as Samuel, Elijah, Moses and Jesus, appear similar to their earthly forms[12]) but also by our intuitions of what it would look like if we were disembodied ("I" would still think of myself in masculine terms, and my wife tells me she would do likewise in feminine terms). Moreover, since human bodies are distinguished by their sex (I leave difficult cases of sexual brokenness to the side for the moment), it seems that human spirits are sandwiched between God and angels – gendered spirits – from above, and sexed bodies from below. Very likely, then, we should think of ourselves, in our inner self, spirit or soul as being essentially gendered, either masculine or feminine.

WHAT GENDER IS TO SOUL, SEX IS TO BODY

Gender, then, appears to be an ontological given – an essential property in the substance or spirit. Moreover, because a general principle in both the Bible and Nature seems to be that the higher guides, controls or affects the lower, the human spirit, which is higher, would guide, control or affect the lower aspect or physical body. Thomas Aquinas's formulation of the soul-body interaction seems to me to be more or less the correct one here.[13]

In terms of gender and sex, what this means is that if your soul has the essential property "being masculine," then your soul, which guides the development of your body, would see to it that your body develops the corresponding sex, which is male. You are masculine and your body will likely reflect this insofar as you have male parts. Or again, if your soul has the essential property of being feminine, then your body will likely have female biology. You, then, would be feminine, and your body would be female.

---

11   For a defense of this claim, see J. P. Moreland and Scott Rae, *Body & Soul: Human Nature & the Crisis in Ethics* (Downers Grove, IL: IVP Academic, 2000), 17-47.
12   1 Samuel 28:11-15, Matthew 17:1-13, John 20:25-27, and Revelation 11:1-12.
13   Thomas Aquinas *Summa Theologica* pt. 1, q. 76, art. 6-8.

General biological differences, including general brain differences, are then determined by the soul.[14]

And something similar is probably true of other spirits as well. In Genesis 6:1-8, the "sons of God" – which the Old Testament always refers to as angels[15] – appear to have taken on a biological form and had sex with "the daughters of men," producing the "nephilim" or giants. Even in the case of Spirit Himself, we can reason that if God is Masculinity, then it makes perfect sense that His incarnate body would be male. This is to say, that it's not at all accidental that Jesus was born a man.

But to return to human beings: What can we say about those with an ambiguous sex? What about those that appear both male and female? Orthodox Christianity has always maintained that because of the falls (the angelic fall and the human fall), nature, including human bodies, have been damaged, though not all in the same way nor to the same degree. Cancer, handicaps and physical death to name a few are probably effects of the human fall. And if so, why would we be surprised that occasionally there would be sexual irregularities? These wouldn't be indicators that all is well (that we've discovered new sexes), but rather that these human bodies are broken, and need fixing. We don't have a perfectly satisfactory way of deciding whether a body with an ambiguous sex suggests a masculine or feminine soul, but we can make attempts to discover this by asking the person what they think, in their best estimation, they are more like. Who do they think they really are? Based on this best guess, then, the appropriate sex operation could be performed.

Of course, all of these comments should only be applied to those with an ambiguous sex. Those whose sex is clear should be thought of as having

---

14 That the sexes have biological – including brain – differences is a scientific fact. Feminists usually don't take issue with this nor need they, for no one is saying boys are smarter than girls or girls are smarter than boy in an absolute sense. *Generally speaking*, they are smarter (if that's even the right word) in different ways. There are important biological differences between males and females in non-nervous system physiology, in the peripheral nervous system, in the limbic system, and in cerebral organization. Of course, hormone imbalances and gene manipulation can affect this all to some extent. Moreover, even if a man is more focused in his brain use (while a woman is more broad), the man who hasn't been trained to focus likely won't excel as well as the woman who has been, and a woman who hasn't been trained to take in the broad details of her environment might not excel as well as a man who has been.

15 Consider "Now there was a day when *the sons of God* came to present themselves before the Lord, Satan also came among them" (Job 1:6); "Again there was a day when *the sons of God* came to present themselves before the Lord, and Satan came among them to present himself before the Lord" (Job 2:1); and "Where were you when the morning stars sang together, and all *the sons of God* shouted for joy?" (Job 38:7).

the corresponding gender. It's no good for a man to say he feels that he is really a woman inside (i.e. that his soul is feminine). To come to this kind of conclusion, we must attribute his confusion to another kind of brokenness: brokenness in the soul.

We are all born with both natural (God-designed) and unnatural (sinful) desires: we are all born with the good desire for God, Truth and Justice on the one hand, and also, because of original sin, for the self-above-all, falsity and injustice on the other hand. Thus, we shouldn't be surprised to hear some people say they were "born gay" or something to that effect.[16] Probably they were. But being born in a certain way is hardly evidence of God's design or that such things are good. Don't get me wrong: I don't think a sinful disposition makes a person guilty of sin (in need of Christ's forgiveness), but I do insist that we consider these dispositions broken or unnatural (in need of Christ's healing). Moreover, we are all born with sinful, unnatural desires – selfish desires, lustful desires, vain desires and so on – and so why should we be surprised if some are born with gay desires? True, the best evidence suggests that nurture plays an enormous part in people engaging in homosexual activities (which do need Christ's forgiveness),[17] but I'm not sure why we'd need to stake everything on saying homosexuality is due purely to nurture any more than we'd need to say that theft, adultery or lying is purely due to nurture. Most (I don't say all) sinful actions seem to come about due to a person choosing to do so based largely on sinful dispositions, certain biological dispositions, the way a person has been raised, and circumstance. But I digress. The point here is that confusion about one's gender is not hard to explain, even if it is hard to heal.

THE MEANING OF MASCULINITY AND FEMININITY

Throughout I've assumed that most of us know what masculinity and femininity are, but it's now time for a definition. John Piper defines masculinity as "a sense of benevolent responsibility to lead, provide for and protect women in ways appropriate to a man's differing relationships," and femininity as "a freeing disposition to affirm, receive and nurture strength and leadership

---

16 Cf. Leonard Sax, *Why Gender Matters* (New York: Broadway Books, 2005), 217.
17 Based on twenty years of researching lesbian adoptions, two University of California sociologists concluded both that a significantly greater proportion of young adult children raised by lesbians had engaged in a same-sex relationship (6 of 25 interviewed) than those raised by a heterosexual mother (0 of 20 interviewed), and, importantly, that those raised by lesbian mothers were also more likely to consider a homosexual relationship. "Professors Take Issue with Gay-Parenting Research," *The Los Angeles Times*, April 27, 2001, http://www.narth.com/docs/docs.html (accessed October 8, 2011).

from worthy men in ways appropriate to a woman's differing relationships."[18] I think these definitions are pretty good, but the trouble is that Piper takes an essential property that belongs to spirit and restricts it only to the human, biological realm. Thus, instead of saying that masculinity has within it the disposition to "protect women," we should rather say that it has within itself the disposition to "protect the feminine," and instead of saying that femininity seeks to strengthen "worthy men," we should say that it seeks to strengthen "the worthy masculine."

In respect to the angels, we don't know for certain that there are feminine ones, but if there are, then it seems likely that the masculine ones would generally feel inclined to protect them. Or again, God is the Eternal Masculine and so defines Himself partly through His eternal idea of the feminine. This literal truth is often expressed metaphorically when we talk about God's relation to Israel or the Church. God the Masculine protects the creation, which, metaphorically, is feminine in relation to Him (His "wife" or "bride"), but these, as I said, are metaphors. God is essentially and literally masculine, but He isn't literally a husband or bridegroom. In fact, if we push this metaphor too far, we get the very distasteful, somewhat homoerotic notion (sometimes expressed in well-meaning praise songs) that though I myself have literally a masculine soul, I am still literally to imagine myself as feminine in relation to God. But this is to confuse what is literal with what is metaphorical. God is essentially and literally masculine; the creation is metaphorically feminine in relation to him. I am essentially and literally masculine and my wife is essentially and literally feminine, but we are metaphorically feminine in relation to God. Nevertheless, these metaphors are valuable and do agree with my revised Piper definition of masculinity and femininity, namely, that the masculine has a sense of benevolent authority over, and responsibility to protect, that which is feminine, while the feminine has the sense of submission and the responsibility to strengthen and ennoble that which is masculine.

Because the ramifications of these gender distinctions both in general and in the human realm are too many to discuss here, I'll restrict myself to a few loose comments about how masculine and feminine beings – in our case, incarnate human beings – should interact.

In general, and all things being equal, men can flourish as men insofar as men have a sense of benevolent responsibility toward women. A man doesn't have to be married to show chivalry to a woman: my two-year son can hold the door open (if he can) for his mom, and thereby demonstrate his budding masculinity. My three-year old daughter, of course, could do the same, and it

---

18 John Piper, "A Vision of Biblical Complementarity," in *Recovering Biblical Manhood and Woman*, ed. John Piper and Wayne Grudem, 31-59 (Wheaton, IL: Crossway, 1991), 35-36.

would be polite and nice, but it would have no effect on her *femininity*, which is to "nurture strength and leadership in the masculine." Or again, a young man's masculinity would flourish if on a date he and his girlfriend were being robbed and he put himself between her and the robber: here he would be taking care of the woman. But if, on the same date, the woman put herself between the man and the robber, she might flourish in respect to her bravery and love, but not in respect to her *femininity*. Since gender is designed by God and should be exercised according to His design, we can say that in either of these two scenarios it would be better for the guy to act than for the girl. And we can say that if this is the case and if moral action should be based on *all* considerations, then the woman would act more justly ("treat each as they ought to be treated") if she refrained from action.

Of course, if it were two men or two women being robbed, then gender isn't really a factor: a man can still be masculine by following or protecting another man, and a woman can still be feminine by strengthening or leading other women. Men who follow other men aren't any less manly than the men who lead them, and the women who are encouraged by other women aren't made less feminine thereby. Sometimes we *talk* as if "bravery" or "leadership in general" were equivalent to "masculinity," but this is a mistake: bravery and leadership in general aren't absolutely linked to one gender – the masculine has to do with "protecting and leading the *feminine*" and femininity with "nurturing strength and leadership in the *masculine*." Maximus isn't manly because he leads other men, but rather is manly because he leads his wife and family.

To elaborate on this, Piper gives us a few helpful guidelines. He suggests that the feminine should have about it (in girls or women, unmarried or married, weak or strong) a sense of submission and a disposition to ennoble men around her, while the masculine should have about it (in men or boys, married or unmarried, healthy or crippled) a sense to protect and take care of the feminine. In *Gladiator*, Maximus is an excellent example of masculinity not because he is a physically strong warrior, but rather because he is so concerned about protecting his family. If, for example, Maximus had been injured in the Germanic war such that he could no longer walk or earn money, he would still be able to demonstrate his masculinity in his concern for, and intention to take care of, them. Masculinity, like femininity, comes from the inside.

Does this mean that if a man doesn't act masculine he is no longer such? No; gender is an essential property, not an accidental one. Commodus is a *man* even though he enslaves and abuses women ("You *will* love me" he tells his sister). Commodus is a *man* but is a bad man for taking away a woman's freedom rather than preserving it ("I have been living in a prison of fear everyday because of him" his sister says of him). Commodus is a *man*, but doesn't act in keeping with his true nature as a masculine spirit. Commodus and Maximus are both *men*, but Maximus is more self-actualized in his masculinity than Commodus because he cares for women. Marriage, of course, is beside the point.

Healthy gender relationships, whether in everyday interaction, dating, marriage or the church, depend on keeping an eye on how the masculine and feminine can flourish therein. In situations where a woman, for example, has personal and direct authority over a man, the woman *qua* woman and the man *qua* man will likely not flourish. Female drill sergeants are a case in point. Mothers, of course, will be in this relationship with their young sons, but even there a mother ought to take care to help her son flourish in his masculinity, perhaps by letting him open the door for her, for example.[19] If we are concerned about raising our children justly and holistically, then we need to pay attention to gender differences.

So, the types of jobs that males and females pursue as well has how they pursue these jobs are important. Let's consider three more examples just to drive home the point.

A single, highly educated mother may become the CEO of a company to help her to take care of her children and to increase the company's profits, and both of these are generally good things. However, if, for example, her secretary were a man, then very likely their respective genders wouldn't flourish in their direct interactions. The secretary could, of course, try to be chivalrous toward her in small things, and she, of course, would be feminine in receiving these gestures, but on the whole, this situation isn't ideal. Nevertheless, what's ideal isn't always what's possible, and on the whole the female CEO might rightly reason that staying in this job is the correct course of action. Yet even so, she shouldn't pretend that she is flourishing optimally as a *woman*.

Or in the church, Paul, though no clear writer, does make it clear in principle that though feminine participation in services is good and desirable, nevertheless, such service must be done with a submissive attitude to the male authorities: prophetesses may prophesy in church, but males, in keeping with their authority over females – and not as a sign of their intelligence or worth – must evaluate. Female pastors and priestesses, who would take it upon themselves to expound God's word both directly and personally to adult men, are, all things being equal, rightly denounced by Scripture.

And all of this is doubly true in marriage. Males are the "heads" of their house in keeping with their masculine essence, and females are to love, nourish and support this headship in keeping in with their essential femininity. If a man is unwilling to lead, protect and take care of his family, he acts unjustly, not only in respect to himself and God, but also in respect to his wife, who,

---

19 Cf. Leonard Sax, *Boys Adrift* (New York: Basic Books, 2007).

because she has to take more responsibility to lead, can't flourish as much in her femininity. If a man can't do this because of some physical handicap (recall my Maximus example), he can still act justly in respect to his masculinity insofar as he *wants* to take care of and lead, yet even so, his wife's femininity will likely suffer some because she must take on certain male responsibilities; thus, the single mother Lucilla tells Maximus, "I'm *tired* of being strong." Of course, not all women who must, *reluctantly* take on masculine responsibilities. Some women covet these. But if a wife actively desires these responsibilities, then her thoughts are unjust, and if her husband isn't physically unable to lead, then insofar as he is drawn into conflict with his wife about this, she wrongs him.

Before moving on, one final comment is in order. New research has shown that a man who is in an intimate relationship with a woman experiences a decrease in his testosterone.[20] Does this make him less a man and thus contradict what I've just argued? Precisely the opposite. Masculinity is about protecting the feminine, not about who's got the largest sex drive. On the whole, women are better protected by a man whose sex drive has decreased somewhat. Men with a slightly lower sex drive are slightly less likely to cheat on their wives, and thus are slightly more likely to stick around, protect and provide. Of course, testosterone remains a biological disposition and nothing more. A man with decreased testosterone might fail to act manly and vice versa. But dispositions do matter, and the ones that God has given us are for the purpose of upholding His good design, in this case, His good design for the sexes.

MARRIAGE IN THE AFTERLIFE

Based on what's just been said (not to mention a generally cynical attitude toward marriage nowadays), some might say that even if marriage in the next life were possible, who would want such? To these, I have nothing to say. I assume marriage is a good thing (though I don't say it's better or worse than being single), and understand Maximus's desire to be reunited with his wife in the next life. The question, however, is, is such even possible?

Herein I've shown that it's very likely that our souls are essentially gendered, and because I believe our souls continue to endure after we die (and will be reunited with a new body), that we, "like the angels," will continue to be gendered in the afterlife. Moreover, I take it as obvious that insofar as a man's wife is saved by Christ that he will know and recognize her in the next life. But what will this relationship be like?

Jesus tells us "they will neither marry nor be given in marriage," which is

---

20 Micah Toub, "Bye-bye, Dear Testosterone," *The Globe and Mail* September 30, 2011.

to say that there will be no *new* marriages in the afterlife. Nowhere does Jesus actually deny that some marriages from this life will continue to exist in the next, so it seems perfectly possible to imagine a man such as Maximus (let's say that Jesus accredited his faith to Him) being reunited to his wife in the next life. The biological aspect of that relationship will be transformed (probably to a higher type of biology *qua* the new body), but I don't see why the rest would be so different.

Some, like Kierkegaard, seem to suggest that in the next life we'll love all people equally and therefore all relationships of preference and intimacy will be done away with.[21] But I find this dubious. A general moral principle that God reveals to us is that all things being equal we should prefer kin and those closest to ourselves to others. For example, if I had only one indivisible unit of food and I had two little girls in front of me who were identical to each other in every way except that one had the property "being my daughter," then it would be *just* for me to give the food to my daughter and *unjust* to give it to the other girl. And because *agape* perfects justice rather than doing away with it, I conclude that every Christian father ought to think likewise. This is *not* emotional weakness, but rather clear moral reasoning. But the point: since general moral principles aren't arbitrary creations but rather flow from God's nature as the Righteous and Good, the moral principle that commands us to, all things being equal, prefer kin to others, will almost certainly still be true in the next life. Coupled with the fact that we will almost certainly carry with us our memories of this life (purified by greater knowledge to be sure), then my argument goes like this:

> We will likely be gendered in the next life,
>
> We will likely remember the fact that we were married,
>
> We will still have the moral duty to love those closest to ourselves in the next life,
>
> Marriage is a good thing,
>
> God would likely not do away with any good thing, but would rather redeem it,
>
> So, it seems likely that some marriages will continue to endure in the next life.

Of course, marriages that are legitimately dissolved here would also be so in the New Earth, and multiple marriages now would likely, as Jesus pointed out, make the continuation of these in the next life impossible. There is much more that could be said here and much more work that needs to be done;

---

21 Søren Kierkegaard, *Works of Love*, trans. Howard Hong and Edna Hong (Princeton: Princeton University Press, 1995), 53.

nevertheless, this shouldn't blind us to the work that has already been done – to the argument given above. Thus, while a single man or woman might be like a single star in the heavens called God (alone, but never alone), a married couple, like Maximus and his wife, would be like a constellation therein. Truly, "What we do in life, echoes in eternity."

Chapter Eleven

"It's Arbitrary"?
Breaking Bad and the Ethics of Drugs

In one particular episode of the drug drama *Breaking Bad*, Walter White, a chemistry teacher-turned-meth producer, engages in a spirited discussion with his brother-in-law and DEA agent, Hank Schrader, about the legality of drug use, sales and production. Walt, an American, thinks laws that made alcohol illegal during the Prohibition (1920-1933) and current laws that make Cuban cigars and drugs like marijuana and meth illegal are "arbitrary."[1] Hank dismisses this with an *ad hominem* argument, "You ought to visit lockup; you hear a lot of guys talking like that."[2] The effect is that we are left feeling that Walt is probably right: that alcohol, cigars and other drugs like meth are more or less the same, and that the legality or illegality of any of these is based on mere social whimsy.

Although all laws are grounded in what society deems lawful or unlawful, the really important question has to do with the morality that lies behind, and informs, society's sense of lawfulness or unlawfulness. Here I'm not so much concerned with the precise relationship between the laws of state and morality so much as morality itself and what it has to say about drugs. I'm not so much interested in whether it was lawful for booze to have been illegal during the Prohibition or for Cuban cigars and illicit drugs to be illegal at present so much as whether producing, selling and using drugs – be it alcohol, cigars, caffeine, aspirin, marijuana or meth – is moral or immoral. In this chapter, I will explore the morality of drug use, sales and production vis-à-vis *Breaking Bad*.

WHAT IS A DRUG ANYWAY?

Before exploring the morality or immorality of drugs, it's important to have a working definition of a "drug." One dictionary says a drug is "a chemical substance that affects the processes of the mind or body."[3] Another says it's

---

1 *Breaking Bad* season 1, episode 7.
2 *Breaking Bad* season 1, episode 7.
3 *The Free Dictionary* http://medical-dictionary.thefreedictionary.com/drug (accessed on

"a substance used as medication or in the preparation of medication" or, alternatively, "an illegal substance that causes addiction or marked change in consciousness."[4] Of course, it doesn't take the keen mind of a Walter White or an Aristotle to see that none of these definitions are particularly helpful. Since salt mixed in water is, on the first definition, a "chemical substance," should we thus consider it a drug? Or, on the second definition, if water is used as medication, does this, then, make it a drug? And what about in a country like Saudi Arabia, where pornography, an addictive substance for many, is illegal: should it be considered a "drug" there?

While it's apparent that no perfect definition of a "drug" is forthcoming, I think we can work with the first general definition: "a chemical substance that affects the processes of the mind or body." Subsequently, we can divide these chemical substances into drugs that cloud the mind and drugs that don't. Why this distinction is preferable as a preliminary division between drugs than, say, "medical drugs" and "recreational drugs," requires a bit of argumentation, beginning, as is proper, with basic moral principles.

THE PRINCIPLE OF GENERAL BENEFICENCE

The Natural Law or universal moral law has many basic precepts that all rationally-developed, properly functioning people can understand. Walt Jr. understands the basic principle that, all things being equal, he should respect his superiors, which is what he does when he sets up a website to help his dad, who is dying of cancer. Or again, Hank understands that, all things being equal, he shouldn't lie, which is why he didn't when he had to give his statement about what happened when he assaulted Jesse Pinkman. More to our purpose, all rationally-developed, properly functioning people can know that, all things being equal, they should keep the principle of general beneficence or the principle that says "do no harm." Because some may misunderstand the universal moral law and its precepts, it's important, before elaborating on the principle of general beneficence, to be clear about my phrase "all things being equal."

Moral reasoning begins with basic moral principles to be sure, yet these principles don't necessitate a clear solution to every moral problem. Most of the basic moral principles of the Natural Law are objective, generally binding principles rather than absolute or inviolable ones, meaning that every particular moral situation requires all relevant moral principles and facts to be gathered together in order to determine the solution that is likely the best: moral reasoning, as virtue ethicists would say, requires *wisdom*. For example,

---

July 27, 2011).
4 *Merriam-Webster* http://www.merriam-webster.com/dictionary/drug (accessed on July 27, 2011).

just because Walt Jr. ought to respect his father, it hardly follows that he has to respect his father in all things. Walt Jr. would be wise not to respect his father when Walt Sr. lies since Junior's piety should be qualified by another moral principle, namely, "Don't lie." Or again, Hank is wise for not lying about his assault on Jesse, not only because he did, in fact, assault Jesse ("It wasn't the right thing to do," he says plainly[5]), but also because there were no stronger moral principles or group of principles that would trump this one. Yes, Hank could keep his job by lying, but the good of keeping his job isn't a moral good since Hank could get another job by which he could take care of his wife, Marie, thus adhering both to the principle of special beneficence (the principle that obligates us, all things being equal, to favour our family over others) and the principle of care for subordinates (the moral principle that obligates the strong to take care of the weak[6]).

In the same way, the principle of general beneficence or the "do no harm" precept is an objective moral principle that requires wisdom when applied to particular moral situations. Because the application of moral principles isn't a straightforward matter, rational people can disagree, though, of course, some solutions are better than others. Here is how I believe the principle applies to drugs.

THE CLEAR-HEADEDNESS INJUNCTION

To do no harm means to do no harm to everything, including plants, animals, human beings, God and so on. Although all of these are important to the question of drug use, sales and production, harm to human beings, especially the self and society, is the most crucial consideration.

Now most would agree human beings have the potential to become better than they currently are, where "better" refers chiefly, though not exclusively, to moral characteristics like courage, self-control, justice and wisdom. Moreover, most make becoming better, especially in the moral sense, a moral imperative: a person *should* strive to become brave, temperate, just and wise; a person should strive, if we were to reduce all of these to the principle of justice, to treat each as it ought to be treated. Thus, after Hank assaulted Jesse, he says

---

5   *Breaking Bad* season 3, episode 7.
6   When I speak of "subordinates" or "the weak," I mean this, of course, in a general, qualified sense. Marie is a "subordinate" or "the weak" in the statement above primarily in the sense of being under the headship and protection of her husband, rather than being less valuable, intelligent, physically strong, competent or what have you. The world is full of just inequalities, which morally obligate the "strong" to take care of the "weak." Marie is "the strong" when she physically takes care of the injured Hank, but Hank is "the strong" insofar as he is the head of his house (a position that can't be reduced to his physical strength, earning power, and so on).

to Marie, "I'm supposed to be better than that."[7] Conversely, a person who doesn't try to improve himself – a person who doesn't care about virtue and self-actualization in this sense – is generally considered morally negligent. In the language of justice, such a person is unjust since he doesn't treat himself, and those connected with the proper actions of the self, as they ought to be treated.

Although there are many ways a person may fail to act virtuously and against his proper destiny, one way is to engage in activities that intentionally obstruct wisdom and clear thinking. Of course, while engaging in such activities need not always be unjust and immoral, generally they will be. Given the principle of general beneficence and our moral duty to try to live virtuously, then, we can deduce what I'll call "the clear-headedness injunction," which generally obligates us to shun activities that cloud our minds and engage in activities that illuminate them. This injunction, as a mere derivative of the universal moral law and not a principle itself, is contentious; nevertheless, in its various forms, it's acknowledged by important thinkers as diverse as the Buddha, Mohammed, and Jesus.

DRUGS THAT CLOUD THE MIND AND DRUGS THAT DON'T

"Then God said, 'I give you every seed-bearing plant on the face of the whole Earth and every tree that has fruit with seed in it. They will be yours for food.'"[8] What I take away from this verse is that, among other things, there is goodness in all things, even if this goodness has been, and can be, distorted and abused. Opium poppies can be chewed to soothe a toothache, coca can be munched on to stimulate an unfocused mind, psychedelic mushrooms are an ancient anaesthetic, and alcohol is a natural sedative found in over-ripe fruit. Thus, we can well imagine Hank, the homebrew king, saying with the Psalmist, "Oh praise the LORD, O my soul. . . . He makes grass grow for the cattle, and plants for man to cultivate – bringing forth food from the Earth: wine that gladdens the heart of man, oil to make his face shine, and bread that sustains his heart."[9] Because this is so important, it's well worth emphasizing: such drugs, usually in fairly unrefined states, are good. This is why the ancient Greeks sacrificed to Dionysius, the god of wine, Shinto priests still pour out

---

7 *Breaking Bad* season 3, episode 7.
8 Genesis 1:29.
9 Psalms 104:14-15. Of course, not all alcoholic drinks are equal: red wine is probably the best of them since, in addition to alleviating stress and hypertension, it also helps prevent heart disease and eases stomachaches; thus, even an ancient layman like St. Paul insists, "Stop drinking only water, and use a little wine because of your stomach and your frequent illnesses" (1 Timothy 5:23).

libations of sake every New Year's, and Yahweh required, on certain occasions, "half a hin of wine as a drink offering."[10]

But if some drugs that cloud the mind can be used for good purposes, how can we reconcile this with the clear-headedness injunction? Wisdom bids us pay attention to all factors involved in every particular situation, rather than to be too quick to absolutize. For instance, let's say for argument's sake that when Hank was shot, the doctor had the choice to give him an anaesthetic that would cloud his mind, such as marijuana, or an anaesthetic, like metoclopramide, that wouldn't. Obviously, insofar as the doctor can more fully obey the law of general beneficence (alleviating his patient's pain *and* not clouding his mind), he should do so. Thus, metoclopramide is better than medical marijuana, for example. However, if, for some reason, the doctor only had a bag of Jesse's weed, then I believe it would be better for Hank to smoke the weed and have a cloudy mind than not to be anaesthetized at all. The reason for this is not only that alleviating serious, unnecessary pain is a general moral duty, but also that if Hank were not anaesthetized, he would likely wrong those around him – nurses, doctors and visitors – with flaying arms, curses and so on. To appropriate the proverb: "Give beer to those who are perishing, wine to those who are in anguish; let them drink and forget their poverty and remember their misery no more."[11] Obviously, my argument isn't a defense of medical marijuana – especially since we have drugs that don't cloud the mind and are more medically efficient – but rather a very particular case where a mind-clouding drug might be justly used.

It should be apparent, then, why I favour separating drugs into those that cloud the mind and those that don't, rather than into medical drugs and recreational drugs. Marijuana – or Walt's bottle of tequila, for that matter – can have a medical purpose. Indeed, if we start dividing drugs into medical and recreational, we are faced with a whole host of problems: Is Viagra a medical drug or a recreational one? What about red wine? Better to make our distinction at drugs that cloud the mind and drugs that don't, even if this distinction shouldn't be taken to imply that drugs that cloud the mind are always bad and drugs that don't are always good. Life is too messy for this kind of absolute division.

Nevertheless, because of the clear-headedness injunction, we do have a general rule that helps us to say why in most cases it's unjust and immoral to use, sell and produce drugs that cloud the mind. Alcohol in moderate doses, aspirin and coffee don't cloud the mind, and can also do some good, such as alleviate stress, relieve pain and stimulate a tired mind: Hank relaxes with his margaritas, Skylar takes an aspirin when she has a headache, and Walt

---

10 Numbers 15:10.
11 Proverbs 31:4-5.

drinks coffee every morning to help him wake up. But LSD, peyote, ecstasy, cocaine, pot, heroin, and, of course, meth are in virtually all cases taken for no other reason than to cloud the mind, thus leading to a distorted, unjust form of enjoyment.[12] Biochemically speaking, these illicit drugs impair short term memory in the temporal lobe, disrupt communication between the limbs and the cerebellum, and cause the pleasure part of the brain (the nucleus accumbens), the emotional part of the brain (the amygdala) and hormonal part of the brain (the hypothalamus) to overrule the self-control part of the brain (the lateral habenula by way of the fasciculus retroflexus). Heavy drinking can kill cells in the fasciculus retroflexus in a matter of months to a few years, cocaine in a few weeks to a month, and meth in a few days to a week. But cloudy thinking, whether for a few hours at a party (pot) or for a lifetime through regular abuse (meth), prevents a person from acting justly both toward himself and to those around him. Through mind-clouding drugs, reason and wisdom are overthrown by mere instincts, at best lowering man to the level of the beasts (seeking base pleasures above superior ones), and at worst reducing man to a zombie, where nothing else matters but a "bump" to increase a spike of dopamine in his brain. As William Bennett says, "Drug use is wrong because it is immoral and it is immoral because it enslaves the mind and destroys the soul."[13]

THE ADDICTION AND ABUSE FACTOR

While the cloudy-mindness factor is the first factor to consider when examining different types of drugs and their misuse, it's not the only factor. Abuse and addiction are two other important factors, and are best looked at in four distinct cases: coffee, alcohol, cigarettes and meth.

Coffee is likely good in and of itself, but it can be addictive and misused. For example, if Walt couldn't control his coffee intake, then he would be acting intemperately or unjustly since his higher self (his will) should be able to control and regulate his lower self (the desire for coffee). Moreover, because caffeine

---

12   I leave aside the issue of religious uses of mind-clouding drugs since even if I were willing to concede that piety to the gods is a more important moral principle than clear-headedness, I find it very dubious that the gods, who presumably are even more intelligent than ourselves, would require us to become stupider in order to honour, and commune with, them. Surely when we are told to be humble before God and to "be like children" this is a call to moral purity rather than to give ourselves over to foolishness.

13   William Bennett, John Dilulio, Jr. and John Walters, *Body Count* (New York: Simon & Schuster, 1996), 140-141. James Wilson is also right when he says that heavy drug use is "destructive of human personality" and "destroys the user's essential humanity." James Wilson, *Thinking about Crime* (New York: Basic Books, 1975), 156.

can be addictive, Walt the coffee drinker needs to be ever-vigilant to make sure that he, and not coffee, is in charge. Nevertheless, while coffee abuse can hurt Walt (spiritually, insofar as he wouldn't be able to control himself, and physically, insofar as too much caffeine hurts the body), the abuse of coffee isn't likely to seriously affect others around him.

Alcohol, especially red wine, in small doses is good in and of itself, yet it can be misused and is addictive as well. Although not all agree what "drunkenness" is, I think we are safe to follow the standard medical practice of measuring BAC or Blood Alcohol Content. A person with .000-.029% BAC is normal, while a person with .030-.059% will enjoy mild euphoria and relaxation. For a generally healthy adult (alcohol is always harmful to children), neither of these blood alcohol levels would constitute intemperance, and the latter would likely constitute the proper blessing of "wine that gladdens the heart." In concrete terms, a man of Walt's body weight (body weight mattering a great deal in determining BAC) might enjoy two fingers of scotch, a pint or so of beer or a glass or two of wine without intemperance, while a man of Hank's body weight could enjoy a bit more. However, because anything in excess of .06% probably counts as drunkenness or cloudy-mindedness, such alcohol abuse would thus be unjust or "wicked."[14] Moreover, just because a person like Walt might not get drunk on two glasses of wine, it doesn't mean that this is good for his *body*: science shows us quite the opposite, and wisdom, importantly, tells us to treat our bodies justly. Nevertheless, if over-drinking-but-not-getting-drunk (that is, Walt having two glasses of wine) isn't a regular occurrence (that is, a non-addictive habit), this might well be justified on some occasions, such as at a party or after a particularly stressful day at work: there are many more important factors than the body's optimum health. Also, because those who abuse alcohol, compared to those who abuse coffee, are much more likely to hurt others around them through brawling, making unwanted sexual advances, drunk driving and so on,[15] its benefits are more controversial than those of coffee. Finally, alcohol is also a potential "gateway" to drugs that are bad in and of themselves, and so needs to be temperately used in order to disassociate it from such drugs.[16]

Cigars – one of Hank's favourite drugs – aren't obviously good in and of themselves since smoked tobacco is carcinogenic; however, because most who

---

14 1 Samuel 1:13.
15 "Wine is a mocker and beer a brawler; whoever is led astray by them is not wise" (Proverbs 20:1). "Be very careful how you live – not as unwise but as wise, making the most of every opportunity for the days are evil. . . . Do not get drunk on wine, which leads to debauchery" (Ephesians 5:15-18).
16 "All food is clean, but it is wrong for a man to eat anything that causes some to stumble. It is better not to eat meat or drink wine or to do anything else that will cause your brother to fall" (Romans 14:20-21).

smoke them do so with great pleasure and only on very special occasions – as Hank does to celebrate the birth of Holly – they aren't obviously bad either (perhaps no worse than a slice of decadent cake on a birthday). But this isn't true of Skylar's favourite drug: cigarettes, which, while good insofar as they both facilitate group acceptance and don't cloud the mind, are still largely bad. The nicotine in them makes them very addictive, leading to intemperate behaviour (including, as with all addictions, financial intemperance), and the carcinogens that a smoker inhales makes lung cancer an increased probability, constituting obvious moral neglect since a person has a general moral duty to preserve his life – for his own sake and for the sake of others who he has a duty to benefit. Second-hand smoke, moreover, is harmful to all.

Lastly, meth – *Breaking Bad*'s drug of choice – has really no proper benefit, and has a string of serious problems surrounding its use. Dopamine is the neurotransmitter in the midbrain that mediates communication between the personality centers, the emotional centers and the motivational centers of the brain. It's the primary transmitter in the nucleus accumbens (the pleasure center of the brain), and increases with certain stimuli. While a just or proper pleasure such as that which comes from a delicious meal or an orgasm cause synaptic levels of dopamine to increase around 200-300%, meth – the drug with the highest dopamine spike, especially if it's Walt's 99% pure ice – can cause increases of up to 1200%.[17] When the relevant cells are depleted of dopamine, the person crashes. Because the relevant brain cells are still fairly healthy in a first time user, the person experiences mild depression for a few days; however, because the pleasure is so intense, it's extremely addictive, and as use continues and the brain can't keep up, the crash becomes more intense to the point where nothing can satisfy but the pleasure brought on by the crystal: food that once tasted good now tastes bland and conversation with friends no longer gives joy. The addictive nature of meth (and many other illicit drugs) ultimately causes a person not only to violate the moral injunction against cloudy-mindedness, but also causes him to treat *everything* around him unjustly. Eventually, not only does he fail to take proper pleasure in food, drink, sex and so on (that is, he fails to treat these and the pleasure they give justly or as they ought to be treated), but he also becomes so fixated on his next hit that he both breaks moral laws to get money for drugs (through theft, prostitution and murder) and also neglects important moral obligations, in particular, to his family.[18] Thus, in season two, episode six, we see Spoonge

---

17 Mary Holley, *Crystal Meth: They Call It Ice* (Mustang, OK: Tate Publishing, 2005), 48.
18 In Oregon, meth use is the leading problem of property crimes (85% in the state) and the leading reason children are sent into foster homes (50%). *The Meth Epidemic*, written and produced by Carl Byker (PBS, 2006).

and his woman completely unconcerned with each other's proper good and, most importantly, completely unconcerned with the proper good of their small child, who is dirty and hungry and forced to entertain himself with infomercials on TV. In another episode, this incident causes Jesse to say with righteous indignation, "What kind of mother gets wasted when she has a little kid to take care of?"[19] Consequently, while some of the chemicals in meth have legitimate or just uses, meth itself has really no just use, which means that meth sales and production are largely unjust as well.

"RUIN LIVES"

Philosopher Douglas Husak is right when he says that those who condemn illicit drug use as immoral or unjust "rarely offer a reason in support of their vehement moral condemnation."[20] It's my hope that in this chapter I've met Husak's challenge as well as that of Walt's, which would have us believe that there is no compelling moral reason or foundation to oppose the legalization of drugs like marijuana, cocaine or meth. In response, I've argued two key things in respect to the ethics of drug use, sales and production: that drugs that cloud the mind (like pot and meth) are, for the most part, immoral since such violate the clear-headedness injunction, a derivative of the Natural Law, and that drugs that lend themselves strongly to addiction (such as cigarettes and meth) are likely immoral as well since a just person is one who is also self-controlled. In this way, I agree with Hank, who lucidly sees that mind-clouding and addictive drugs "ruin lives."[21]

---

19 *Breaking Bad* season 3, episode 11.
20 Douglas Husak and Peter de Marneffe, *The Legalization of Drugs: For & Against* (Cambridge: Cambridge University Press, 2005), 74.
21 *Breaking Bad* season 1, episode 3.

Chapter Twelve

"The Gods Hate Incest": Nature and Consanguine Unions in *A Game of Thrones*

"The gods hate incest," says a nameless knight in the fictitious land of Westeros.[1] That the knight is nameless is important since his sentiment is nearly universally acknowledged in *A Game of Thrones*. People as diverse as Stannis Baratheon, Tywin Lannister, and Catelyn Stark all agree that consanguine unions, incest, or, crudely, a sexual union between a near relative is an "abomination,"[2] a "disgusting [thing],"[3] and "a monstrous sin to both old gods and new."[4]

To their credit, then, the old gods and new of Westeros and Essos are perhaps like Plato's true gods or Judeo-Christian angels, who, as powerful, but not all-powerful, beings, command what is good simply because it's good. This implies, firstly, that none of these gods are themselves identical to the Moral Good, and, secondly, that there must be a Supreme Moral Good or a supreme God, who, at once transcendent and immanent, commands what is good, natural or just because such is in keeping with His perfect nature as the Good. Additionally, the supreme Good in *A Game of Thrones*, who is everywhere known and never clearly acknowledged, seems, if their world is at all like ours, to be intimately connected with the creation of that world. In ours, and likely in theirs, all created things have a proper nature and such act naturally when they act in accordance with their respective natures. Lower animals and insects act rightly by natural, God-designed instincts, but human beings, as spirits possessing physical bodies, have not only natural instincts but also, more importantly, the Natural Law or basic moral principles which can be applied to particular circumstances to discern, in varying degrees, correct action.

Nevertheless, given the popularity of Freudian psychology, relativistic ethics and the countless cases or hints of incest in *A Game of Thrones* – from Jamie and Cersei, to Caster and Gilly, Viserys and Daenerys, Arnolf and Alys,

---

1   George R. R. Martin, *A Clash of Kings* (New York: Bantam Books, 2011), 260.
2   Martin, *A Clash of Kings*, 158.
3   George R. R. Martin, *A Storm of Swords* (New York: Bantam Books, 2011), 265.
4   Martin, *A Clash of Kings*, 497.

Walder and his brother's wife, Theon and Asha, Loras and Margery, and a host of others – many will still find it hard to believe that there's anything like a *natural* instinct against, and a *natural* command forbidding, incest. This, consequently, is what will need to be shown in this chapter. Thus, using *A Game of Thrones* as my example, I will argue that incest is, indeed, unnatural and will attempt to answer challenges to the contrary.

JAMIE, FREUD AND THE WESTERMARCK EFFECT

Jamie and Cersei Lannister are full-siblings and lovers. Born twins, they saw in each other their own reflection and their own other half: "You are me," Cersei says to Jamie, "I am you."[5] From their earliest days, they pushed the boundaries of gender and sex norms, cross-dressing "for a lark,"[6] imagining themselves of the opposite sex ("If I were a woman, I'd be Cersei"[7]) and even in their early childhood expressing erotic feelings for each other:

> As children, they would creep into each other's beds and sleep with their arms entwined. . . . Long before his sister's flowering or the advent of his own manhood, they had seen mares and stallions in the fields and dogs and bitches in the kennels and played at doing the same. Once their mother's maid had caught them at it . . . he did not recall just what they had been doing, but whatever it was had horrified Lady Joanna. She had sent the maid away, moved Jamie's bedchamber to the other side of Casterly Rock, set a guard outside Cersei's, and told them they must *never* do that again.[8]

However, once Jamie and Cersei's mother died, the two were free to continue to explore their increasing erotic attraction toward each other to the point where they eventually became full-blown lovers. Indeed, their young adult devotion to each other was so intense that Jamie gave up his inheritance as the future lord of Casterly Rock to be part of the kingsguard so that he could be closer to his sister, who had then become queen of the seven kingdoms. Likewise, Cersei risked much for her love, cheating on her husband – King Robert Baratheon – and bearing three children to Jamie – Joffrey, Tommen and Myrcella – who were passed off as Robert's heirs.

The cross-dressing and incest led to adultery, which in turn led to Jamie attempting to murder seven year-old Brandon Stark, who had seen the two secretly fornicating, and which also led Cersei to have a hand in murdering Jon Arryn and Eddard Stark, which subsequently led to civil war and, among other

---

5   George R. R. Martin, *A Feast for Crows* (New York: Bantam Books, 2011), 179.
6   Martin, *A Clash of Kings*, 849.
7   Martin, *A Storm of Swords*, 294.
8   Martin, *A Storm of Swords*, 286-287.

things, tens of thousands of lives lost. In the midst of this, Jamie was adamant that he wanted to wed his sister ("Marry me, Cersei"[9]), yet eventually he discovered that she had been unfaithful to him, having had another incestuous affair with their cousin Lancel while Jamie was imprisoned. But perhaps more importantly, while Cersei's depravity only became more marked – having a lesbian fling to see what it felt like to be a man and plotting against the wife of her son[10] – Jamie's encounter with the noble knight Brienne stirred his conscience, compelling him to keep his oaths and do justice.[11] Their morality began to diverge and with it, their relationship, including their erotic one. Nevertheless, never once did either Lannister imagine incest to be morally wrong. For them, it was natural; as Jamie says, "I'm not ashamed of loving you, only of the things I've done to hide it."[12]

Sigmund Freud would have loved this odd take on the Lancelot-Guinevere story. The famed Viennese psychotherapist is renowned for reducing distinct forms of love, such as *storge* or affection, *eros* or sexual attraction, *philia* or friendship and *agape* or sacrificial love, largely to *eros*. Building on the assumption that all norms are social constructs (meaning that norms forbidding consanguine unions are relative and can be overturned if need be), Freud argued that people are largely sexual beings who only control their sexual urges to keep society working, and not because there is anything inherently wrong with any sexual act or expression. In particular, Freud believed that sons have a "natural" sexual desire for their mothers (the Oedipus Complex), that daughters feel likewise about their fathers (the Electra Complex), and so on. As he says, "psychoanalytic investigations have shown beyond the possibility of doubt that an incestuous love choice is in fact the first and regular one."[13] Jamie and Cersei couldn't agree more.

Nevertheless, nowadays we know that Freud's theory is, as he himself often hinted, more autobiographical than fact: "I have found, in my own case too, falling in love with the mother and jealousy of the father, and I now

---

9   Martin, *A Storm of Swords*, 852.
10 Martin, *A Feast for Crows*, 692 and 929.
11 After hanging a guilty man, Jamie thinks to himself, "It felt good. This was justice." Martin, *A Feast for Crows*, 571.
12 Martin, *A Storm of Swords*, 1002.
13 Sigmund Freud, *A General Introduction to Psychoanalysis*, trans. Joan Riviere (New York: Pocket Books, 1953), 220-221. Sir James Frazer is a famous expositor of this Freudian idea, writing, "Instead of assuming from legal prohibition of incest that there is a natural aversion to incest, we ought rather to assume that there is a natural instinct in favour of it, and that if the law represses it, as it represses other natural instincts, it does so because civilized men have come to the conclusion that the satisfaction of these natural instincts is detrimental to the general interests of society." J. G. Frazer, *Totemism and Exogamy*, vol. 4 (London: n.p., 1910), 97-98.

regard it as a universal event of early childhood."[14] Though Freud's theories are popularly known, few psychologists and philosophers accept his theory of incest, and the reason for this is due in part to Edward Westermarck.

In a nutshell, Westermarck argued that inbreeding has deleterious consequences (high rates of genetic disorders), and that because of this, many species, including human beings, have natural aversions to sexual relationships with early childhood associates:

> I must confess that the attempts to prove the harmlessness of even the closest inbreeding have not shaken my opinion that there is convincing evidence to the contrary. And here I find, as before, a satisfactory explanation of the want of inclination for, and consequent aversion to, sexual intercourse between persons who from childhood have lived together in that close intimacy which characterises the mutual relations of the nearest kindred. We may assume that in this, as in other cases, natural selection has operated, and by eliminating destructive tendencies and preserving useful variations has moulded the sexual instinct so as to meet the requirements of species.[15]

Christians can take or leave the macroevolutionary account, but in either case accept the scientific evidence for the Westermarck Effect or "the remarkable absence of erotic feelings between people living closely together from childhood."[16]

Thus, where George R. R. Martin would have us imagine Jamie and Cersei's incestuous relationship as *developing* from early childhood instincts, Westermarck would say that this is extremely unlikely, and he's backed in this by two key studies.

First, primatology has shown that there is indeed a natural instinct in apes and others to avoid consanguine unions, especially when those related are sexually mature: "Nonhuman primates provide abundant evidence for an inhibition of sexual behaviour among closely related adults. . . . The primate data supports Westermarck's theory that familiarity during immaturity is a

---

14   Sigmund Freud, *The Psychopathology of Everyday Life*, in *The Standard Edition of the Complete Psychological Works of Sigmund Freud*, vol. 1, trans. James Strachey and Anna Freud (London: n.p., 1953), 265. It's agreed by most that Freud himself was "a literary character" in most of his own writings. See Sherwin Nuland, "Blow to the Ego," a review of *An Anatomy of Addiction: Sigmund Freud, William Halsted and the Miracle Drug Cocaine* by Howard Markel, *The New York Times Book Review* Sunday, July 24, 2011.
15   Edward Westermarck, "Recent Theories of Exogamy," in *Three Essays on Sex and Marriage* (London: Macmillan, 1934), 158-159.
16   Edward Westermarck, *A Short History of Human Marriage* (London: Macmillan, 1926), 80.

major reason for this avoidance."[17] Insofar as our DNA is very similar to apes (I make no judgement whether this is due to common ancestry or simply common design), we should expect that many of our *instincts*, including our sexual instincts, would be similar to the apes.

Second, studies conducted of Taiwanese *simpua* ("little daughter-in-law") marriages, where a girl is adopted by her future husband-in-law's family and raised alongside her future husband, show (1) that out of five hundred and fifty *simpua* marriages studied, these marriages had a 40% lower fertility rate than other marriages, (2) that such couples were three times as likely to end up divorced, and (3) that spouses were twice as likely to have extramarital affairs.[18] If the couple had been raised together before the age of three, the Westermarck Effect was extremely sensitive, if they were raised together before the age of eight, the tendency was still very strong, and if they were raised after the age of eight, the effect gradually became less sensitive, though was by no means absent. This means that because Jamie and Cersei (not to mention Margery and Loras[19]) were raised closely since birth, readers should probably conclude either that that the twins are instinctually malformed or that their relationship is unconvincingly written.

Yet whatever conclusion one prefers, there are other incestuous relationships in *A Game of Thrones* that are more convincing given the Westermarck Effect. In the case of parents and children, we know that parents who spend quality time with their young children and participate in raising them also develop natural sexual aversion to their offspring, though for parents this is strengthened not merely by strong affection or *storge* from birth but also by a natural caregiver instinct. Thus, if a parent is absent a lot or, for whatever reason, has little affection for his or her child, the Westermarck Effect is weakened and incestuous relationships become much more likely: "Incest occurs, overwhelmingly, in grossly disturbed families in which neglect, abandonment and physical abuse are also common."[20] So, when Black Walder

---

17   Anne Pusey, "Inbreeding Avoidance in Primates," in *Inbreeding, Incest and the Incest Taboo: The State of Knowledge at the Turn of the Century*, ed. Arthur Wolf and William Durham, 61-75 (Stanford: Stanford University Press, 2004), 71.
18   Arthur Wolf, "Explaining the Westermarck Effect, or, What Did Natural Selection Select for?" in *Inbreeding, Incest and the Incest Taboo*, ed. Arthur Wolf and William Durham, 76-92 (Stanford: Stanford University Press, 2004), 77.
19   "What of our brave Ser Loras? How often does he call upon his sister?" "More often than any of the others. . . . Her brother is devoted to her, they share everything with . . . oh . . . I have had a most wicked thought, Your Grace." Martin, *A Feast for Crows*, 586. cf. 830.
20   Mark Erickson, "Evolutionary Thought and the Current Clinical Understanding of Incest," in *Inbreeding, Incest and the Incest Taboo*, ed. Arthur Wolf and William Durham, 161-189 (Stanford: Stanford University Press, 2004), 171.

took his brother's wife, even while he was alive, this, instinctually speaking, is fairly believable since Black Walder was, in addition to being an evil man, neither raised alongside, nor raised, his brother's wife. Likewise, when Littlefinger passionately kissed Sansa Stark, his wife's niece, his Westermarck instinct wasn't malfunctioning since, once again, he was neither raised alongside Sansa nor was he her guardian throughout early childhood. Perhaps something like this is also true of Shae and her father,[21] and Castor and Gilly, and it's certainly true, on the sibling level, with Theon and Asha Greyjoy, who, though raised together from birth, were then separated for ten years, such that when Theon returned, he didn't recognize her and made sexual advances toward her,[22] only soon after to discover who she really was, causing him to see his actions, quite naturally, as the actions of an "appalling fool."[23]

Of course, as with all theories, Freud's has some basis in truth. First, nature is wounded and doesn't always act optimally, meaning that there may be a few couples like Jamie and Cersei who are born with malfunctioning instincts. Second, incestuous dreams at night do occur, but probably have nothing to do with repressed sexual desire (they need not be the beast awakening in man, as Plato imagined,[24] since even the beasts have a natural aversion to incest!). Third, a few mothers are sexually aroused while breastfeeding – perhaps Lysa Arryn would be a candidate[25] – yet they need not take it as a sign of sexual interest in their offspring since biology often acts very much on its own, as the phenomenon of "morning boner" testifies. Fourth, most children are naturally attracted to people who are similar to their parents since studies in "optimal outbreeding" have shown that children unconsciously choose mates who are a balance between what is familiar (*storge* and developed preference would explain this) and yet still different (in keeping with the Westermarck Effect).[26] And Fifth, though an instinctually malformed or simply an evil parent or sibling could take advantage of a child or a younger sibling sleeping in their proximity, for the most part, studies have shown that *storge* is *storge* and *eros* is

---

21 Martin, *A Clash of Kings*, 642.
22 Martin, *A Clash of Kings*, 378.
23 Martin, *A Clash of Kings*, 390.
24 "In sleep when . . . all that belongs to the calculating, tame and ruling part . . . slumbers . . . the beastly and wild part, gorged with food and drink . . . seeks to go and satisfy its dispositions . . . and it doesn't shrink from attempting intercourse, as it supposes, with a mother or with anyone else at all." Plato *Republic* 9.571.
25 Cf. *Game of Thrones* season 1, episode 8.
26 While inbreeding causes an unusually high number of genetic deformities, excessive outbreeding has its own problems as well. If a man with a big jaw and teeth married a woman with a small jaw and teeth, it's possible that their grandchild might end up with a small jaw and big teeth, which would be, biologically speaking, problematic.

eros and that "Contrary to expectations, children who coslept with their parents were *less* likely to have been treated in a mental health clinic for emotional and behavioral problems."[27]

NATURAL COMMANDS AND NATURAL ROLES

But this is only half the story. So far I've only discussed natural instincts and why people like Jamie and Cersei should be seen as thus malformed. In other words, I've only shown that Jamie and Cersei's instincts need to be *healed*, and I've yet to show why their incestuous actions need to be also *forgiven*.

Animals and lesser creatures are given natural instincts that help them to function according to God's design for them. As things now stand, these instincts don't always function perfectly, and it's not always easy to determine what is natural and what is not (were apes designed to be polygamous or monogamous?). But such is life on our grey planet. Perhaps there is some truth to the old tales about demons partially corrupting animal design in a manner similar to how the Serpent tempted and corrupted the First Men; these would then be Tyrion's "monstrous gods" who (because God has given them free will and largely respects their usage of it) "torment us for their sport."[28] Yet whatever the precise truth may be, human beings both have instincts designed to function properly but don't always do so and have reason, which allows us to understand moral commands in order to determine, though not always perfectly since we aren't perfectly wise, what is natural and just.

So do we have such a command forbidding incest? The near universal agreement in Westeros, Essos and Earth seems to be yes, though I think that this command is perhaps more derived from self-evident principles rather than being itself self-evident. Combining the general moral prohibition "do no harm," the general moral principle "take care of the weak," the general moral precept "respect our superiors," and the general moral principle "favour one's family over others," an incest prohibition is readily deduced in at least three ways.

First, it didn't take knowledge of advanced genetics for people to discern that inbreeding often results in unhealthy children who suffer and thus cause their parents and society to suffer as well: the ancient Arabs knew "the seed of relations bring forth feeble fruit"[29] and the Toradjas that such children "will be

---

27 Erickson, "Evolutionary Thought and the Current Clinical Understanding of Incest," 179.
28 George R. R. Martin, *A Dance with Dragons* (New York: Bantam Books, 2011), 763-764.
29 In Edward Westermarck, *Marriage Ceremonies in Morocco* (London: Macmillan, 1914), 55.

weak, sickly or idiotic and quickly die."[30] Dwarfism, by the way, is a common result of incest, though we have no reason to suspect that Tyrion the imp is a product of this! Whatever the case, we must say that inbreeding is usually harmful and has little or no benefit, and so in most cases it unnecessarily harms everyone considered and is thus unjust.

Second, if endogamy – marriages in a small group – were the norm, then society would be further harmed since it would prevent the glue of marriage from bonding people into the larger society. If the Lannisters didn't marry the Baratheons or the Starks the Tullys, then there would be less solidarity in the seven kingdoms. Indeed, even the wildlings know, "A true man steals a woman from afar, t' strengthen the clan. Women who bed brothers or fathers or clan kin offend the gods, and are cursed with weak and sickly children."[31] Extreme endogamy, then, also does unnecessary harm to society and is thus, in most cases, unjust.

And third, recent findings in psychology confirm what most of us have always known, namely, that the nuclear family – one father, one mother and their children – is the natural organization of human beings, the goal, from the point of view of biology, being primarily to breed and raise optimally healthy children, and the goal, from the point of view of spirit, to further develop the higher virtues, in particular, *agape* or sacrificial love.[32] Since the notion of a natural family presupposes natural *roles* within the family, each family member must be aware of his or her role therein. Because a basic moral principle teaches the strong to take care of the weak and the weak to respect the strong, parents – here, the strong – are aware of a natural moral command to take care of their children, and children understand it as quite natural to obey their parents. Moreover, since people also know that they ought to favour their own family over others (that is, it would be better for someone else's daughter to starve than your own), parents understand that they have a very strong obligation to help their children, and children to obey and respect their parents. But since incestuous relationships confuse roles and expectations in the family, domestic happiness is impaired: sons who sleep with their mothers might see themselves as their fathers' equal in position and authority, for example, and

---

30   In N. Adriani and A. Kruyt, *The Bare'e-speaking Toradja of Central Celebes*, vol. 2 (Amsterdam: N. V. Noord-Hollandsche Uitgevers Maatschappiji, 1951), 11. In a study conducted in Czechoslovakia, it was discovered that "Overall, 43% of the incest offspring revealed severe physical problems, compared to with 11% of the control group." Jonathan Turner and Alexandra Maryanski, *Incest: Origins of the Taboo* (London: Paradigm Publishers, 2005), 35.
31   Martin, *A Storm of Swords*, 365.
32   Such has also strengthened the hand of those who argue against polygamous, polyandrous and gay marriages.

fathers who have sexual relations with their daughters betray their daughters' natural expectation for parental care.[33] For these reasons, incest should be seen as harmful, unnatural and unjust.

But what about cases where incest is encouraged such as with the biblical Cain and his sister and the Targaryens of Westeros and Essos? Don't such exceptions prove that incest isn't an absolute moral principle? Yes they do, but this is precisely what I've said: incest *isn't* an absolute, inviolable moral principle, but rather is a strongly derived general moral prohibition that most rational men and women, in most cases, will agree with. However, let's look at these two examples just to be clear.

Cain must have married his sister since both sprang from the mitochondrial Eve, the original mother. If the biblical record is at all accurate, Cain would have been quite a bit older than his sister, and so likely would have had a much diminished Westermarck instinct. Furthermore, there was no larger society for Cain and his wife to wrong through endogamy, and because God guided humans to this point and endowed them with His image, the Creator, in His goodness, would likely have directly acted to prevent genetic deformities in any children born of the consanguine union. Thus, it seems nearly undeniable that the good of perpetuating the human race – another God-given general moral command, I should add – would have trumped the other weakened considerations. Nevertheless, when incest was no longer a necessity, the force of this argument would have been greatly reduced and reasons for incest would, in most other cases, face my three previous objections.

Indeed, such is the case with the Targaryens, who wed brother to sister to keep the "bloodlines pure."[34] Baelor married Daena for this reason, and Daenerys was expected to do so with either her brother Rhaegar[35] or her brother Viserys[36] or, when neither were an option, her nephew, Aegon.[37] In our world, this was also practiced by some Roman Egyptians and Hawaiian kings, and it's easy to appreciate that such unions could help, for a time, to preserve status, wealth and lands thereby keeping, in one respect, the moral command to prefer the good of one's own family over the good of another. Yet there is also an irony in this. Inbreeding leads, literally, to the weakening of bloodlines. Indeed, we are told that the Targaryens are plagued by a "taint" of madness,[38] which, when it runs its course, will ultimately end up destroying the bloodline as was almost the case when Aerys was murdered and his throne

---

33 Turner, *Incest: Origins of the Taboo*, 41.
34 George R. R. Martin, *A Game of Thrones* (New York: Bantam Books, 2011), 485.
35 Martin, *A Storm of Swords*, 587.
36 Martin, *A Dance with Dragons*, 73.
37 Martin, *A Dance with Dragons*, 280.
38 Martin, *A Dance with Dragons*, 153.

taken from him and his family. Thus, the preservation of bloodline argument is flawed, and the practice of incest for this reason should be seen as largely immoral and unnatural.

But even more sinister and unnatural is the hint that the Targaryens, like the Greek gods, Egyptian pharaohs and Japanese emperors, simply thought themselves above, rather than bound by, the Natural Law and all derived injunctions against incest. Catelyn Stark believes that the Targaryen's practiced incest since they "answered to neither gods nor men,"[39] and Jamie wants to marry his sister, thus showing "the realm that the Lannisters are above their laws, like gods and Targaryens."[40] This blasphemy and hubris is obviously immoral and unnatural, and incest on this basis can't be justified.

"ABOMINATIONS BORN OF INCEST"?

In this chapter, I've argued that consanguine unions or incest is, by and large, unnatural, and that we're aware of this through both natural instincts and reasoning from the Natural Law. If not "in defiance of *all* the laws of gods and men,"[41] it's certainly in defiance of *most*. Nevertheless, what needs to be added is that children born of incest – children such as Gilly's baby, Joffrey, Tommen and Myrcella, not to mention the biblical Isaac – aren't quite the "abominations" that they're often thought to be.[42] It's true that biologically speaking, many children born of incest will be deformed and in this sense "abominations," but what is also true is that such children didn't choose to be born thus and it would be wrong to judge them as if they had. Joffrey is an abomination, not because he was born of incest (he isn't even physically malformed), but rather because of poor parenting and, most importantly, because he chose to ignore the commands of the Natural Law.

---

39 Martin, *A Clash of Kings*, 498.
40 Martin, *A Storm of Swords*, 287.
41 Martin, *A Dance with Dragons*, 247.
42 Martin, *A Clash of Kings*, 158.

Chapter Thirteen

"All of This Is Wrong": Roman Thoughts on Slavery and *The Hunger Games*

The Hunger Games trilogy is packed with allusions and images meant to call to mind the Roman Empire: it's filled with Latin names (Cinna, Portia, Claudius, Caesar, Flavius, et al.); it talks about the Capitol, which controls Panem or all that remains of North America (Rome was called "The Capital of the World"); and, of course, it centers around the Hunger Games (a unique take on the Roman gladiatorial games). The trilogy, moreover, makes it clear that "All of this" – the Rome-like Capitol and its games – "is wrong."[1] Nevertheless, well-grounded ethical reasons condemning the Capitol and its Hunger Games are lacking in the novels.

Consequently, in this chapter I will endeavor to articulate such reasons vis-à-vis two of the greatest Roman thinkers, Seneca (not to be confused with Seneca Crane, the first Head Gamemaker in *The Hunger Games*) and St. Paul. Both men were contemporaries (pseudonymous letters purport they knew each other[2] and biblical evidence makes it clear that St. Paul knew Seneca's brother[3]), both were, and still are, renowned for their wisdom and virtue, and both died during the reign, and by the hand, of the Roman emperor Nero, who, like President Snow in *The Hunger Games*, was powerful and evil. Seneca and St. Paul, therefore, should be able to help *Hunger Games* heroine, Katniss Everdeen, formulate clear reasons why the Capitol and its slave practices, including the Hunger Games, are wrong, and what, generally speaking, is the right way of living.

APPROACHING THE CORNUCOPIA OF HAPPINESS

Although Seneca is a Stoic and St. Paul, a Christian, both Romans agree that the happy life is that which conforms to God's ways, which, above all, calls for people to become virtuous or godly.

---

1 Suzanne Collins, *The Hunger Games* (Toronto: Scholastic, 2009), 24.
2 *The Epistles of Paul the Apostle to Seneca, with Seneca's to Paul.*
3 Seneca's brother Gallio is mentioned in Acts 17:12-17 as the official before whom St. Paul was arraigned.

Seneca, who also speaks of God as *Logos* (Divine Reason) and Nature, insists that God's purpose in creating the world is "goodness,"[4] in particular, desiring that the jewel of creation, human beings, become His true children by them living according to the divine image – "reason"[5] – within: "The good man is God's pupil, His imitator and true offspring."[6] Though some Stoics are pantheists (postulating that human beings are a part of God), Seneca appears not to have been, even though he does insist that God lives in our rational faculties and consciences, telling us what is good and what is bad: "God is near you, He is with you, He is within you. A holy spirit dwells within us, one who marks our good and bad deeds, and is our guardian. . . . Indeed, no man can be good without the help of God."[7] The divine voice in us will tell us, if only we "seek understanding first before anything else,"[8] of God's or "Nature's law,"[9] which are the basic moral principles that first convict us of wrongdoing ("The knowledge of sin is the beginning of salvation"[10]) and then compel correct moral behaviour. If virtue is pursued – and this is no easy task ("Real joy is a stern matter"[11]) – then, with God's help, people can "rise to the highest human happiness."[12]

St. Paul agrees with Seneca that God is good and that we are made in His image, and, in fact, he goes so far as to quote approvingly from Aratus the Stoic's *Phenomena*, "'In Him we live and move and have our being. . . . We are His offspring.'"[13] St. Paul also agrees that the purpose of human creation is to

---

4 "God has within Himself these patterns of all things, and His mind comprehends the harmonies and the measures of the whole totality of things which are to be carried out; He is filled with these shapes which Plato calls the 'ideas' – imperishable, unchangeable, not subject to decay. . . . The pattern is doubtless the model according to which God has made this great and most beautiful creation. The purpose is His object in so doing. Do you ask what God's purpose is? It is goodness. Plato says, 'What was God's reason for creating the world? God is good and no good person is grudging of anything that is good. Therefore, God made it the best world possible.'" Seneca *Epistles* 65.
5 "The Divine Reason is set in supreme command over all things, and is itself subject to none; and this reason which we possess is the same, because it is derived from the Divine Reason." Seneca *Epistles* 92.
6 Seneca *On Providence* 1.6.
7 Seneca *Epistles* 41.
8 Seneca *Epistles* 17.
9 Seneca *On Mercy* 1.18.
10 Seneca *Epistles* 28.
11 Seneca *Epistles* 23.
12 Seneca *Epistles* 44.
13 Acts 17:28. Cf. "God, who is over all and through all and in all" (Ephesians 4:6).

be "reconciled"[14] with God insofar as "all are called to righteousness."[15] This righteousness or goodness is something that all can discern, for God testifies into our consciences and speaks to us by the laws of nature:

> When the Gentiles, who do not have the [Mosaic] law, do by nature things required by the law, they are a law for themselves, even though they do not have the law, since they show that the requirements of the law are written on their hearts, their consciences also bearing witness, and their thoughts now accusing, now even defending them.[16]

Moreover, and in partial agreement with Seneca again, St. Paul insists that though human beings can know what is good and virtuous, righteous or virtuous character isn't something that can be achieved by man's efforts alone but requires God's help since imperfect man can't erase his acts of injustice or past sins: "All have sinned and fall short of the glory of God and are justified freely by His grace through the redemption that came by Jesus the Christ. God presented Him as a sacrifice of atonement, through faith in His blood. He did this to demonstrate His justice."[17] Thus, the virtuous or righteous person is he who speaks justice, acknowledging his own sins and that God, by Jesus, can make him right,[18] and then, with God's further aid, "goes into strict training"[19] to produce "character"[20] in keeping with virtue, first, the virtues of justice,[21] and second, the virtues of love ("Love always protects,"[22] we are told, it always "forgives"[23]). To become like God – to be declared good, righteous or virtuous – is to achieve real happiness.[24]

Katniss Everdeen doesn't talk about God, wisdom or even virtue as such, nor does she ever mention what she thinks the purpose of life is or how, ideally, she ought to live it. Thus, she isn't in a wonderful position to critique the Capitol. Yet, whether she acknowledges nature as the voice of God or not, nature has certainly taught her some things about virtuous behaviour and she demonstrates, progressively as the trilogy unfolds, a number of virtues that are promising to the good life.

---

14 2 Corinthians 5:18.
15 Romans 9:21.
16 Romans 2:14-15.
17 Romans 3:23-26.
18 Romans 1:17.
19 1 Corinthians 9:25.
20 Romans 5:3.
21 2 Corinthians 7:11 and Philippians 1:20.
22 1 Corinthians 13:7.
23 Ephesians 4:32.
24 Romans 9:1-3, 1 Corinthians 10:24, and Philippians 2:4.

Katniss is "brave,"[25] not just for volunteering to take Prim's place as a tribute, but also for hunting beyond the fence, for defying the Capitol by honouring Rue's death, and for participating in the subsequent rebellion against President Snow. Though initially she has no strong sense of retributive justice, this takes root in her through her trials in the arena; thus, she both promises "to avenge [Rue]"[26] and praises Fulvia for her video clips honouring slain tributes, "This is brilliant. . . . It's the perfect way to remind people why they're fighting."[27] Finally, she has the first fruits of the greatest virtue of all, *agape* or sacrificial love, demonstrating the growth of this virtue on four occasions: first, with Prim when she takes her place in the Hunger Games ("Family devotion only goes so far for most people on reaping day. What I did was the radical thing"[28]); second, and in keeping with the beginning of virtue being repentance, when she feels guilty for not having helped the Avox girl escape from the Capitol ("I'm ashamed I never tried to help her in the woods. I let the Capitol kill the boy and mutilate her without lifting a finger"[29]); third, when she desires to protect her friend Peeta from the Games ("It's my dying wish. Keep Peeta alive"[30]); and lastly, when she protects a stranger like Mags in the arena even though the elderly woman slowed her down and could well have cost her her life.[31]

Our Roman thinkers would praise Katniss for these virtues, but would still exhort her not only to seek to understand ethics in a larger, metaphysical context, but would challenge her to develop aspects of her character that need more work. Though I don't think they would see Katniss as dishonest for deceiving viewers of the Games (this is proper or just deception), though I don't think they would think she is wrong for hunting for food beyond the fence even though it was forbidden by the Capitol (an unjust law is no law at all),[32] and though I don't think they would call Katniss a murderess for killing out of self-defense in the arena or enemy combatants in battle, Seneca and St. Paul would almost certainly think she needs more self-control (when she shoots arrows out of frustration at the Gamemakers), a clearer understanding of her motives for wanting to kill President Snow (revenge? justice?) and, at least in the case of St. Paul, has to learn to forgive ("I'm not the forgiving type,"

---

25 Collins, *The Hunger Games*, 36.
26 Collins, *The Hunger Games*, 242.
27 Suzanne Collins, *Mockingjay* (New York: Scholastic, 2010), 109.
28 Collins, *The Hunger Games*, 26.
29 Collins, *The Hunger Games*, 85.
30 Suzanne Collins, *Catching Fire* (New York: Scholastic, 2009), 189.
31 Collins, *Catching Fire*, 233.
32 "All forms of stealing are forbidden in District 12." Collins, *The Hunger Games*, 29.

she tells us[33]).

Thus, while Katniss fails to live up fully to the ideals of our Roman thinkers, she is well on her way and because of this does contrast with the corruption that is the Capitol. Nevertheless, to fully appreciate the Capitol's corruption, we still need to supplement Katniss with Seneca and St. Paul.

CAPITOL CORRUPTION

Seneca and St. Paul lived during a period in Roman history known as the Principate, when Roman emperors, and not the people, ruled. Though these emperors did a fairly good job of keeping the peace, this peace – the *pax Romana* – was a mixed bag. On the one hand, criminals on lesser rungs of society, such as pirates, were justly punished by Rome's disciplined forces. But on the other hand, criminals on higher rungs of society – in particular, the emperors – were untouchable, which led, for the most part, to a peace founded on injustice, greed and cruelty: conquest of weaker nations, unreasonable taxes for non-Romans (both *vectigalia* and *tributum*), and brutal force toward all who opposed the emperor's will – including the will to be worshipped as a god – were the orders of the day.

Though he was advisor and tutor to Emperor Nero, Seneca was never afraid to prescribe correct moral behaviour and critique the Emperor when he failed to live up to the Stoic ideal. While Seneca believed that "Nature herself conceived the idea of kingship,"[34] he thought that if the laws of Rome and the Emperor were to be just laws, they must be based on God's will: "Nature wishes our laws to be identical to her own."[35] Moreover, distinguishing between things that are good (virtue), "preferable" (food, power, money) and bad (vice), he criticized the Emperor for focusing on conquest, which is at best a preferable but most often leads to all sorts of vice, including greed, pride and so on: "What does it concern you who conquers? The better man may win; but the winner is bound to be the worse man."[36]

And so often this was the case. Rome's greed for luxury – for expensive clothes, exotic foods and so on – weakened the empire morally: "Much harm is done by a single case of indulgence or greed; the familiar friend, if he be luxurious, weakens and softens us imperceptibly;" thus, Seneca advised, "Eat

---

33 Collins, *The Hunger Games*, 8.
34 Seneca *On Mercy* 1.14.
35 Seneca *Epistles* 30. Cf. "He who has the power to give and to take life away ought to use this great gift of the gods in a noble spirit." Seneca *On Mercy* 1.21:
36 Seneca *Epistles* 14. Cf. "The true goods are those which reason bestows, substantial and eternal. . . . Other things are goods according to opinion . . . 'preferables.' Let us recognize that these are our chattel, not parts of ourselves; let us have them in our possession but take heed to remember that they are outside ourselves." Seneca *Epistles* 74.

merely to relieve your hunger; drink merely to quench your thirst; dress merely to keep out of the cold; house yourself merely as a protection against personal discomfort."[37]

Furthermore, in order to feed Rome's greed, an enormous amount of slaves were required. While Seneca maintained that there were a number of just inequalities between people, he didn't think that people *qua* rational souls, spirits or persons were unequal: "'They are slaves,' people declare, 'Nay, rather they are men!'. . . Kindly remember that he whom you call your slave sprang from the same stock."[38] Indeed, Seneca didn't think that slaves were any *less* slaves than the rest of us were slaves to sin and vice: "Show me a man who is not a slave; one is a slave to lust, another to greed, another to ambition, and all men are slaves to fear."[39] So, while Seneca thought possessing a slave was only acceptable provided that the slave, as an acknowledged equal in worth (and in moral incompleteness), agreed to it, slave owning was, even then, still dangerous since it tempted those in authority to be "excessively haughty, cruel and insulting."[40]

And nowhere was this clearer than in the gladiatorial games, which were fought exclusively between slaves. The gladiatorial games, which were largely instigated to distract the masses from rebellion, were, according to Seneca, "pure murder."[41] The emperors corrupted themselves by holding the games ("Who that is pleased by virtue can please the crowd? It takes trickery to win popular approval"[42]); the crowds corrupted themselves by watching the organized murder ("Nothing is so damaging to good character as the habit of lounging at the games. . . . I come home more greedy, ambitious, more voluptuous and even more cruel and inhuman"[43]); and the gladiators, though they could learn "courage of soul" and were often just in defending themselves, were typically corrupted by fear of dying rather than fear of killing another.[44] Because of opinions such as these – opinions that aimed at the heart of immoral Roman practices – Emperor Nero, who "was corrupted by every lust, natural

---

37   Seneca *Epistles* 7. Cf. "Add statues, paintings and whatever any art has devised for the satisfaction of luxury; you will only learn from such things to crave still greater." Seneca *Epistles* 16.
38   Seneca *Epistles* 47. Cf. "All men, if traced back to their original source, spring from the gods." Seneca *Epistles* 44.
39   Seneca *Epistles* 47.
40   Seneca *Epistles* 47. Cf. "Riches have shut off many a man from the attainment of wisdom. . . . No throng of slaves surrounds the poor man – slaves for whose mouths the mast must covet the fertile crops of regions beyond the sea." Seneca *Epistles* 17.
41   Seneca *Epistles* 7.
42   Seneca *Epistles* 29.
43   Seneca *Epistles* 7.
44   Seneca *Epistles* 30.

and unnatural," ordered Seneca to commit suicide, which later generations came to see as "an atrocity" of the first order.[45]

Like Seneca, St. Paul acknowledges that kingship is natural, though this is primarily in terms of God's kingship.[46] In further agreement, St. Paul insists that "everyone must submit himself to governing authorities,"[47] though this is only insofar as they are agents of justice – "to bring punishment on the wrongdoers"[48] – and not insofar as they are unjust (indeed, St. Paul himself refused to worship the emperor as a god and even escaped from, rather than submit to, the unjust King Aretas[49]). While St. Paul wouldn't have thought the Stoic distinction between "goods" and "preferables" is meaningful (preferables are just lesser goods[50]), he certainly agrees that virtuous character is more important than luxury and power; thus he says that "Those who use the things of the world, should act as if not engrossed in them,"[51] that "I want women to dress modestly with decency and propriety, not with braided hair or gold or pearls or expensive clothes, but with good deeds,"[52] and that "People who want to get rich fall into temptation and a trap and into many foolish and harmful desires that plunge men into ruin and destruction."[53]

As for slavery and the games, St. Paul was again like Seneca. The Apostle emphasized that the slave, just as much as the freeman, is made in the image of God and the slave, just as much as the freeman, is saved by trust in Jesus: "We were all baptized by one Spirit into one body – whether Jews or Greeks, slave or free."[54] While St. Paul, like Seneca, emphasized that Nature – the voice of God – teaches us certain just inequalities (such as the inequality of authority between parents and children and husbands and wives), St. Paul, as with Seneca, was aware that other inequalities in society, such as the authority between masters and slaves, is a mere social construct and can be abolished if necessary.

But is the abolition of slavery morally necessary? Yes and no. Just as much as for St. Paul as for Seneca, St. Paul thought the most important thing in life

---

45 Tacitus *The Annals of Imperial Rome* 15.38.
46 1 Timothy 1:17 and 6:15.
47 Romans 13:1. Cf. Titus 3:1.
48 Romans 4:1.
49 2 Corinthians 11:32-33.
50 Unlike Seneca and the Stoics, St. Paul does seem to imply that being in "rags," "homeless," "hungry and thirsty" and being "brutally treated" are *bad*, rather than merely *not to be preferred* (1 Corinthians 4:11-12).
51 1 Corinthians 7:31.
52 1 Timothy 2:9-10.
53 1 Timothy 6:9.
54 1 Corinthians 12:13. Cf. "Here there is no . . . slave or free, but Christ is all, and is in all" (Colossians 3:11).

is righteousness. Yes, freedom to decide what you want to do in the morning is good, but the greater good is to be self-controlled; yes, freedom to marry is good, but freedom to show *agape* is greater. Thus, the slave shouldn't focus all his energy on being free but should rather focus on being moral: "Slaves, obey your earthly masters with respect and fear, and with sincerity of heart, just as you would obey Christ. . . . Serve wholeheartedly, as if you were serving the Lord, not men, because you know that the Lord will reward everyone for whatever good he does, whether he is a slave or free."[55] Nevertheless, because St. Paul says the act of *slave trading* is an evil on par with murder ("We know that the law is made . . . for the ungodly and sinful . . . for murderers . . . slave traders . . ."[56]), this strongly suggests that in a perfect world there would also not be any *slave owners*. Since being physically free, then, is a good (even if not a good on par with virtue), "if you can gain your freedom," St. Paul writes to some slaves, "do so."[57] Of course what this also entails is that if masters also want to be moral they must treat their slaves "with what is right and fair,"[58] and, in fact, if they understand God's ideal vision for the world – seeing a slave as "a dear brother"[59] – we can guess that they would give their slaves the freedom to choose to serve, rather than forcing them. It goes without saying, then, that any association with the slave games, which perversely delight in "men condemned to die in the arena," is something all the virtuous will shun.[60]

As with Rome, North America went from a republic to an empire.[61] Though the Capitol's empire helped to establish order in the post-apocalyptic world of Panem, it came at the terrible price of ubiquitous injustice and cruelty. Not everyone in, or working for, the Capitol is bad, of course: witness Plutarch Heavensbee and Madge's father, the Mayor of District 12 (and not all in the districts are good, hence Alma Coin of District 13); however, most in the Capitol are correctly labeled "Capitol-loving, Games-hungry, bloodthirsty."[62]

---

55 Ephesians 6:5-9.
56 1 Timothy 1:10.
57 1 Corinthians 7:21.
58 Colossians 4:1. Cf. Ephesians 6:5-9, 1 Timothy 6:1-2, and Titus 2:9-10.
59 Philemon 1:16.
60 1 Corinthians 4:9. St. Augustine wrote more than St. Paul about the games, calling them "a miserable pastime," and speaking of his friend Alypius "fatally doting upon the circus," a "filthy" place "excited with inhuman sport." St. Augustine *Confessions* 6.7-8.
61 "Frankly, our ancestors don't seem much to brag about. I mean, look at the state they left us in, with the wars and the broken planet. Clearly, they didn't care about what would happen to the people who came after them. But this republic idea sounds like an improvement over our current government." Collins, *Mockingjay*, 84.
62 Collins, *Catching Fire*, 256.

President Snow smells like "blood and roses,"[63] suggesting cruelty and luxury, and is called a "fanged viper,"[64] who says plainly, "I'm not above killing children."[65] His "peacekeepers" are instruments of a false peace, and the "Justice Buildings" to be found in every district are perversely named since it's in front of them where the reaping – the selection of children to be murdered in the Hunger Games – takes place. The voice of Nature – God – is ignored in these respects just as it was in the Roman Empire under Nero.

Furthermore, while some of the districts of Panem eat mice, squirrels and pig intestines, those in the Capitol "are vomiting for the pleasure of filling their bellies again and again. Not from some illness of body or mind, not from spoiled food. It's what everyone does at a party. Expected. Part of the fun."[66] While those in the Capitol enjoy the luxury of cosmetics and fashion, the "barbarians"[67] from the districts – "barbarian" being a word the Greco-Roman world used to dehumanize non-Greeks or Romans – don't even have proper medicine. Of course, it's not that fashion and fine dining are bad in and of themselves – thus, Peeta could well be echoing both Seneca, who thinks such are "preferables," and St. Paul, who would say they are lesser goods, when The Boy With Bread says, "Having an eye for beauty isn't the same thing as a weakness."[68] Nevertheless, Katniss's warning is in accordance with our Roman thinkers when she tells Peeta, "They would lure you into their Capitol ways and you'd be lost entirely."[69]

Although the word "slavery" isn't used in *The Hunger Games*, each of the districts in Panem are surrounded by high electrical fences which the Machiavellian Capitol says is to keep the wild animals out but which are actually meant to keep the people pent in; indeed, the fact that President Snow removed all the tracker jacker nests from around the Capitol, but didn't around the districts, makes this clear.[70] The people of the districts are under laws – as we all are – but most are so unreasonable, such as the law forbidding hunting in the woods or the law making it a capital offence to possess a basic weapon, that for all intents and purposes these are laws for people with no rights. Yet if these conditions aren't clearly those of slaves, Darius and Finnick are both

---

63 Collins, *Catching Fire*, 20.
64 Collins, *Catching Fire*, 18.
65 Collins, *Mockingjay*, 356.
66 Collins, *Catching Fire*, 80.
67 Collins, *The Hunger Games*, 74. After plucking all of Katniss's body hair, Flavius, a cosmetician, says, "Excellent! You almost look like a human being now!" Collins, *The Hunger Games*, 62.
68 Collins, *Catching Fire*, 211. Cinna, who is good, is also called a "fashion hero." Collins, *Catching Fire*, 40.
69 Collins, *Catching Fire*, 211.
70 Collins, *The Hunger Games*, 186.

explicitly called "slaves,"[71] and Katniss admits to having been one, not just because she was forced against her will to go to the Hunger Games but also – and here in keeping with Seneca's "slave to fear" or St. Paul's "slave to sin" – because she didn't refuse to participate: "I am [a slave]. . . . That's why I killed Cato . . . and he killed Tresh . . . and he killed Clove . . . and she tried to kill me. It just goes around and around, and who wins? Not us. Not the districts. Always the Capitol."[72]

Finally, we know that the enslaved districts of Panem provide the *"panem"* – the Latin word for "bread" – "and circuses,"[73] which distract them from the fact of their own slavery and provide ample entertainment for the citizens of the Capitol. Of course, the fact that the districts actually watch the Games is evidence that they need to heed Seneca and St. Paul's emphasis on wisdom and understanding, for to sponsor a tribute in the arena may show that individual tribute a kindness, but, unless it's food or medicine, such gifts aggravate the problem since they're still playing the Capitol's corrupt game. Indeed, even when a tribute gets a sponsor he or she usually does so by prostituting themselves before the cameras, pretending to be something that they aren't; as Katniss says, "All I can think is how unjust the whole thing is, the Hunger Games. Why am I hopping around like some trained dog trying to please people I hate?"[74]

Thankfully, however, Katniss and others eventually came to recognize the systemic problem and so justly rebelled against the corrupt Capitol, eventually overthrowing it. And although many rebels, such as Coin and Gale,[75] were more than willing to exchange cruelty for cruelty (ignoring the higher and lower virtues), Katniss and others weren't; indeed, what Peeta says of the Hunger Games, so it could be said of war, "To murder innocent people? It costs everything you are."[76] Seneca and St. Paul would applaud.

"NO ONE BENEFITS IN A WORLD WHERE..."

By focusing on the Roman allusions throughout *The Hunger Games*, I proposed to critique the Capitol and its practices by way of two of the most famous Roman thinkers, Seneca and St. Paul. These, I demonstrated, insisted that the happy life is the life lived according to God's laws, which teach us that virtue is to be prized above all else – be it exotic foods or power, as with the Capitol, or even physical freedom, as with the rebels of Panem. While all, not just the

---

71 Collins, *Catching Fire*, 218. Collins, *Mockingjay*, 171.
72 Collins, *Mockingjay*, 215.
73 Collins, *Mockingjay*, 224.
74 Collins, *The Hunger Games*, 117.
75 Collins, *Mockingjay*, 31 and 369.
76 Collins, *Mockingjay*, 23.

Capitol, can learn to love virtue more, some love it more than others, and it's these that are the hope of Panem, for it's these who stand firm like Peeta, saying, "I don't want them to change me in there. Turn me into some kind of monster that I'm not,"[77] and it's these who recognize with Katniss that "no one benefits to live in a world where [evil rules]."[78]

---

77   Collins, *The Hunger Games*, 141.
78   Collins, *Mockingjay*, 377.

Chapter Fourteen

"Make What You Can of It If You Are a Philosopher": Sherlock Holmes Investigates Necromancy

Whereas Sherlock Holmes is by all accounts "super-rational,"[1] "scientific . . . [and] passion[ate] for definite and exact knowledge,"[2] his creator, Sir Arthur Conan Doyle, is often seen as nearly the opposite due to his support for Spiritualism or the belief system which asserts, among other things, the reality of necromancy or that the spirits of the dead can provide mediums with information about the afterlife. On the one hand, in the late 1920s, Doyle has Holmes say in no uncertain terms, "This agency stands flat-footed upon the ground, and there it must remain. The world is big enough for us. No ghosts need apply."[3] But on the other hand and during the same time period, Doyle himself admits to having seen spirits firsthand and declares himself "a firm believer in the truth of Spiritualism."[4] Most agree with Doyle biographer Andrew Lycett that this is a paradox of the highest order – of rationality and irrationality deeply polarized in one and the same man. Most people, however, are wrong.

Although I'm mindful of the looming "personal heresy" (that is, seeing a work of art as nothing but the reflection of the artist's own personal beliefs),[5] I do think that if one takes the time to understand Doyle's approach to, and reasons for his belief in, necromancy and Spiritualism, one can see his creation, Holmes, in a new light; indeed, it's significant that Doyle was always willing to give *reasons* for why he supported Spiritualism and even challenged his

---
1   Andrew Lycett, "The Odd Spiritualism of Sir Arthur Conan Doyle," *More Intelligent Life* (Summer 2009), http://moreintelligentlife.com/story/conan-doyle-spiritualism (accessed on October 30, 2010).
2   Arthur Conan Doyle, *A Study in Scarlet*, in *The Penguin Complete Sherlock Holmes*, 15-84 (London: Penguin, 1981), 17.
3   Arthur Conan Doyle, *The Case Book of Sherlock Holmes*, in *The Penguin Complete Sherlock Holmes*, 984-1122 (London: Penguin, 1981), 1034.
4   Arthur Conan Doyle, *The History of Spiritualism*, vol. 1 (San Diego: The Book Tree, 2007), 160.
5   C. S. Lewis and E. M. W. Tillyard, *The Personal Heresy: A Controversy* (London: Oxford University Press, 1965), 5.

readers, saying, "Make what you can of it if you are a philosopher."[6]

In this chapter, I will argue that while Doyle, both directly and indirectly through Holmes, can be somewhat justified in his Spiritualist beliefs, he, nevertheless, is unwise to engage in Spiritualist practices for moral reasons, the Bible declaring, "Do not turn to mediums or seek out spirits, for you will be defiled by them."[7]

KNOWLEDGE OF EVIL AS A GOOD THING

Doyle was raised a Catholic Christian, and though unfortunately he later came to reject many of the church's teachings, including its prohibition against necromancy, he never ceased associating himself with some form of Christianity; indeed, according to the best sources, he favoured what was then called "Christian Spiritualism."[8] Given this, I believe Doyle's approach to Spiritualism is best seen against the backdrop of a general Christian understanding of philosophy and rationality.

Christianity typically asserts that true philosophy comes with the desire *to know something for its own sake*. In the first few chapters of Genesis, we're told that God, who is the perfection of all things, including Knowledge, Logic, Morality, and so on, made man. Why did He do this? Being the perfection of Love, God wanted to expand the scope and depth of His love, which is to say, among other things, He wanted to enter into more friendships. However, a rational being, such as God, can't have friendship or achieve the highest forms of love with non-rational creatures: the only type of love achievable between a rational and a non-rational being is what the Greeks call *storge* or we, in English, call affection or the sense of being comfortable with someone or something (for instance, Holmes's affection for his pipe, or his dog's affection for Holmes's slippers). Since God wanted real friendship with His creation, He had to make part of His creation – at the very least the human part – rational. Rationality, here, doesn't refer simply to the ability to reason, but rather to the rational soul, spirit or person – "the image of God." Within the rational soul or spirit are different faculties, including the rational faculty (intuition, logic and so on), the free will (the ability for the individual to act as its own first-cause) and also the higher affections or desires.

In particular it's worth noting that because God *desired* to make man, man, as the image of God, also has desires, the chief of which is a *desire* for God. This said, this desire for God is not always – indeed, is rarely – for God *qua* God (that is, the totality of all that God is), but is often a desire for some aspect of God, such as for God *qua* Justice or, more to the point, God *qua*

---

6 Doyle, *The History of Spiritualism*, vol. 1, 154.
7 Leviticus 19:31.
8 Leslie Price, "Did Conan Doyle Go Too Far?" *Psychic News* (2010): 4037.

Knowledge or Truth. Since God is Omniscience (the totality of all knowledge) and Truth, we can say that God has made man with a desire for truth or with a desire to want to know things, primarily, though not only, for their own sakes. For instance, man should want to know if there is something called "ectoplasm" firstly because to know the answer to this is good in itself, and only secondly, because this knowledge might be used for some other end. God is called the perfection of all-knowledge and part of what makes Him perfect in this respect is that He knows about all the horrible things in the world. If God is our model, then, all things being equal, knowing about evil is, in itself, a good thing.

Because man is made in the image of God, man has a desire – insofar as he is functioning properly – to want to know something for its own sake. "For its own sake," of course, doesn't exclude "for man's happiness" since man was designed both to want to be happy and to want to know things, and both of these have their root in God, who is the source of all Happiness and Knowledge. In other words, to know something for its own sake – for instance, to know whether it's possible for the dead to communicate with the living – is, all things being equal, to simultaneously increase one's own happiness. Moreover, because God is *Logos* or the perfection of Logic, man, when he is functioning properly, delights in logical thinking and, though his ability to reason is limited (that is, there are mysteries which the human mind can't grasp in its current state), he – as the image of God – always seeks to stretch his thoughts.

"A SCIENCE OF RELIGION"

Doyle's understanding of philosophy and rationality, I will now show, was largely shaped by the Christian understanding of these, even though we should bear in mind he used these beliefs to reject other important Christian claims and ultimately to formulate his own Christian Spiritualist position.

In respect to his approach to philosophy, Doyle agreed with the Christian tradition that knowledge should be pursued for its own sake. Thus, we have the sheer fact that he dedicated a tremendous amount of time gathering evidence for necromancy and Spiritualism – evidence which eventually was published in his two volumes on *The History of Spiritualism*.

Pragmatists in respect to knowledge would likely not make the effort to write such a work, for their interest is *only* in results for their own immediate use, not to make the belief system more respectable nor to convince others of its truth value; indeed, the pragmatist rejects the very notion of objective truth.

In *The History of Spiritualism* we have many statements that suggest that Doyle was primarily interested in Spiritualism for its own sake. Hence he speaks about "the *truth* of this new philosophy [i.e. Spiritualism];"[9] he admits that he was "at first disposed to doubt the genuineness of the phenomena" but later was moved to consent because of "convincing evidence;"[10] he quotes approvingly scientist Sir W. M. Crookes's reasons for becoming interested in Spiritualism, "For my own part, I too much value the pursuit of truth, and the discovery of any new fact in Nature, to avoid inquiry because it appears to clash with prevailing opinions;"[11] and has no trouble admitting that many who claim to be mediums are frauds and that all Spiritualist claims must be examined honestly and in a "sober" and "sane" mind.[12]

Yet although Doyle did, in general, appear to love truth for its own sake, he is probably best seen primarily as a lover of truth for practical ends. This is *not* pragmatism in respect to knowledge, which, as I said, rejects the very notion of truth, but rather is an acknowledgement that there is truth, that it's valuable for its own sake, but is also valuable insofar as it can make the world a better place. Thus, after refuting his critics who accused him of simple emotional reasons for endorsing necromancy and Spiritualism (the death of his son), Doyle emphasized a practical-because-it's-true approach to Spiritualism, saying,

> If for a moment the author may strike a personal note he would say that, while his own loss had no effect upon his views, the sight of a world which was distraught with sorrow, and which was eagerly asking for help and knowledge, did certainly affect his mind and cause him to understand that these psychic studies, which he had so long pursued, were of *immense practical importance* and could no longer be regarded as a mere intellectual hobby or fascinating pursuit of novel research.[13]

Because Doyle thought Spiritualism was largely true and that this truth – above all – had practical results, many critics of Doyle have been tempted, as we saw in the introduction, to dismiss him with a single stroke of the *ad hominem* brush. Although I myself think Doyle gets some of the facts wrong and makes some errors in his reasoning, he was far from an irrational, blind believer. His love of logic, which he inherited from the Christian tradition, is felt on many occasions, and is best seen in how he refutes three typical fallacies.

The first fallacy Doyle deals with is the genetic fallacy, which sees his critics attacking his psychology or psychological state rather than dealing with the facts of the matter. These critics, as I mentioned before, usual dismiss

---

9   Doyle, *The History of Spiritualism*, vol. 1, 78 (emphasis mine).
10 Doyle, *The History of Spiritualism*, vol. 1, 160.
11 Doyle, *The History of Spiritualism*, vol. 1, 232.
12 Doyle, *The History of Spiritualism*, vol. 1, 120, 121.
13 Arthur Conan Doyle, *The History of Spiritualism*, vol. 2 (San Diego: The Book Tree, 2007), 227 (emphasis mine).

Doyle's interest in necromancy or Spiritualism *simply* or *only* as a result of his son's death and the subsequent "trauma" that resulted; but Doyle soundly deals with these critics, saying,

> It has been said, too, by these unscrupulous opponents that the author's advocacy of the subject . . . was due to the fact that [he] had a son killed in the war, the inference being that grief had lessened [his] critical faculty and made [him] believe what in more normal times [he] would not have believed. The author has many times refuted this clumsy lie, and pointed out the fact that his investigation dates back as far as 1886.[14]

The second fallacy that Doyle deals with is the special case fallacy, which falsely argues that because something is true in a special case, it is simply true. Doyle's example is to point out the logical error of critics who completely dismiss necromancy because one particular medium is shown to be a fraud. Although it's true that fraud weakens the credibility of Spiritualism and certainly of the individual medium who practices the fraud, it hardly warrants dismissing the entire belief system as *certainly* false in its *entirety*. Doyle remarks, "We must not argue that because a man once forges, therefore he has never signed an honest cheque in his life."[15]

The third fallacy Doyle spends a great deal of time refuting is that of begging the question, which is typically accompanied by the fallacy of selective evidence. Begging the question has to do with assuming the truth of that which you want to prove and then proceeding to "prove" it, and selective evidence, as its complement, has to do with ignoring evidence that doesn't support one's case. According to Doyle, the worst offenders in these respects were the materialist scientists of his day. Doyle insists from the start that his interest in Spiritualism is motivated by love of truth, especially truth as it produces practical results; his approach is that everything that can be should "be checked by *reason*,"[16] and his goal is to help establish Spiritualism as a kind of "science of religion."[17] Since there was, and still is, no evidence that *disproves* a spiritual dimension, Doyle – like a Victorian Fox Mulder – was perfectly in keeping with his intellectual rights to pursue questions about the apparent spiritual dimension of reality. Materialist scientists and philosophers who dismiss all questions about spiritual matters from the get-go illogically limit the scope of their investigations since there was, and still is, no compelling or conclusive evidence against such a realm: "Speaking generally, it may be said

---

14 Doyle, *The History of Spiritualism*, vol. 2, 225.
15 Doyle, *The History of Spiritualism*, vol. 1, 305.
16 Doyle, *The History of Spiritualism*, vol. 1, 34, 35 (emphasis mine).
17 Doyle, *The History of Spiritualism*, vol. 2, 248.

that the attitude of organised science during these years was as unreasonable and unscientific as that of Galileo's cardinals, and that if there had been a Scientific Inquisition, it would have brought its terrors to bear upon the new knowledge."[18]

Doyle, of course, isn't always above logical reproach. He uses hyperbole on more than one occasion, such as when he says of a particular case having to do with spirits pressing themselves into moulds, that it's "inconceivable that any normally endowed man" could "doubt" it,[19] and he often commits the black and white fallacy when he implies that readers must *either* accept his interpretation of the facts *or* the materialists' interpretation of the facts. Nevertheless, suffice to say, Doyle's largely Christian approach to philosophy and rationality is quite laudable and, as such, should help us better understand Holmes's approach, to which I now turn.

THE SOCRATIC DETECTIVE

When we first encounter Sherlock Holmes, he is seen as "eccentric," as a man who "has amassed a lot of out-of-the-way knowledge," and who is, for many, "too scientific... [approaching] cold-bloodness."[20] Although he might appear to be the very description of a philosopher, Holmes's "ignorance was as remarkable as his knowledge. Of... philosophy... he appeared to know next to nothing."[21] The reason for this, we are told, is because Holmes emphasizes the practical: he is of the opinion that the brain is like an empty attic into which you can only put so much furniture before it becomes too crowded. "Holmes's smallest actions were all directed towards some definite and practical end,"[22] we are told, and "as a practical man of affairs it is acknowledged that [he] stand[s] alone."[23]

For many, including Lycett, this is a clear indication that Holmes is a materialist pragmatist – a man who, because materialism has eliminated the concept of objective truth, only cares about immediate, pragmatic results. *This* Holmes, of course, would be very much out of step with Doyle and his largely Christian understanding of rationality. However, this understanding of Holmes is mistaken.

For one thing, though it's true that Holmes, like his creator, emphasized results, the detective, again like his creator, was also able to value a thing for its

---

18 Doyle, *The History of Spiritualism*, vol. 1, 182.
19 Doyle, *The History of Spiritualism*, vol. 2, 170.
20 Doyle, *A Study in Scarlet*, 16.
21 Doyle, *A Study in Scarlet*, 21.
22 Doyle, *A Study in Scarlet*, 31.
23 Arthur Conan Doyle, *The Hound of the Baskervilles*, in *The Penguin Complete Sherlock Holmes*, 668-768 (London: Penguin, 1981), 673.

own sake. For instance, he is able to appreciate music simply for what it is (he calls the concert he attends in one adventure "magnificent") and even made a point to remember for no practical or pragmatic end but simply for its own sake Darwin's theory of music predating speech.[24]

Moreover, Holmes makes it clear on more than one occasion that he is concerned not with results simply speaking (as per the pragmatist who doesn't care about questions of truth or falsity), but is concerned about results insofar as they are *true*. Hence, his "business [is] to *know* what other people don't know"[25] (where knowledge is grounded in *truth*); and he works for "love of his art rather than for the acquirement of wealth," where his art "is an impersonal thing – a thing beyond [the] self,"[26] which suggests the Christian understanding of rationality, which has man desiring something beyond the self, namely, truth. Consequently, Holmes largely agrees with Doyle that truth is valuable both for its own sake and for practical (not merely pragmatic) ends.

Furthermore, since acknowledgement of, and love for, truth implies, of course, the *existence* of truth, it should be clear that *if* Holmes is a metaphysical materialist (as Lycett seems to imply), then he is logically inconsistent, for by maintaining the existence of truth – objective truth – he is asserting the existence of something that *isn't* material but rather is immaterial or spiritual. Two more things can also be added in order to make it clear that Holmes should not willy-nilly be seen as materialist, and, indeed, should, like his creator, be seen as open, for logical reasons, to the immaterial or spiritual realm.

First of all, nowhere, as it is sometimes implied, does Holmes *deny* there is a spiritual realm. It's true that in a few of his cases, such as *The Hound of the Baskervilles*, "The Adventure of the Sussex Vampire," and, of course, the latest Hollywood movies, Holmes refutes unusual explanations (such as ghost hounds, vampires or magic) which are forwarded to explain certain mysterious phenomena. However, what's vital to see is that even though, for instance, the hound of the Baskervilles is shown to be a fraud, it hardly follows that Holmes believed that ghost hounds were logical impossibilities.

In order for them to be logical impossibilities, the spiritual realm would either have to be shown not to exist or it would have to be understood in its entirety such that one knows that there are no ghost hounds in it. Holmes doesn't assert either of these positions: all he does say is that he has very modestly confined his "investigations to this world"[27] – and so he can't be seen challenging the logical possibility of ghost hounds. What we do see

---

24 Doyle, *A Study in Scarlet*, 37.
25 Arthur Conan Doyle, *The Adventures of Sherlock Holmes*, in *The Penguin Complete Sherlock Holmes*, 161-334 (London: Penguin, 1981), 255.
26 Doyle, *The Adventures of Sherlock Holmes*, 257, 317.
27 Doyle, *The Hound of the Baskervilles*, 681.

Holmes doing is what every rational man – every image of God – would do: first, reasoning that a ghost hound being the cause of a series of deaths is highly improbable given what we know about the normal workings of the world around us; second, recognizing that since such is improbable, it's more rational to consider some other explanation for these deaths, namely, human volition; and yet third, still leaving open the *logical possibility* of an atypical, in this case, spiritual, cause:

> There are two questions waiting for us at the outset. The one is whether any crime has been committed at all; the second is, what is the crime and how was it committed? Of course, if Dr. Mortimer's surmise should be correct, and we are dealing with forces outside the ordinary laws of Nature, there is an end of our investigation. But we are bound to exhaust all other hypotheses before falling back upon this one.[28]

Second of all, even though Holmes may not have thought spiritual knowledge (including, if we like, knowledge attained through necromancy) valuable for his immediate cases, it hardly follows that he thought such knowledge would be worthless for all cases: there may be cases in the future, for instance, where such knowledge would be valuable. Holmes, we must remember, is supremely logical, which means he only asserts what he knows with certainty ("$1 + 1 = 2$"), probability ("I have a mother and father") or possibility ("I ate pizza for lunch two months ago") and he only absolutely denies what he knows with certainty not to be the case ("$1 + 1 \neq 3$"). Those who see Holmes as a materialist, therefore, need to pay closer attention to his *modus operandi*, which is logical and balanced.

"I WILL SET MY FACE AGAINST THE PERSON WHO..."

So if, as I have argued, Doyle largely maintained a Christian understanding of rationality – valuing truth both for its own sake and for practical results – and if this is also Holmes's understanding of these, then how do we deal with the suggestion, mentioned in the first paragraph of this chapter, of an apparent radical divide between the irrational, spiritualist Doyle on the one hand, and the rational, materialist Holmes – the Holmes who says, "No ghosts need apply" – on the other? This, I believe, should be seen as an instance of Lycett and those like him arguing fallaciously, for when Holmes appears to deny ghosts, he is in fact neither denying ghosts (there is nothing in the sentence that suggests ghosts don't exist) nor is Holmes's point even about ghosts in this context but rather is a general comment about the supernatural in general, and vampires in particular. Thus, we may assert with both Doyle and Holmes that ghosts – or any spiritual being, thing or state of affairs for that matter – *may*

---

28   Doyle, *The Hound of the Baskervilles*, 684.

apply, provided that their existence and presence is logically warranted.

Nevertheless, while the existence of non-human spirits may be rationally believed, and while knowledge of them, even the most horrible spirits, is good in and of itself (or else God wouldn't be Omniscience), we still must ask whether our God-given desire for knowledge should be *absolutely pursued* or *generally pursued*. This is to ask whether we should seek out knowledge in a qualified or unqualified manner.

According to orthodox Christianity, to which Doyle doesn't subscribe, it's quite clear that the pursuit of knowledge is a qualified or general good. Some knowledge should not be pursued, or at least not *at this time* or *in this manner*. For instance, I wouldn't let my preteen son read Nietzsche's *Anti-Christ*, but when he is older, and, more importantly, discerning, then I would – and, indeed, would encourage it since it's good to know about a thing both for its own sake and for the sake of apologetics, for example. Or again, for a man tempted by pornography to look at pornography simply to *learn* about what is going on is a bad idea since this knowledge can be gained without looking at pornography and without the risk of corrupting his soul.

That authentic necromancy and Spiritualism can give us knowledge I do not doubt: the Witch of Endor used necromancy to raise the spirit of Samuel and the knowledge that the spirit communicated to Saul was in fact knowledge.[29] God, of course, allowed the witch to raise the spirit, but insofar as necromancy is an abomination to God, we must maintain that He didn't desire the witch to do this. Somehow, probably through a pact with a fallen angel or demon, she was able to do so, and God, respecting our free wills, allowed her and the demon to do this. But the *how* isn't as important as the *that*: necromancy – and magic in general (hence the sorcerers battling Moses in Egypt) – does work and can give us knowledge. But the Bible also makes it clear that while knowledge is good in and of itself, attaining any knowledge through necromancy is bad: "'I will set My face,' says God, 'against the person who turns to mediums and spirits to prostitute himself by following them.'"[30]

Adam and Eve gained experiential knowledge of evil by eating the fruit, but did they have to eat the fruit in order to understand evil? Clearly not. God understands evil, but is Himself perfect Goodness and, indeed, is incapable of evil. Should we say that God, therefore, doesn't understand evil? Surely He does, but He understands it in the right way – through eternal deduction, for example, or foreknowledge. Humans, too, can understand evil – and this is, as I said, a good thing – but need to do so at the right time and in the right way. God made us, including Doyle, to be in relationship with Him – to be His sons and daughters – and as a True Father, He wants us to become knowledgeable,

---

29 1 Samuel 28:3-24.
30 Leviticus 20:6.

Above All Things

but He wants us to pursue knowledge *wisely*.

Chapter Fifteen

Is a Tattoo a Sign of Impiety?

In many ways my wedding was a meeting of two worlds: my family and friends come from European backgrounds, while my wife's family and friends come from Asian – largely, Korean – ones. My side of the family has, for the most part, a Christian worldview, while my wife's, despite a number of them being Christian, live within a Confucian ethos. Yet in spite of these differences, nearly all at my wedding would have shared one thing in common: some degree of discomfort with my best man's heavily tattooed arms. Of course, this "one thing in common" actually springs from sharing *two* things in common: *piety* (a form of justice emphasizing respect for one's superiors) and *ignorance* in respect to what piety looks like in particular circumstances.

That is, both the Judeo-Christian tradition and the Confucian one insist that it's just or pious that both God and one's parents / ancestors be deeply respected: the reasoning being that since justice means treating each as it ought to be treated, and since God and one's parents occupy elevated positions, justice demands they be treated piously. None of this I have a problem with. The trouble, however, is that in both the Bible and the *Hsiao King*, there are statements linking tattoos, or rather, choosing to get a tattoo, with impiety – the body of the inferior belonging, in a sense, to the superior: be it one's Heavenly Father (the Bible) or one's earthly father (the *Hsiao King*). Because neither the uncontextualized Bible verses condemning tattoos nor Confucian philosophical reasoning in respect to tattoos are properly understood, the result is a Christian Confucian confusion over the ethics of tattooing. My goal herein is to dispel this confusion.

"YOU SHALL NOT MAKE...ANY MARKS UPON YOURSELVES."

Jews and Christians alike accept that the Torah, or the books of "Moses" in the Old Testament, is a part of Scripture or instances of what theologians call "special revelation." What this means exactly is far from clear; however, what is agreed is that these books and their content – taken either in minute detail or in a more general sense (depending on who you talk to) – have been sanctioned or approved by God. Jews and Christians often claim to be rationally justified in believing the Torah (and for Christians, the Bible) primarily, though not exclusively, on the basis of faith. In order for faith to be rationally justified, some Jews and most Christians maintain two things. First, the existence of God – in one shade or another, either as the Creator, the Good, Heaven, Truth, Love, or a combination of these and others – *can* be known by all such that all who *want* to know God, can know Him. Second, those who want to know God are open to hear His voice, and so when they read the Torah or Bible, they can hear God testifying to them, saying in effect, "these are my words." The testimony of God (a person who exists) to the reader (another person who exists) is a form of knowledge by acquaintance – what the French call *connaitre* – and this knowledge, when held on to, is what Jews and Christians mostly mean when they talk about "faith": faith is holding on to things you have good reason to believe are true. Thus, when Jews and Christians read Leviticus 19:28 – "You shall not make any cuttings in your flesh on account of the dead or tattoo any marks upon yourselves: I am YHWH" – Jews and Christians claim to have gained knowledge, specially revealed knowledge, about an ethical command.[1] Consequently, on pain of both ignorance and impiety (i.e. ignoring the commands of a superior) neither Jews nor Christians are safe to ignore this passage about tattooing. However, few things in ancient writings – Scripture included – are clear to modern readers, so the context needs to be unpacked.

Prior to the writing of Leviticus, Israel had been chosen by God to be a nation "set apart." It wasn't that only Israel could know of God's existence nor that only Israelites could be reconciled with God after man's fall from grace (which will be discussed later); rather, Israel, as a "pure" nation, was to be a sign to all nations of the perfect Holiness, Righteousness or Justice that is God. Indeed, some non-Israelites were more pious and better than some Israelites: Abraham, the grandfather of Isaac (later named Israel), paid tribute to Melchizedek, the priest-king of a Canaanite city-state, and even Jesus is identified with this non-Israeli priest. Thus, the point of Israel being set apart was for it, as a nation, to reflect perfect doctrinal, and from this, moral, purity.

Furthermore, because the nations surrounding ancient Israel practiced either self-laceration (as a means to remember the dead, such as in Canaan) or tattooing (as in Egyptian fertility cults) as part of their impure religious teachings, Israel was forbidden to practice these. Indeed, because in nearby Mesopotamia being tattooed was also associated with being owned by a cult (Mesopotamian temple slaves were tattooed), there was a strong sense that

---

1   Deuteronomy 14:1 and 1 Kings 18:28 re-enforce this command.

Israel, as belonging to YHWH, ought not to be "owned" by a lesser god and thus be associated with these unjust practices (unjust, of course, because to honour a lesser god over the greatest God is not to treat each as it ought to be treated). Israel, as a doctrinally pure nation, was to be the metaphorical bride-wife of YHWH, who is pure Righteousness or Righteousness itself.

Two things follow from this. First, nothing in Leviticus implies that tattooing *in and of itself* is immoral or unjust. And second, what is equally as clear is that insofar as impure belief systems make tattooing a part of their practice, Israel is forbidden to engage in such practices: distinctions, it seems, need to be both visible and invisible. It's for this reason that Orthodox Jews, even to this day, see those who choose to get tattoos as immoral or impious and hence are usually forbidden burial in a Jewish cemetery.[2] For Christians, the case is a bit different. Because Israel was to be a *sign* of purity to all nations, the spirit, not the letter, of the law in Leviticus is what really matters: in other words, it's not obvious from the Old Testament that a person would necessarily be impious for choosing to get a tattoo – the Christian's attitude toward God and impure religious practices being what matters the most. Nevertheless, there are still some passages in the New Testament that cause some Christians confusion over tattoos.

"HONOUR GOD WITH YOUR BODY"

The majority of Christians throughout history have erroneously understood the prohibition against tattooing in Leviticus as being true to the letter for all time. Their mistaken understanding of this verse is reinforced by further misunderstanding another verse, this time in 1 Corinthians 6:19-20 of the New Testament, which reads: "Do you not know that your body is a temple of the Holy Spirit, who is in you, whom you have received from God? You are not your own; you were bought at a price. Therefore honour God with your body." Of course, there is nothing in this passage that explicitly forbids tattoos and thus would link them with impiety. In fact, if a person reads this passage properly, that is, from within its proper context, it's clear that God via St. Paul is talking about what happens when a man engages in sexual relations with a temple prostitute of an impure religion. Ink on one's skin is a red herring; the point, as in the Old Testament, is to preserve sanctity and the argument for this is as follows.

God created the first man, Adam, and gave him authority over the entire planet. Adam was created in a just state, but because he was given the faculty of free will, he was able to choose between justice and injustice: treating the

---

2   Of course if a Jew is tattooed against his or her will, such as when the Nazis branded six million of them, such Jews are not considered impious or unjust.

greatest thing (God) as the greatest thing, or treating a lesser thing (such as Eve) as the greatest thing (God). Adam chose the latter and hence "fell." Because anyone who chooses to act unjustly even once can't enter into the presence of the burning purity that is perfect Justice or Righteousness (God), *all* who act unjustly even *once* are consigned – as the most ancient Hebrews,[3] Mesopotamians,[4] Greeks,[5] and even Japanese[6] knew – to the underworld or the land where the spirits of the dead dwell. Yet even if man can't save himself, insofar as God became man and dwelt among us as the Christ, He can. But how?

Jesus can represent all people. For God as God to forgive man for his sins might call into question God's justice since God can't just pretend that sin didn't happen: injustice needs to be dealt with. For the same reason that an animal can't bear man's injustice (an animal isn't a man), God as God probably couldn't bear man's injustice (God isn't a man). Hence, God probably needed to become a man – to descend to man's ontological level, to be identified with man and his guilt – in order to make forgiveness possible. Moreover, since Jesus as God is Adam's elder, Jesus can represent all men, just as Adam could: insofar as Adam, our first father, could pass on the curse of original sin (the disposition to prefer injustice to justice), Jesus, as the "Second Adam," can take all under His authority and pass on forgiveness by virtue of his humanity, authority and, of course justice. This latter point is especially important since if Jesus hadn't lived a perfectly just life, He, no more than any of us, could enter the presence of the Father so-to-speak and be in harmony with Him. And insofar as people speak justly, confessing both that they can't save themselves (they can't remove all the stains of their injustice) and that the Christ can, these people, by the graciousness and authority of the Christ, can be accredited as just or righteous and hence be reconciled with the Father, who is perfect Joy.

Thus, when 1 Corinthians says, "you are not your own" it refers to those who have freely acknowledged the authority of God over all of what they are, including their bodies. Taking care of one's body as God has ordained bodies to be taken care – here in respect to sexual matters ("The body is not meant for sexual immorality"[7]) – is an act of justice, and because God is one's superior,

---

3 Philip Johnston, *Shades of Sheol: Death and Afterlife in the Old Testament* (Downers Grove, IL: InterVarsity Press, 2002), 77.
4 See *Nergel and Ereshkigal* and *Adapa*, in *Myths from Mesopotamia*, ed. Stephanie Dalley (Oxford: Oxford University Press, 2000).
5 Thus, in book eleven of Homer's *Odyssey*, even the noble Achilles dwells in the underworld.
6 In the *Kojiki*, the sacred text of Shinto, the land of *Yomi* is explained to be "an underworld, . . . the habitation of the dead, . . . the land whither, when they die, go all men, whether noble or mean, virtuous or wicked." See *Kojiki* 1.9.
7 1 Corinthians 6:13.

it's also an act of piety. Nonetheless, there is nothing at all here that says getting a tattoo is a form of misusing one's body and hence acting impiously.

"WE MUST NOT INJURE OUR BODIES"

Confucius lived around five hundred years before the birth of the Christ. As a self-confessed "lover of the ancients," he sought to align his teachings with the most ancient Chinese sages and to make their vague instructions more deliberate (hence Confucianism is often called "the deliberate tradition"). The teachings of these sages can be traced back to the beginning of Chinese civilization, which began around 2700 B.C. At this time, the first Chinese emperor, Huang Di, built a temple to the One Supreme God, known to the Han Chinese as Shang Di (later also called Tian or Heaven[8]). There never was, nor is to this day,[9] an image made to represent Shang Di since He is beyond all representation. This was the beginning of Chinese religious practice and the subject with which the sages of the ancient world were most concerned.[10]

Thus, when Confucius complied *The Classic of History*, which describes the oldest accounts of the Middle Kingdom, he is careful to note not only that Shang Di is the Supreme Lord on High, but also that "It is virtue that moves Heaven"[11] and that "His will extends everywhere;"[12] we are told, "But Shang Di sent down calamities on the Xia Dynasty. The ruler of Xia had increased his opulence. He would not speak kindly to the people, and became utterly immoral and foolish. He was unable for a single day to bring himself to follow the path marked out by Shang Di."[13] Mencius, the second greatest Confucian after the Teacher himself, thus perfectly agrees with the ancients when he writes, "It is by the preservation of one's heart and the nourishment of one's character that man is able to serve Heaven."[14] Shang Di or Heaven – God, we can say – was the source of true morality and justice, and the goal for the ancients, as for the earliest Confucians, was to look to Heaven to discern how

---

8   Zheng Xuan, a scholar of the Han Dynasty, comments, "Shang Di is another name for Tian. The spirits do not have two Lords." *Historical Records, Han History, and Zi Zhi Tong Jian*, Sima Qian, Historical Records, vol. 28, book 6, p. 624.
9   Even to this day, the Temple of Heaven complex in Beijing has no image of Shang Di in it.
10 Scholars, of course, continue to debate the origins of China and its religious practices, and so it's possible to get different interpretations, even radically different interpretations, of these. For example, compare Chan Kei Thong's *Finding God in Ancient China* (Grand Rapids, MI: Zondervan, 2009) with David Noss's *A History of the World's Religions*, 12th ed. (Upper Saddle River, NJ: 1999).
11 *The Classic of History*, The Book of Tang, The Counsel of Great Yu, paragraph 21.
12 *The Record of Rites*, Xian Ju, verse 29.
13 *The Classic of History*, Chronicles of Zhou, Duo Fang, 3.
14 Mencius *Mencius* 3.1.

to act on Earth. Piety, then, was "the root of all virtue."[15]

Of course, Confucians, just as much as Jews and Christians (and many others), saw the scope of created reality not merely as an ontological hierarchy between God and man, but also as a hierarchy taking into account differences of age, gender, ability, character, rank and so on. On the top was Shang Di and below Him were those belonging to the created heavens (lower case "h") – the *shen* or nature spirits and the *zu xian* or the spirits of the blessed ancestors[16] – and below these were those belonging to Earth – first and foremost the just emperor and then a myriad of hierarchies encompassing gender, age, ability, character and rank distinctions. Piety – the form of justice concerned with treating a superior as a superior – ought to be shown first and foremost to Shang Di and then, down the ranks, to one's father.

Confucius's *Hsiao King* or treatise on filial piety is the text often cited when discussing the impiety of tattoos. The piety discussed in this book is towards one's father, though since to honour one's father is to honour the way of Heaven,[17] Heaven itself is honoured when fathers are honoured: "In filial piety there is nothing greater than the reverential awe of one's father. In the reverential awe shown to one's father there is nothing greater than making him the correlate of Heaven."[18] In this vein it should be pointed out that even minor acts of injustice – minor when comparing one's father to God – offend Heaven and bring about trouble: "Shang Di will pour down calamities on those who do evil. We must not neglect to do small acts of righteousness because it is by the accumulation of these that the nations celebrate. We must not neglect to avoid acts of unrighteousness because it is by the accumulation of these that an entire generation is corrupted."[19] This, then, leads us to the question as to whether getting a tattoo was, or, more importantly, ought to have been, considered an act of impiety according to Confucius and early Confucians.

In *Hsiao King*, Confucius remarks, "Our bodies – to every hair and bit of skin – are received by us from our parents, and we must not presume to injure or wound them: this is the beginning of filial piety."[20] Here we should immediately note two things. First, Confucius doesn't explicitly mention

---

15   Confucius *Hsiao King* 1.
16   Supreme among the blessed or virtuous ancestors are the virtuous sage-emperors who have died: "King Wen lives above, his virtues shine in heaven. Though our Zhou nation is old, Shang Di's Mandate is still with us. The Zhou nation was not established when the time of Di's Mandate had not arrived. King Wen's soul is active and he lives in the presence of Shang Di." *The Classic of Poetry*, Da Ya, Anecdotes of King Wen, King Wen, verses 1-2.
17   Confucius *The Doctrine of the Mean* 1.1.
18   Confucius *Hsiao King* 9.
19   *The Classic of History*, Book of Shang, Instructions of Yi, paragraph 8, verse 2.
20   Confucius *Hsiao King* 1.

tattooing. And second, injuring or wounding one's body is only a *prima facie* prohibition since to wound one's body to protect one's family or in service of the emperor would have been praised, not condemned, and even suicide to remove the shame of a misdeed plaguing one's family was, and still is, generally accepted by Confucians. So, why, then, have Confucians linked tattooing with injuring one's body and thus with dishonouring one's father?

Racism is the likely explanation. Because the Han Chinese tended to look down on the ethic minorities in their kingdoms, and because many of these minorities practiced tattooing (such as in Quanzhou and Taiwan), tattooing was associated with uncivilized peoples. Because of this, if a son were to get a tattoo, he would, in effect, shame his father by linking himself, and thus his father, with what they thought were lesser peoples and lesser practices. Moreover, because the minorities living in Han kingdoms were treated as inferior peoples, they couldn't get the best jobs and so were often forced into criminal activities. Tattoos, inferior people and criminals were thus linked in the mind of the ancient Chinese and so it was easy for Confucians to interpret their master's prohibition against wounding one's body as a prohibition against tattooing.

But notice this: just as much in Confucianism as in Christianity, tattoos themselves aren't really the problem: the problem is what they are associated with and the subsequent embarrassment they can cause one's parents; if tattoos weren't associated with lower status or immoral people (criminals), then it's not clear that they would be a source of shame to one's parents. Indeed, legend has it that the mother of the famous Chinese general Yue Fei tattooed on her son's back the words "serve the country loyally," which suggests that getting a tattoo for the right reasons – namely, out of pious obedience (as Yue Fei submitted to his mother's needle) or as a reminder to be pious (as the words on Yue Fei's back implore) – may have had some legitimacy in ancient China and so among the earliest Confucians. Of course, just as much for a Confucian as for a Jew or a Christian, if one's superior – one's father, in this case – thought that getting a tattoo is a sign of disrespect, then, insofar as the son or daughter owes the father respect in this matter, that is, insofar as they are still under the father's authority, they must not get a tattoo, for to get one would be considered impious and unjust and thus an offence against Heaven itself.

THE CHRISTIAN CONFUCIAN CONFUSION

In this chapter I agreed with Christians and Confucians that piety – the justice shown towards one's superiors – is indeed admirable and proper, yet I disagreed with what many Christians and Confucians have understood piety to look like, particularly in respect to remaining free of tattoos. I argued that neither the Bible nor the works of Confucius allow us to say that tattoos in and of themselves are bad, and, indeed – though I didn't argue it – could be good, not only for aesthetic reasons but also, as we saw with Yue Fei, for didactic purposes as well. Nevertheless, because justice is more important than both aesthetics and mere reminders to be just, if a person finds himself under a *legitimate* superior who has, in that relationship, a *legitimate* claim to one's obedience, then to disobey the moral or non-moral commands of that superior would be impious and unjust.[21] Thus, if a child living under the roof of a Christian or Confucian parent forbade that child from getting a tattoo (or from dying his or her hair, getting a piercing and so on), then it would be impious of the child to disobey: as Confucius says, "When a youth is at home, let him be filial."[22] However, when the child moves out and is no longer under the authority of the parent (I don't say, no longer owes the parent respect and certain duties), then the child – the man or woman – may legitimately opt for ink: Heaven, very likely, doesn't have a problem with this.

---

21 Although some imagine Confucius and the early Confucians accepting absolute obedience to one's superiors, this is probably not true. Obedience is owed only when the command is either moral or non-moral, never when it is immoral since an immoral command is a command against God or Heaven, who has greater authority than fathers and emperors. "He who has a moral duty," Confucius insists, "should not give way even to his master." Confucius *Analects* 15.35.
22 Confucius *Analects* 1.6.

Chapter Sixteen

Winnie the Pooh and the Four Loves

In *Winnie the Pooh* stories there are no lovers, yet there are plenty of persons who love. Or better, there is no discussion of what the Greeks call *eros* (attraction, especially sexual attraction), but plenty of discussion about *storge* (affection), *philia* (friendship), and *agape* (sacrificial love). If one's subject is "lovers," it might seem odd for *Winnie the Pooh* stories to come up; however, this is strange only if we think of lovers as persons of *eros* and nothing more. Yet this understanding, I believe, is mistaken since perfect lovers – and here I'm taking inspiration from, and extending, *Pooh* – must have not only *eros* but also *storge*, *philia* and *agape* as well. Moreover, the basis of these loves is, according to *Winnie the Pooh*, individuality.

In *A Very Merry Pooh Year*, Rabbit becomes so infuriated with Tigger, Piglet, Pooh and Eeyore that he expresses his distaste for – in a non-technical sense – the traits or characteristics that make the other four unique: Tigger's love for bouncing, Piglet's timidity, Pooh's love for honey, and Eeyore's pessimism. Out of love for Rabbit, the four try to change these intimate features about themselves; however, when Rabbit finds himself in a bind and only the original traits or characteristics of his friends can help him (especially Tigger's bounce), Rabbit realizes that he doesn't want them to change their most defining characteristics in order to remain friends with him; rather, it's their most defining characteristics that form the basis, and perhaps even one of the goals, of friendship and love in general. As Pooh wisely reflects, "If you weren't you, then we'd all be a little less we."

Taking cue, and using examples, from *Winnie the Pooh*, I will argue that a perfect lover is a person who, respecting and desiring the individuality of the other lover, shows the other not just *eros* – which of course needs to be addressed herein – but *storge*, *philia* and *agape* as well. The perfect lover is not one, but four-dimensional.

Above All Things

STORGE

Storge or affection is the most basic of loves and can be enjoyed by virtually anyone. A young boy like Christopher Robin may share it with his inanimate teddy bear; two students in the same class may share it simply by being in the same class; and a man may feel this way toward his favourite sweater or brand of scotch. This kind of love can also be seen between a woman and her pet (it's often confused with *philia* or friendship) and can even be seen between two pets, such as a dog and a cat raised together. Love of one's race, ethnicity and country (patriotism) are forms of *storge* since the criteria for this love is very simple: the object of this love must simply be familiar.

Storge is the least discriminating and broadest of the loves. It's homely, comfortable, humble and familial. It can be seen when Kanga baths Roo, Pooh (mis)spells the word "hunny," Piglet puts an ornament on the Christmas tree, Tigger bounces through Rabbit's garden, and, tellingly, when Rabbit scolds Tigger for doing so. Even Gopher, who seems to have no particular interest in anyone but himself, is, in the Hundred Acre Wood, "good old Gopher." *Storge* says with Pooh, "As long as we are apart together, we shall certainly be fine."

Lovers enjoy *storge* when they watch their favourite shows together, when they take comfort in just knowing the other person is in the house, and when they give each other pet names, such as Sweetheart or Dear. C. S. Lewis (no stranger to the four loves) once said he felt that Falstaff's fat was more an essential quality than an accidental one. Though the metaphysics of this statement is questionable, the sentiment is indisputable. Eeyore *ought to* be slouchy; Pooh *must* wear red T-shirts; and Owl *has to* speak some Latin. In fact, women and wives, who I may safely say are less aesthetically demanding than men and husbands, may be quite satisfied with their man's bald head and hairy back just because of *storge*. Aspects such as these, which we may find objectively distasteful, we may love – or better, *come to love* (since *storge* takes time) – simply because they are ours.

But lovers must also be careful of unjust or perverse *storge*. While affection is certainly natural and good in its proper place, a lover can't always be expected to feel it to the degree that the other lover would like nor when they would like to feel it. How many husbands complain that their wives aren't home to cook them a meal even when their wives may very properly deserve an outing with their friends? How many girlfriends complain about their boyfriends not wanting to talk on the phone 24/7? And how many lovers ridicule each other's interests simply because they don't include the other? *Storge* is quite proper when it enjoys the individuality of a familiar presence, but it's distorted when it wants to subsume the other into one's self. There is no selfishness, egotism or inordinate love of self in wanting to feel affection from those around one's self; but there is much selfishness in wanting to be loved by the familiar at all costs, even at the cost of robbing the other person of their freedom, identity and proper enjoyment of things other than the lover. Jealousy, then, isn't unique to *eros*, and the feeling of suffocation brought on by the other's sense of abandonment is a common feeling one has when *storge* sours.

But suffocation isn't the only perversion of *storge*. A couple may feel bored with each other because they have only *storge* and none of the other types of loves. They may feel things are dull or uninteresting when *storge*, the humble servant, is inordinately elevated to the king of the loves. Or again, rudeness is often a corrupt form of *storge* because people, including lovers, often confuse being *comfortable* with being *uncouth*, being *casual* with being *free from manners*. This, of course, is another instance of *storge* being elevated above its correct station, or better, being untempered by justice. The home may be a place where a man can take off his tie and a woman can take off her makeup, but the home is still under the sovereignty of Goodness. Morality should never be taken off not only because it is good in and of itself, but also because proper comfort and relaxation *require* the higher love. We feel *storge* when Tigger bounces Rabbit not because jumping on people against their will is good, but because this familiar situation is tempered by Tigger's genuine good intent toward "Old Long Ears."

PHILIA

Philia or friendship is probably the least understood of the loves. "Friending" on Facebook is more an effect than the cause of a predominate confusion between *storge* and *philia*. *Storge* will be felt in some measure between all who spend enough time together. Acquaintances in a class, colleagues at work, and even comrades who endure many hardships together share *storge*, yet all of these may not, as such, share *philia*. A person can become an acquaintance, a colleague and even a comrade or teammate quite effortlessly – time spent together being the key ingredient. However, time spent together is not sufficient for friendship. Common loves and interests – not just common situations and circumstances – are what's needed.

And here is the test: If you think a person is your friend, try spending some years apart; then, meet up again and see how things go. If, after the initial excitement brought on by reminiscing, things become a bit uncomfortable and you find there is little for you to say to each other, then you *may have been* friends, but now, having few ideas or interests in common, are simply aquaintances, colleagues or comrades. However, if you find that reflecting on "the good old days" to be fun but almost beside the point – if you feel a hunger to get on to talk about the things that the two of you have in common, in particular, ideas (be it of war, art, Dickens novels, video games, cooking or whatever) – then there is a very good chance that you are still friends, for *philia* typically stands side by side and looks at a third object in common, while *storge* has no interest in such third objects.

Because *eros* is necessary for people to be begotten and *storge* is necessary for people to be *reared* and *preserved* through herd instinct, these two loves can be found among both animals and human beings.[1] However, *philia* isn't necessary in these ways at all. Because shared loves, in particular, of ideas, is what is central to *philia*, such is beyond non-rational animals, and, in fact, belongs very much to the rationally-endowed: human beings, rational stuffed animals and the like. Moreover, such shared love of ideas in no way implies that all ideas must be shared: *philia* may very properly develop between two people who disagree on nearly everything so long as they both share the same love of discussing the ideas in common. In fact, what makes the conversation better is precisely the differences of each in the group. Individuality is vital: one friend asserts what he thinks and the other does likewise and through the meeting of two different persons, a single beautiful friendship emerges. As Pooh tell us, "It's much more friendly with two."

And perhaps with three or four as well since *philia*, often unlike *storge* and *eros*, is not jealous when another friend or two enters the mix. Thus, in *A Very Merry Pooh Year*, although Tigger, Rabbit and Piglet enjoy discussing with each other their shared love of Santa, theatre, and how to hunt heffalumps, they still feel impoverished when Pooh, the fourth member of their group, is missing. Each of the four is different, and yet all are united in a common love of the topic before them and have become richer – far richer than non-rational animals – because of friendship. This is why Confucius, Aristotle and most of the ancients elevated *philia* to a position of honour in life's feast.

Lovers, then, ought to make friendship one of their aims. The old saying about finding a girlfriend who is a friend first is a good saying, yet the order may not be as important as the desire to see *eros* and *philia* meet. Although most couples begin their relationship with *eros* and end it with *storge*, a couple that doesn't share some of the same interests, in particular, interests requiring discussion, remains – leaving *agape* aside for now – all too animal. Since human beings aren't merely animals, this is often a sad state of affairs.

And speaking of which – that is, of being more than animals, of being spiritual beings – one of the reasons (not the only reason) why persons of different worldviews are less inclined to date and marry those of other worldviews is because of *philia*. While love of the same object demands *within itself* individual differences, if there is no love of the object *itself* in common

---

1   C. S. Lewis, *The Four Loves*, in *C. S. Lewis: Selected Book* [Long Edition] (London: HarperCollins, 1999), 39.

(for instance, if a Jew cares nothing for the Hindu's most cherished belief, such as that of the doctrine of *atman*, or if a secular humanist thinks the Muslim's Qur'an poetic nonsense), then one of the most central roots upon which *philia* can grow is absent and, worse yet, severed. Of course, *philia* may develop by the two discussing other interests they may have in common, such as travel or food, yet because even these interests are sometimes contextualized by a larger worldview, the soil for friendship here isn't always fertile.

Moreover, just as *storge* and *eros* require justice, so too does *philia*. An evil couple, such as Paul Bernardo and Karla Homolka, may share many of the same interests with each other (for instance, how to rape and murder), and in this sense can be seen as friends, and indeed their friendship can even give each other strength – for this is one of the glories of *philia* – to achieve goals unimagined individually. However, in another, more profound sense, Cicero is right when he says there can be no friendship between evil men. Why? If the two do not love goodness and justice *first* – that is, if they don't desire to love or treat all people as they ought to be loved or treated, namely, as individuals of inherent worth and dignity – then there is nothing to stop the two villains from ultimately seeing the other not as individuals to be respected for his or her own sake, but rather as a means to an end: friendship is expendable for those who are not true friends. Thus, here again is where the lack of a shared worldview – or better, the lack of a shared worldview which sees justice as good for its own sake and *agape* as the king of the loves – matters. "A little consideration, a little thought for others," Pooh tells us, "makes all the difference" – in friendship, as in all the loves.

EROS

We cannot conceive of perfect lovers without *eros* or sexual love. The phrase most associated with *eros* is "being in love," which may be thought of either in a very high-minded fashion (as teenagers often do with their first love) or in a very base, animalistic fashion (as those with more experience of this love often do). Both understandings of *eros* are correct, yet are ideally joined. A middle-aged couple that has become disenchanted with romance or even never experienced it to begin with (as is the case with most arranged marriages) is impoverished since *eros* as romance sees the object of its desire in an ennobled – and, in a sense, its truest, most uncorrupted – form and treats it accordingly: songs are written, wars are fought, lives are given to protect the treasured other. This doesn't mean that *eros* doesn't see the flaws, but rather that it desires the beloved despite them. Yahweh, metaphorically speaking, saw Israel in this light. Subsequently, a couple needs to become re-enchanted with each other – wives must not carelessly let their looks go, and husbands must keep things interesting – since the energy of life, the adventure of seeking out the mystery in the other, and the beauty spurred on by *eros* is certainly something good in and of itself: how wonderful it is that a young man in love would *truly* rather kiss his beloved than have sex with her; how wonderful it is to see a man quest for the woman he loves and for the woman to desire to uncover the mysteries of her would-be lover. Nevertheless, young people or people who remain wildly romantic can also commit the error of making *eros* a god, when, in fact, he is also part animal. Perfect sex requires the mind and imagination, to be sure, but it also requires other, more physical parts.

While *storge* simply wants the other around, and *philia* stands side by side with a friend to discuss a common object, *eros* stands face to face with the lover. And here is where we need some insight from *Pooh* again. In its perfect form, *eros* is tempered by justice and *agape* such that it sees and wants the other to be his or her true self. Individuality is the key to proper *eros* since the lover wants to go on admiring the splendour of the other, especially in his or her physical form. True *eros* says truly, "I would have you above any other." Of course, this ought to mean "I would have you above any other *woman or man*" not "above any other *period*" since *eros*, even more than *storge* and *philia*, needs to remember that it can only love truly when it loves justice and *agape* first. We may admire Romeo and Juliet's passion for each other, yet to commit suicide out of despair is an act lacking wisdom.

But let's return to *eros* and individuality, wherein a beautiful mystery lies, namely, that though the man and the woman must remain themselves in order for *eros* to be true, they must also become one. Nevertheless, here we must be careful since mystery is not the same as paradox or nonsense. Perverse *eros* sees this oneness as the dissolution of the other's individuality into the self. Or better, such *eros* desires not the other – the beloved woman, for instance – but merely the pleasures that she can give him. In a very real sense, perverse *eros* does not want the woman herself, but the feeling of sexual excitement and release that she, quite beside the point, can provide. This is why without justice a husband may cheat on his wife even with a woman (or a computer image of a woman) who is less attractive than her. This malformed *eros* is a black hole.

We may see, then, that the proper union of the two individuals in *eros* is when each, loving justice and *agape* more than each other, elevates the other, as persons, equal to, or above, themselves. Moreover, because each respects the individuality of the other, this relationship is freely entered into and the cage, so to speak, remains open. Of course, perfect lovers never fly out, or, rather, they never fly out alone, since they want to be together; they want *each other* and they want each other *forever* – this is why some talk of soul-mates and others, including Christians, hope for some kind of continued union in the next life. Polygamy is animalistic; monogamy is divine.

And finally, while this relationship ought to be freely entered into and the individuality of the other must be respected at all times, there is no sense, in *eros*, that the lovers must in *everything* be thought of as equals: equals as rational souls and persons, yes, but not as gendered beings. Chivalric knights very properly lay down their lives for their ladies, and their ladies, very properly, receive this: women want a champion – not just a man – who will shelter them when the storms of life are too much. None of this, of course, is to say that a woman can't rescue a man or that a man can't find comfort in a woman's arms; but such moments are the exception, not the rule: women rightly like a man who can talk about his feelings, but none desire a man who cries at the slightest hardship. This is part of the truth in the old saying "girls love bad boys." If the individuality of persons matter, then the gender differences of each matter as well. Only a mistaken understanding of gender as a social construct rather than a given, and justice as equality, rather than as treating each as they ought to be treated, would say otherwise. Even in *Pooh*, the hierarchical differences, not of gender, but of intelligence, physical strength and so on matter very much to the relationships between the individuals: Owl is *wiser* than Pooh; Tigger can bounce *higher* than Piglet; and Gopher digs *better* than Rabbit. And they, as we, properly delight in this.

AGAPE

Throughout this chapter, I have alluded to the fourth and final love – the king of the loves – *agape* or sacrificial love. Even more than *philia*, it takes rational souls, spirits or persons to comprehend and practice this love. A doe may sacrifice herself for her fawn but she does so out of non-rational instinct and *storge*. Bull elephants may fight to the death for a mate, but they do so out of bare *eros*. Justice and its bloom, *agape*, complete each of these loves and *philia* as well. None of the loves can be perfect without justice and *agape*, and so perfect lovers simply cannot *be* without understanding and implementing these. Good lovers are, first and foremost, good people.[2]

In its purest form, *agape* is a love that values the other more than is required by justice or risks itself for another. It makes itself deeply vulnerable to others, and thus can be hurt. That is what Pooh means when he says, "Some people care too much; I think it's called love."

Nevertheless, because of its costly or risky nature, some philosophers have failed to see its value: Epicurus thought it foolishness since it entails the potential to be hurt, and the Buddha made the rejection of *agape* his central argument: life is suffering, suffering is caused by desire, so try to extinguish all desires, above all, a love that may entail suffering. But most have sided with

---

2 Lewis, *The Four Loves*, 73.

Pooh on the importance of *agape* – even Mahayana Buddhists quickly found the Buddha's dethronement of this love too rash.

If justice loves each thing as it ought to be loved, then *agape* perfects this: it loves each thing, in a proper sense, *more* than it ought to be loved. Since this is not straightforward, let's take an example from Christianity. Justice demanded that Adam love Eve more than the animals and the rest of nature, but less than God (lovers take note). Adam could have acted unjustly by either loving an animal (a lesser thing) equal to, or more than, his wife (a greater thing), or by loving her (a lesser person) equal to, or more than, God (the greatest person). Now, when I say that *agape* loves each thing "*more* than it ought to," I do not mean that *agape* contradicts justice in this sense. Rather, as the perfection of justice, *agape* should be seen as going beyond the call of duty – of helping those who have no claim to be helped, showing mercy to those who have no claim to be shown mercy, forgiving those who have no claim to be let off the hook. Justice is always present and acknowledged – thus, the important phrase "has no claim to" – but justice itself allows that individuals have the freedom to pay the price for someone else's injustice or to suffer something that they don't deserve to suffer on behalf of another. This supremely free, giving love is *agape*. Justice demanded that God love his creation, including Adam and Eve, to some degree, but not to the extent of giving His life, which is greater than all of creation, for it and them.³ Likewise, when Tigger ruins Rabbit's garden, Rabbit is wronged and Tigger is morally to blame. Rabbit could ask Tigger to compensate him for the injustice he suffers and justice would demand Tigger comply; however, Rabbit usually takes the injustice upon himself and, through *agape*, forgives Tigger and frees him from his proper blame. Good lovers ought to imitate actions such as these in all things.

---

3   Of course, while it's *agape* that moves God to try to save Adam and Eve, it's not simply *agape* – it's also justice – that moves God to try to save Adam and Eve's children. If the children of man were born into a world where they had no potential to desire, choose and be in a relationship with God – if damnation was their only option – then God's Justice can't be maintained. Thus, because God is bound by His own nature as the Just, we must say that God has some duties toward the children of man, including the duty to make it *possible* for man to desire and choose Him. For example, if my mother were to give birth to me and then leave me on the street to die, we rightly think she wrongs me. And something similar is true of God though to a much higher degree since while earthly mothers are imperfect in both knowledge and morality, God is the perfection of these. God can't do injustice; He can't wrong anyone. Thus, we have two biblical truths: "that all are *able* to be saved" ("God *is not willing* that any should perish" 1 Peter 3:9) and "that few are saved" (not all will choose God; Hell is real).

"HUGGABLE, LOVABLE..."

Inspired by *Winnie the Pooh* and using examples from it throughout, I have argued that perfect lovers – and not just lovers in general – need four types of love: *storge* or affection, *philia* or friendship, *eros* or attraction, and *agape* or sacrificial love. While all of these loves are unique, the first three loves – *storge*, *philia* and *eros* – require that *agape*, the perfection of justice and the defender of individuality, be properly acknowledged as the king of loves if these other loves are to be their proper selves. Lovers, as we may extend Pooh to be saying, need to be not just romantic, but also familiar, friendly, just, merciful and forgiving: "huggable" and "lovable" – stuffed with fluff or not.

Above All Things

INDEX

Abortion, 88
Abrams, J. J., 54, 57, 61
Addiction, 122, 126, 128-129, n133
Adultery, 114, 131
Aesthetics, 94, 168, 170
Agape, 68, 80, 108, 119, 132, 143, 147, 169, 171-177
Alcohol, 121, 124-127
Analogy, 10, 108
Angel, 38, 71, 77-78, 98, 107-108, 110-113, n111, 115, 118, 130, 139, 194
Anthropocentric, 2
Apologetics, 6, n8, n19, 159
Aquinas, Thomas, 44, n44, 94, 112, n112
Aristotle, n14, 24, 49, 55, 58, 64, n84, 122, 172, 192
Arminian, 12-14, 16
Atheist, 3, 8, n8, n31, 41, n41
Augustine, n6, 9, n18, n55, n147
Authority, v, n6, n8, 33, 40, 49, 52, 64, 67, 71, 111, 115, 117, 137, 145-146, 163-164, 167-168
Autonomy, 24-25, 29
Avengers, 69, n69, 70, 72, 74-82, n74-n82

Bartholomew, Craig, n18
Bible, 10, 12, 26, 33-34, n59, 63, 71, 77-78, 80, 97, 109-112, 152-159, 161-162, 167
Big Bang, 23, 30, 33, 41, 72
Big Bang Theory (TV), 30, n32-n33, n39, n43
Biology, 113, 119, 135, 137
Black Widow, 74, 76-77, n77, 79-81, n81
Bravery, see Courage
Breaking Bad, 121, n121, n123-n124, 128, n129
Brunner, Emil, 5
Buddha, 94, 124, 175-176, 192

Calvinism, 1, 4, 12, 15, 18, n19, n20, n21
Calvin, John, 2, n5-n6, 8, 10, n10, 12, 16, 17
Catholic, 11, 152
Certainty, 158
Church, 18, n18, 97, 110, n110, 115, 117
Cigarettes, 57, 126, 128-129
City of God, 17
City of the World, 17
Coffee, 125-127
Collins, Francis, 37, n37, 40, n40
Common ancestry, 30-33, 37, 40
Common design, 40, 134
Compatibilist, v, 9
Confucius, n9, 25, 45, 48, n48, 165-168, n166, n168, 172
Consanguine unions, see Incest
Cosmological argument, 5
Courage, 65-68, 93, 100, 116, 123, 145, 194
Covenant, 4, 12
Creation, 2-7, 12, 16, 18-19, 23, 33-34, n35, 38, 41, 70-71,

73, 78, 95-96, 105, 109, 115, 130, 144, 151-152, 176
Creational laws, 3, 5-6, 10, 18, n55, 62
Creator, 2, 7, n26, 34, 41, 46, 56, 65, 67, 70, 77, 82, 84, 138, 151, 156-157, 162
Cross-dressing, 131
Cultural mandate, 4
Cultural relativism, 93

Darwin, Charles, 39, n39
Dating, n35, 117
Democratic, n13
De Monarchia, 62, n62-n66, n68
Dennett, Daniel, 40, n40
Descartes, René, 25, 45
Desire, 6, 9-10, 12, 14, 26, 37, 57, 60-61, 67, 94, 114, 118, 126, 132, 152-153, 159, 172-176
Dinosaurs, n34, 35-36, 38
DNA, 40-41, 85-86, 89, 134
Dooyeweerd, Herman, 19, n19-n20
Doyle, Sir Arthur Conan, 151-159, n151-n152, n154-n158
Drug, 85-86, 121-129, n121-122, n126

Eastern Orthodox, 1, 11
Education, 19, 22, n23, 24, n25, 194
Elect, 12, 16, n21, 64, 111
Emotion, 7, 32, n59, 79, 89, 94, 119, 126, 128, 136, 154
Empire, 140, 144, 147-148
Epistemology, v, 8, n8

Eros, 72, 132, 135-136, 169, 171-175, 177
Eternal, 44, 72, 75-76, 110, 115, n144, 159, 194
Ethnicity, 170
Eugenics, 88
Euthyphro Dilemma, n11, 47, n48
Evangelical, 1
Evidence, v, n6, 7, n11, 15, 23, 30-32, 35, n36, 37-42, n59, 63, 88, 101, 111-112, 114, 133, 140, 149, 153-155
Evolution, 30, 33, n35, 38-42, n87, 98
Existence, 4-6, n8, 9, n18, 30, n31, n38, 41-42, n41, 45-46, 62, 67, 72-73, 77-79, 84, 94, 157, 159, 162

Faith, 1, n6, 11, n11, 12, 14-18, n37, n40, 65, 67-68, 100, 105, n109, 119, 142, 162, 191-194
Fall, 2, 6-8, 10, 18, 37-38, n37-n38, 40, 68, 113, n127, 142, 146, 162
Fallacy, 39, 78, 154-156
Falsity, 9-10, 114, 157
Family, 20, 47, 54, 57-59, 63, 80, 97, 105, 107, 116-117, 123, 128, 134, 136-139, 143, 161, 167, 191, 194
Femininity, 110, 114-118
Feminist, 108, n109, n113
Flood, 24, 36, n36
Foreknowledge, 12, 159
Forgiveness, 11, 53, 100, 114, 164
Fossil record, n34, 35
Four Cardinal Virtues, 67

Freedom, n5, 13, n14, 15, 22, 24, n26, 37, 65, 90, 96, 116, 147, 149, 171, 176

Free will, v, 4, 9-10, 12, n15, 16, 25, n26, 31, 37-38, 45-46, 53, 64, 71, 79, 82, 88-89, 111, 136, 152, 159, 163

Freud, Sigmund, 130-133, n132, 135

Galileo, 33, n33, 156

Game of Thrones, 130-131, 134, n135, n138

Gender, v, 107-117, 131, 166, 175

Gender-inclusive language, v

General beneficence, 47, 49, 51, 122-125

Gene therapy, 86, 92

Genetic, 30, 84-86, 91, 133, 135-136, 138, 154

Gladiator, 107, 140, 153

Gladiator (movie), 107, 116

Gnosticism, 108

Goodness, 5, 7, 10, n11, 33, 40, 45, 78-79, 82, 124, 138, 141, n141, 159, 171, 173

Grace, 11-12, n14, 15-16, 65, n134, 142, n162

Grayling, A. C., 102, n102

Greek mythology, 72-73

Guilt, 55, 114, n132, 143, 164, 210

Happiness, 4-5, n4, 14, 46, 53-54, n56, 57-61, 65, 67, 94, 100, 137, 140-142

Hare, R. M., 23-24, n23

Heaven, n1, 6, n6, 18, n18, 25, 36-37, 45, 67-69, 78, 89, 98, 109, n109, 120, 162, n165, 166-168, 189

Heresy, 151, n151

Hesiod, 72, n72

Hierarchy, 63, 166

Hinduism, 23-25, 32, 43-44, 46, 173

Hitchens, Christopher, 42, n42

Holiness, 65, 162

Holmes, Sherlock, 151, n151, 156, n156-n157

Holy Spirit, 12-13, 15, 17, 26, 141, 163

Homosexual, 114, n114

Hope, 9, 22, 29, 40, 47, 54, 65, 67-68, 104, 107, 129, 150, 174, 190

Hulk, 74-80, n75, n79, 83-92, n86-n87, n90-n91

Hulk (movie), n75, n80-n81, 83-84, n83-n84, n86-n87, 87, 89, n89, 90-92, n90-n91

Human, 4-5, 7, 9, 12-13, 18, 23-26, n31, 33, n34, 35-40, 44, 46, 49-56, 60, 62, n69, 70, 74-85, n84, 87-94, 100, 102, 110-115, n112, 123, n126, 130, 133, n133, 136-138, 141-142, 148, 152-153, 158-159, 172-173, 186

Hunger Games, 140, n140, 143-144, n143-n144, 148-147, n148-n150

Hypnosis, 22, 26-27, n26-n27

Image of God, v, 3, 19, 34, n59, 94, n111, 152-153, 158

Immortal, 7, 13, 65, 75-77, 84

Inception, 22, 28-29

Incest, 130-139, n132, n134, n136-n138

Indoctrination, 22-25, n23
Inerrancy of Scripture, 11
Irresistible Grace, 16
Israel, 115, 162-163, 173

Jesus Christ, 2, n19, 103
Joy, n1, n3, 5, n6, 13-14, 113, 128, 141, 164, 191
Jung, Carl, 98
Justice, 3, n3, 5-10, n10, 12-16, n18, 21, 31, 44, 46, 48, 51-80, n55-n59, 98-99, n99, 102-104, 111, 119, 123-124, 132, n132, 142-148, 152, 161-168, 173-177

Kant, Immanuel, 45, 49, 94
Kierkegaard, Søren, 119, n119
Kingdom of God, 18
Knowledge, 4-6, 8, n8, 11-12, 16, 19, 23, n24, n31, 45, 58, 65, 67-71, 74, 77-78, 119, n134, 136, 141, 151-162, 176
Kreeft, Peter, 1, n1
Kuyper, Abraham, 2, n2, 18

Language, v, 3, n5-n6, n37, n40, 53, 60, 66, 86-88, 93, 108-111, n109, 124, 183
Lao Tzu, 47, n47, 94
Law, 6, 8-9, 12, 16, 24-25, 41-55, n55, 58-59, 62, 65, 68, 77, 79
Leadership, 114, 116
Lee, Ang, 83-92, n83-n84, n89
Lee, Stan, 70, 84, n84
Lewis, C. S., 1-21, n1-n21, 25, n25, 37-38, n38, 41, n41, 45, n55, n58, 60, n60, 98, 109, n109, n151, 170, n172, n175, 189-191
Libertarian, 9, 16
Limited Atonement, 12
Locke, John, 31, n31
Logic, 8, 12, 19, n19, 24, 30, 41, 56, 85, 88, 94, 108, 152-159
Logos, 141, 153
Lord's Prayer, 109
Love, v, 3-4, 10, n10, 13-14, n14, 31, 44, 47, 55, 59-72, 79-83, 96-97, 100, 103, 107, 116-117, 119, n119, 131-132, 137, 142-143, 150-157, 162, 169-177, n172, n175, 192

Man, v, n1, 3-11, n6, n9, n11, 13, 15, n15, 17-18, n20-n21, n25-n26, 28-29, 33-34, 37-38, n38, 40, 46, 48, 51-52, 54, n55, 57-58, n59, 61, 65, 67, 69, 76, n76, n78, 84-86, n88, 93-94, 101-107, 111-120, n113, 124, 126, n127, 132, n132, 135, n135, 137, 141-142, 144-145, n145, 151-153, 155-159, 163-168, 170-175, n176
Marijuana, 121, 125, 129
Marriage, 52, 55, 57-58, 107, 110, 117-119, n133, 134, n136, 137, 173
Martin, George R. R., n130, n131-n132, 133-139
Masculinity, 107, 109-118
Materialism, v, 22, 32, 156
Mencius, 45, 165, n165
Mercy, 9-12, 80-81, 95-96, 141, 144, n144, 176

Metaphor, 36, 84-85, 98, 108-109, 111, 115, 163, 173, 190
Metaphysics, 8, 11, n11, 89, 170
Meth, 121, 126, 128-129, n128
Methodological naturalism, 32
Mind, 4, 7, 9-10, n20, 22, 26, 28, 37, 41, n41, 43-45, n45, 62, 66, 74, 79, 89, 91, 99, 121-129, n126, 140-143, 153-154, 167, 174, 192
Monogamy, 174
Moral relativism, 93
Mystery, 16, 59, 101, 174

Natural Law, 3, 25, 44-53, 62, 83, 86, 91-99, 122, 129-130, 139
Natural selection, 37, 40, 133
Natural theology, 5-6
Necromancy, 151-155, 158-159
Neo-Calvinism, 4, 18, n19, 20
Neo-Platonic, n18
New Earth, 18, 119
Nietzsche, Friedrich, 93-96, n94-n95, 98, 100, n100, 105-106, n159
Nihilism, 94

Old earth creationism, 32-43
Omnipotence, 2, 15, 20, 56, 108, 153, 159
Ontology, 37, 55, 69-70, 77
Original sin, 7, 9, 114, 164

Pagan, 4, 9, 14, 18, 94, 107
Paleontology, 38
Patriotism, 51-52, 170
Perseverance of the Saints, 12, 16-17
Philia, 132, 169-177

Philosopher, 8-11, 20-23, 31, 41, 54, 58, 61, 93-95, n95, 98, 102, 107, 129, 133, 151-152, 155-156, 175, 190
Piety, 42, 48, 52, 123, 126, 161-167
Piper, John, 111, 114-116
Plantinga, Alvin, v, 5-6, n5-n6, 8, 10, n10, 16-17, 20, 31
Plato, 6, n6, 18, 24-25, 45, 47, n48, 64, 73, 94, 98, n100, 105, 107-108, 112, 130, 135, n141
Polygamy, 174
Popular culture, v, 26, 192
Pornography, 122, 159
Possibility, 14, 67, 88, 105, 132, 157-158
Postmodern, 22, 45
Pragmatism, 65, 153-157
Presuppositionalist, 8
Priest, 19, 97-98, n97, 102, 104, 107, 110, n110, 117, 124, 162
Probability, 31, 37-38, 78, 86, 111, 128, 158
Prophecy, 26, 93, 102, 104, 117
Providence, 3, n141
Prudence, 55, 65-66, 68

Racism, 167
Rationality, 3, 8-9, n19, 24, 30, 32, 45, 49, 85, 87-88, 108, 111, 151-158
Rational soul, v, 4, 34, 45, 49, 58, 64-65, n77, 84, 86, 108, 110, 112, 145, 152, 175
Reason, 5, 9, 11, 14, n14, 17, 19, 24, 31, 35, 38-40, 49,

58, 62, 67-68, 84, 88, 105, 108-109, 113, 119, 122-123
Redemption, 2, 10, 18, 20, 142, 192
Reformed Epistemology, 8
Regarding Henry, 54
Reincarnation, 23
Religion, 4, n5, n10, 17, 19, n19, 23, 26, n32, n38, n40-n41, 42, 50, 85, 88, n102, n109, 110, 153, 155, 163, n165
Repression, 90
Revelation, 4, 10-11, n10, n18, 19, 25, 33-34, 38, n71, n78, 104, 112, 161
Rights, n3, 27, 50-51, 54-60, n55, 65, 86, 92, 148, 155
Righteousness, see Justice
Romance, 173

Salvation, 9-12, 107, 141
Satan, v, 2-3, 11, 37-38, n38, 77-78, n97, 100, 111, n113
Scientist, 3, 15, 41-42, 89, 154-155, 194
Scotus, Duns, 108
Scripture, 8, 11-12, 15, n18, 20, 48, n48, 77-78, 109, 117, 161-162
Seneca, 140-149, n140-n146
Sex, 66, 107, 109-110, 112-114, 118, 128, 131-138, 157, 163-164, n164, 169, 173-174
Shakespeare, William, 20, 42, 68, n68
Shaman, 26
Slavery, 140, 146, 148-149
Special beneficence, 47, 50, 123
Spider-Man, 69-70, n69-n70, 79

Spirit, 26, 34, 45, n45, 49-50, 58, n59, 84, 86-88, 90, 108-110, n109, 112-113, 115, 117, 137, n144, 146, 152, 159, 163
Spirit of the Age, v
Spiritualism, 151-155, n151, 159
Stoic, 140, 144, 146
Storge, 132, 134-135, 152, 169-177
St. Paul, 4, 13-15, 111, 117, 124, 140-149, 163
Submission, 115-116
Superman, 93-106, n96-n105
Symbol, 81, 93, 100, 102-103, 190

Tao, 25, 47, n47, 83
Tattoo, 161-168, n163
Teaching, 12, 18, 22-26, 48, n48, 152, 162, 165, 190-191
Temperance, 65-68
Theft, 44, 48, 52-53, 114, 128
Theistic evolution, 32, 34, 36-38, 41, 43
Theology, 2, n2, 5-6, n7, 8, n10, 12, n12, 15, 73
Thor, 69, n69, n71, 72, 74-76, n74-n76, n78-n80, 79-80
Total Depravity, 7
Trinitarian, 102, 110
Truth, 5, 7-10, n11, 14, 24-25, 31-33, 45-47, 49, 58-59, 61-63, 65, 67, n77, 85, 87, 91, 98-99, 101-103, 108, 114-115, 135-136, 151, 153-158, 162, 175, 192
TULIP, 1, 7, 12, 16-20

Übermensch, 93-94
Unconditional Election, 12, 14-15
Universal moral law, see Natural Law
Univocity, 108

Van Til, Cornelius, 1, n1, 8-9
Vice, 15, 20, 57, 60, 118, 144-145
Virtue, 10, 15, 47, 49, 58, 60, 65-68, 94, 124, 137, 140-150, 164-166, n166
Virtue ethics, 122
Vollenhoven, Dirk, 19, n19

Walking Dead, 44-53, n45-53
Wasp, 37, 74-81
Westermarck, Edward, 133, n133, n136
Westminster Confession, 4
Will, v, 4, 7-10, n11, 12, n14-n16, 16, 25-29, n26, 31, 37, 45-46, n45, 53, 64, 66, 71, n78, 79, n80, 88-89, 94, 96, 111, 126, 136, 144, 149, 152, 163, n163, 165, 171,
Winnie the Pooh, 169, 177
Wisdom, 9, 36, 48-49, 65-67, n96, 122-127, 140, 142, n145, 149, 174
Wolters, Albert, n3
Wolterstorff, Nicholas, v, 3, 10, n10, 16-18, n18, 20, 54-56, n54-n56, 58-60, n58
Wolverine, n37, 76, n76
World, 5, 7, 9, 12, 17, n18-n20, 19-20, 22-23, 26, 28-29, 31, n31, 33, 37, n38, 40-41, 47, 50, 61, 77, n80, 81, 83, n84, 85, 90, 92, 95-96, 99-100, 102-104, 106-107, n123, 130, 138, 140-141, n141, 146-154, 157-158, 165, n176, 190, 192-194
Worldview, 1, 18, n19, 23-25, 30-32, 161, 172-173

Young earth creationism, 32, 35-37, n35-n37, 40-43

Zarathustra, 95

Other Books of Interest

C. S. Lewis

C. S. Lewis: Views From Wake Forest - Essays on C. S. Lewis
Michael Travers, editor

Contains sixteen scholarly presentations from the international C. S. Lewis convention in Wake Forest, NC. Walter Hooper shares his important essay "Editing C. S. Lewis," a chronicle of publishing decisions after Lewis' death in 1963.

"Scholars from a variety of disciplines address a wide range of issues. The happy result is a fresh and expansive view of an author who well deserves this kind of thoughtful attention."
    Diana Pavlac Glyer, author of *The Company They Keep*

The Hidden Story of Narnia:
A Book-By-Book Guide to Lewis' Spiritual Themes
Will Vaus

A book of insightful commentary equally suited for teens or adults – Will Vaus points out connections between the *Narnia* books and spiritual/biblical themes, as well as between ideas in the *Narnia* books and C. S. Lewis' other books. Learn what Lewis himself said about the overarching and unifying thematic structure of the Narnia books. That is what this book explores; what C. S. Lewis called "the hidden story" of Narnia. Each chapter includes questions for individual use or small group discussion.

Why I Believe in Narnia:
33 Reviews and Essays on the Life and Work of C.S. Lewis
James Como

Chapters range from reviews of critical books, documentaries and movies to evaluations of Lewis' books to biographical analysis.

"A valuable, wide-ranging collection of essays by one of the best informed and most accute commentators on Lewis' work and ideas."
    Peter Schakel, author of *Imagination & the Arts in C. S. Lewis*

C. S. Lewis Goes to Heaven: A Reader's Guide to The Great Divorce
David G. Clark

This is the first book devoted solely to this often neglected book and the first to reveal several important secrets Lewis concealed within the story. Lewis felt his imaginary trip to Hell and Heaven was far better than his book *The Screwtape Letters*, which has become a classic. Clark is an ordained minister who has taught courses on Lewis for more than 30 years and is a New Testament and Greek scholar with a Doctor of Philosophy degree in Biblical Studies from the University of Notre Dame. Readers will discover the many literary and biblical influences Lewis utilized in writing his brilliant novel.

MORE INFORMATION AT WWW.WINGEDLIONPRESS.COM

C. S. Lewis & Philosophy as a Way of Life
Adam Barkman

C. S. Lewis is rarely thought of as a "philosopher" per se despite having both studied and taught philosophy for several years at Oxford. Lewis's long journey to Christianity was essentially philosophical – passing through seven different stages. This 624 page book is an invaluable reference for C. S. Lewis scholars and fans alike

C. S. Lewis: His Literary Achievement
Colin Manlove

"This is a positively brilliant book, written with splendor, elegance, profundity and evidencing an enormous amount of learning. This is probably not a book to give a first-time reader of Lewis. But for those who are more broadly read in the Lewis corpus this book is an absolute gold mine of information. The author gives us a magnificent overview of Lewis' many writings, tracing for us thoughts and ideas which recur throughout, and at the same time telling us how each book differs from the others. I think it is not extravagant to call C. S. Lewis: His Literary Achievement a tour de force."
    Robert Merchant, *St. Austin Review*, Book Review Editor

Mythopoeic Narnia: Memory, Metaphor, and Metamorphoses in C. S. Lewis's The Chronicles of Narnia
Salwa Khoddam

Dr. Khoddam, the founder of the C. S. Lewis and Inklings Society (2004), has been teaching university courses using Lewis' books for over 25 years. Her book offers a fresh approach to the *Narnia* books based on an inquiry into Lewis' readings and use of classical and Christian symbols. She explores the literary and intellectual contexts of these stories, the traditional myths and motifs, and places them in the company of the greatest Christian mythopoeic works of Western literature. In Lewis' imagination, memory and metaphor interact to advance his purpose – a Christian metamorphosis. *Mythopoeic Narnia* helps to open the door for readers into the magical world of the Western imagination.

Speaking of Jack: A C. S. Lewis Discussion Guide
Will Vaus

C. S. Lewis societies have been forming around the world since the first one started in New York City in 1969. Will Vaus has started and led three groups himself. *Speaking of Jack* is the result of Vaus' experience in leading those Lewis societies. Included here are introductions to most of Lewis' books as well as questions designed to stimulate discussion about Lewis' life and work. These materials have been "road-tested" with real groups made up of young and old, some very familiar with Lewis and some newcomers. *Speaking of Jack* may be used in an existing book discussion group, to start a C. S. Lewis society, or to guide your own exploration of Lewis' books.

George MacDonald

Diary of an Old Soul & The White Page Poems
George MacDonald and Betty Aberlin

The first edition of George MacDonald's book of daily poems included a blank page opposite each page of poems. Readers were invited to write their own reflections on the "white page." MacDonald wrote: "Let your white page be ground, my print be seed, growing to golden ears, that faith and hope may feed." Betty Aberlin responded to MacDonald's invitation with daily poems of her own.

"Betty Aberlin's close readings of George MacDonald's verses and her thoughtful responses to them speak clearly of her poetic gifts and spiritual intelligence."
    Luci Shaw, poet

George MacDonald: Literary Heritage and Heirs
Roderick McGillis, editor

This latest collection of 14 essays sets a new standard that will influence MacDonald studies for many more years. George MacDonald experts are increasingly evaluating his entire corpus within the nineteenth century context.

"This comprehensive collection represents the best of contemporary scholarship on George MacDonald."
    Rolland Hein, author of *George MacDonald: Victorian Mythmaker*

In the Near Loss of Everything: George MacDonald's Son in America
Dale Wayne Slusser

In the summer of 1887, George MacDonald's son Ronald, newly engaged to artist Louise Blandy, sailed from England to America to teach school. The next summer he returned to England to marry Louise and bring her back to America. On August 27, 1890, Louise died, leaving him with an infant daughter. Ronald once described losing a beloved spouse as "the near loss of everything". Dale Wayne Slusser unfolds this poignant story with unpublished letters and photos that give readers a glimpse into the close-knit MacDonald family. Also included is Ronald's essay about his father, *George MacDonald: A Personal Note*, plus a selection from Ronald's 1922 fable, *The Laughing Elf*, about the necessity of both sorrow and joy in life.

A Novel Pulpit: Sermons From George MacDonald's Fiction
David L. Neuhouser

"In MacDonald's novels, the Christian teaching emerges out of the characters and story line, the narrator's comments, and inclusion of sermons given by the fictional preachers. The sermons in the novels are shorter than the ones in collections of MacDonald's sermons and so are perhaps more accessible for some. In any case, they are both stimulating and thought-provoking. This collection of sermons from ten novels serve to bring out the 'freshness and brilliance' of MacDonald's message."
    From the author's introduction

Pop Culture

To Love Another Person: A Spiritual Journey Through Les Miserables
John Morrison

The powerful story of Jean Valjean's redemption is beloved by readers and theater goers everywhere. In this companion and guide to Victor Hugo's masterpiece, author John Morrison unfolds the spiritual depth and breadth of this classic novel and broadway musical.

Through Common Things: Philosophical Reflections on Popular Culture
Adam Barkman

"Barkman presents us with an amazingly wide-ranging collection of philosophical reflections grounded in the everyday things of popular culture – past and present, eastern and western, factual and fictional. Throughout his encounters with often surprising subject-matter (the value of darkness?), he writes clearly and concisely, moving seamlessly between Aristotle and anime, Lord Buddha and Lord Voldemort.... . This is an informative and entertaining book to read!"
— Doug Bloomberg, Professor of Philosophy, Institute for Christian Studies

Spotlight:
A Close-up Look at the Artistry and Meaning of Stephenie Meyer's Twilight Novels
John Granger

Stephenie Meyer's *Twilight* saga has taken the world by storm. But is there more to *Twilight* than a love story for teen girls crossed with a cheesy vampire-werewolf drama? *Spotlight* reveals the literary backdrop, themes, artistry, and meaning of the four Bella Swan adventures. *Spotlight* is the perfect gift for serious *Twilight* readers.

Virtuous Worlds: The Video Gamer's Guide to Spiritual Truth
John Stanifer

Popular titles like *Halo 3* and *The Legend of Zelda: Twilight Princess* fly off shelves at a mind-blowing rate. John Stanifer, an avid gamer, shows readers specific parallels between Christian faith and the content of their favorite games. Written with wry humor (including a heckler who frequently pokes fun at the author) this book will appeal to gamers and non-gamers alike. Those unfamiliar with video games may be pleasantly surprised to find that many elements in those "virtual worlds" also qualify them as "virtuous worlds."

Memoir

Called to Serve: Life as a Firefighter-Deacon
Deacon Anthony R. Surozenski

Called to Serve is the story of one man's dream to be a firefighter. But dreams have a way of taking detours – so Tony Soruzenski became a teacher and eventually a volunteer firefighter. And when God enters the picture, Tony is faced with a choice. Will he give up firefighting to follow another call? After many years, Tony's two callings are finally united – in service as a fire chaplain at Ground Zero after the 9-11 attacks and in other ways he could not have imagined. Tony is Chief Chaplain's aid for the Massachusettes Corp of Fire Chaplains and Director for the Office of the Diaconate of the Diocese of Worcester, Massachusettes.

Harry Potter

The Order of Harry Potter: The Literary Skill of the Hogwarts Epic
Colin Manlove

Colin Manlove, a popular conference speaker and author of over a dozen books, has earned an international reputation as an expert on fantasy and children's literature. His book, *From Alice to Harry Potter*, is a survey of 400 English fantasy books. In *The Order of Harry Potter*, he compares and contrasts *Harry Potter* with works by "Inklings" writers J.R.R. Tolkien, C.S. Lewis and Charles Williams; he also examines Rowling's treatment of the topic of imagination; her skill in organization and the use of language; and the book's underlying motifs and themes.

Harry Potter & Imagination: The Way Between Two Worlds
Travis Prinzi

Imaginative literature places a reader between two worlds: the story world and the world of daily life, and challenges the reader to imagine and to act for a better world. Starting with discussion of Harry Potter's more important themes, *Harry Potter & Imagination* takes readers on a journey through the transformative power of those themes for both the individual and for culture by placing Rowling's series in its literary, historical, and cultural contexts.

Repotting Harry Potter: A Professor's Guide for the Serious Re-Reader
Rowling Revisited: Return Trips to Harry, Fantastic Beasts, Quidditch, & Beedle the Bard
James W. Thomas

In *Repotting Harry Potter* and his sequel book *Rowling Revisited*, Dr. James W. Thomas points out the humor, puns, foreshadowing and literary parallels in the Potter books. In *Rowling Revisted*, readers will especially find useful three extensive appendixes – "Fantastic Beasts and the Pages Where You'll Find Them," "Quidditch Through the Pages," and "The Books in the Potter Books." Dr. Thomas makes re-reading the Potter books even more rewarding and enjoyable.

Deathly Hallows Lectures:
The Hogwarts Professor Explains Harry's Final Adventure
John Granger

In *The Deathly Hallows Lectures*, John Granger reveals the finale's brilliant details, themes, and meanings. *Harry Potter* fans will be surprised by and delighted with Granger's explanations of the three dimensions of meaning in *Deathly Hallows*. Ms. Rowling has said that alchemy sets the "parameters of magic" in the series; after reading the chapter-length explanation of *Deathly Hallows* as the final stage of the alchemical Great Work, the serious reader will understand how important literary alchemy is in understanding Rowling's artistry and accomplishment.

Hog's Head Conversations: Essays on Harry Potter
Travis Prinzi, Editor

Ten fascinating essays on Harry Potter by popular Potter writers and speakers including John Granger, James W. Thomas, Colin Manlove, and Travis Prinzi.

Poets and Poetry

Remembering Roy Campbell: The Memoirs of his Daughters, Anna and Tess
Introduction by Judith Lütge Coullie, Editor
Preface by Joseph Pearce

Anna and Teresa Campbell were the daughters of the handsome young South African poet and writer, Roy Campbell (1901-1957), and his beautiful English wife, Mary Garman. In their frank and moving memoirs, Anna and Tess recall the extraordinary, and often very difficult, lives they shared with their exceptional parents. The book includes over 50 photos, 344 footnotes, a timeline of Campbell's life, and a complete index.

In the Eye of the Beholder: How to See the World Like a Romantic Poet
Louis Markos

Born out of the French Revolution and its radical faith that a nation could be shaped and altered by the dreams and visions of its people, British Romantic Poetry was founded on a belief that the objects and realities of our world, whether natural or human, are not fixed in stone but can be molded and transformed by the visionary eye of the poet. Unlike many of the books written on Romanticism, which devote many pages to the poets and few pages to their poetry, the focus here is firmly on the poems themselves. The author thereby draws the reader intimately into the life of these poems. A separate bibliographical essay is provided for readers listing accessible biographies of each poet and critical studies of their work.

The Cat on the Catamaran: A Christmas Tale
John Martin

Here is a modern-day parable of a modern-day cat with modern-day attitudes. Riverboat Dan is a "cool" cat on a perpetual vacation from responsibility. He's *The Cat on the Catamaran* – sailing down the river of life. Dan keeps his guilty conscience from interfering with his fun until he runs into trouble. But will he have the courage to believe that it's never too late to change course? (For ages 10 to adult)

"Cat lovers and poetry lovers alike will enjoy this whimsical story about Riverboat Dan, a philosophical cat in search of meaning."
Regina Doman, author of *Angel in the Water*

Fiction

The Iona Conspiracy (from The Remnant Chronicles book series)
Gary Gregg

Readers find themselves on a modern adventure through ancient Celtic myth and legend as thirteen year old Jacob uncovers his destiny within "the remnant" of the Sporrai Order. As the Iona Academy comes under the control of educational reformers and ideological scientists, Jacob finds himself on a dangerous mission to the sacred Scottish island of Iona and discovers how his life is wrapped up with the fate of the long lost cover of *The Book of Kells*. From its connections to Arthurian legend to references to real-life people, places, and historical mysteries, *Iona* is an adventure that speaks to eternal truths as well as the challenges of the modern world. A young adult novel, *Iona* can be enjoyed by the entire family.

CPSIA information can be obtained at www.ICGtesting.com
Printed in the USA
LVOW13s1931111113

360844LV00002B/24/P